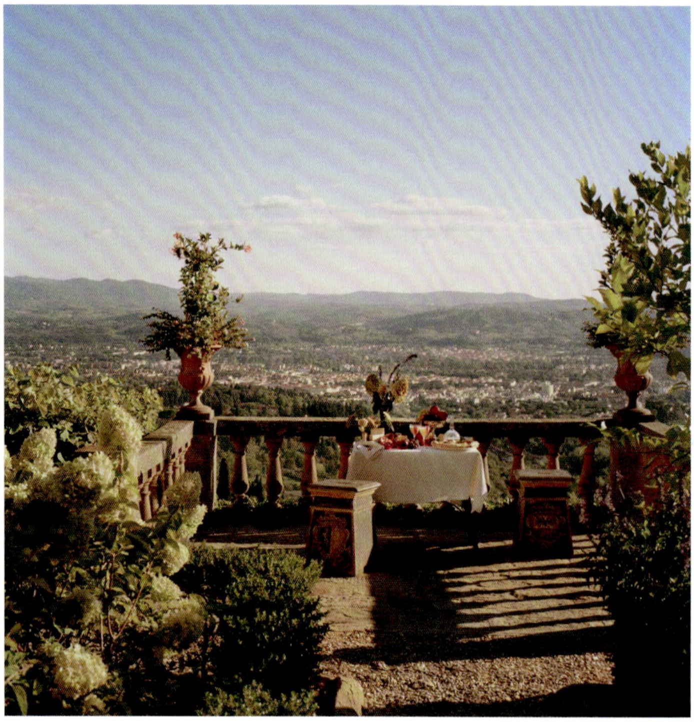

VILLA SAN MICHELE

A BELMOND HOTEL

FLORENCE

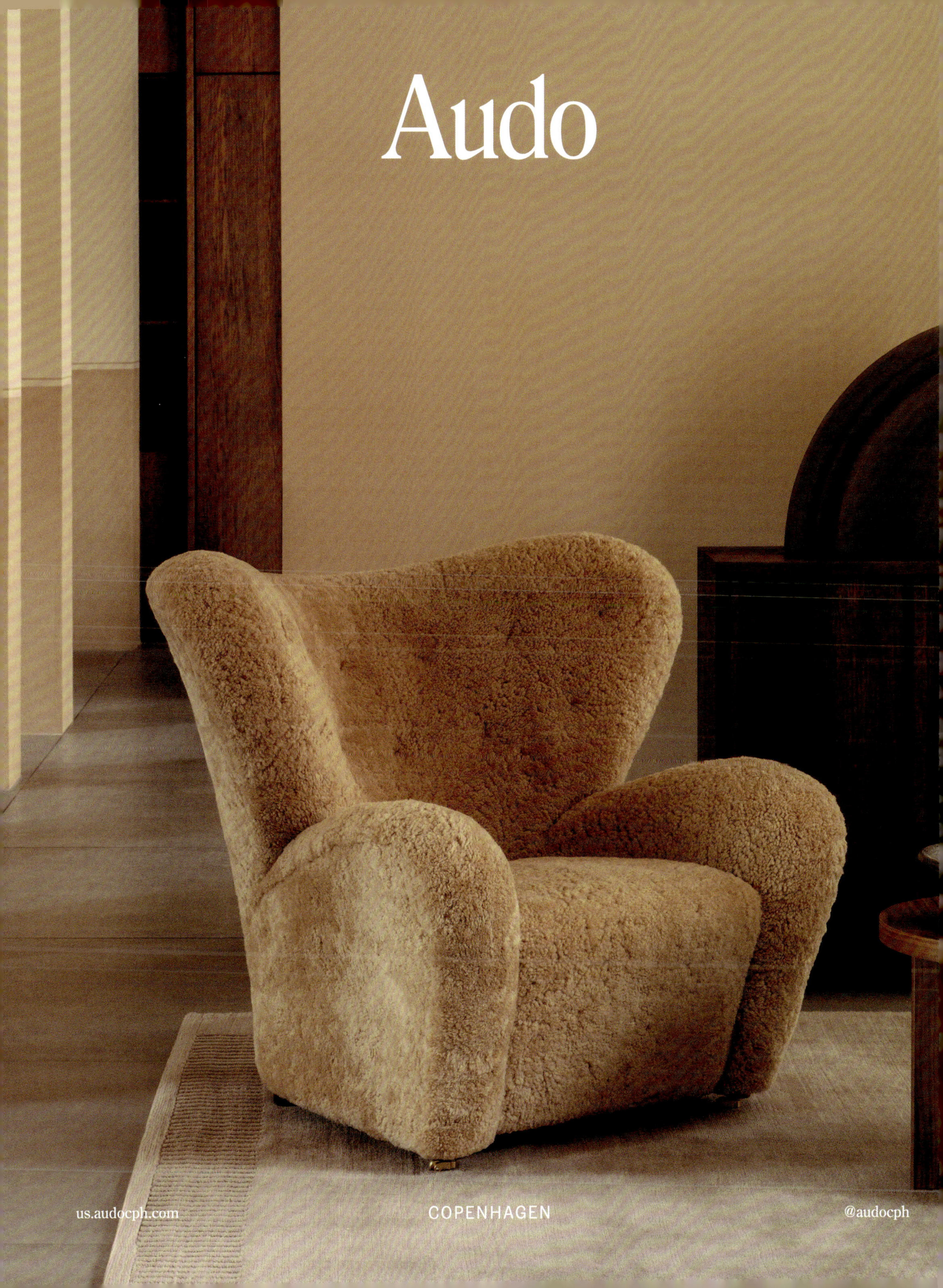
Audo
us.audocph.com
COPENHAGEN
@audocph

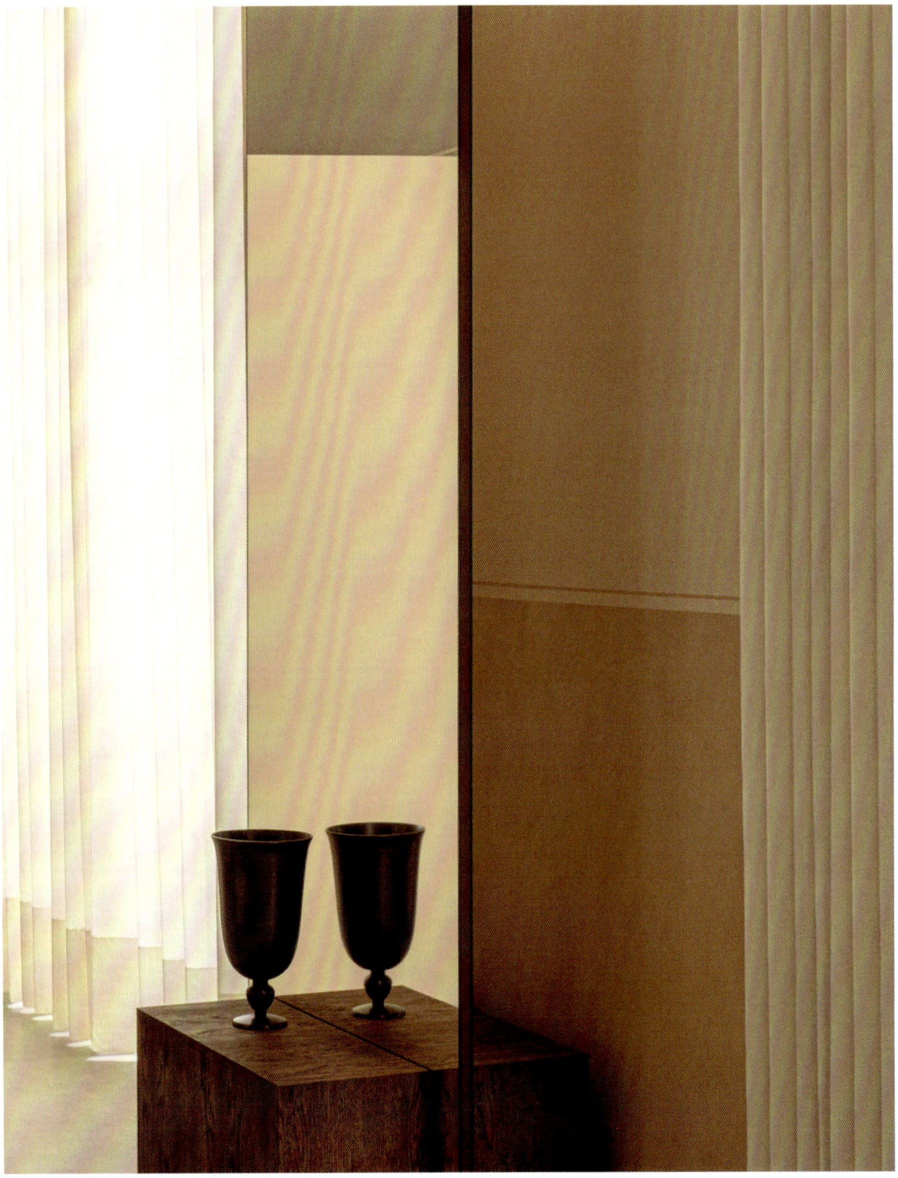

Robert Adams
Diane Arbus
Bernd & Hilla Becher
Elisheva Biernoff
Mel Bochner
Sophie Calle
Cardiff & Miller
Liz Deschenes
Kota Ezawa
Lee Friedlander
Adam Fuss
Nan Goldin
Katy Grannan
Martine Gutierrez
Peter Hujar
Richard Learoyd
Helen Levitt
Christian Marclay
Wardell Milan
Richard Misrach
Nicholas Nixon
Alec Soth
Hiroshi Sugimoto
Richard T. Walker
Carrie Mae Weems
Garry Winogrand

fraenkelgallery.com

FRÆNKEL

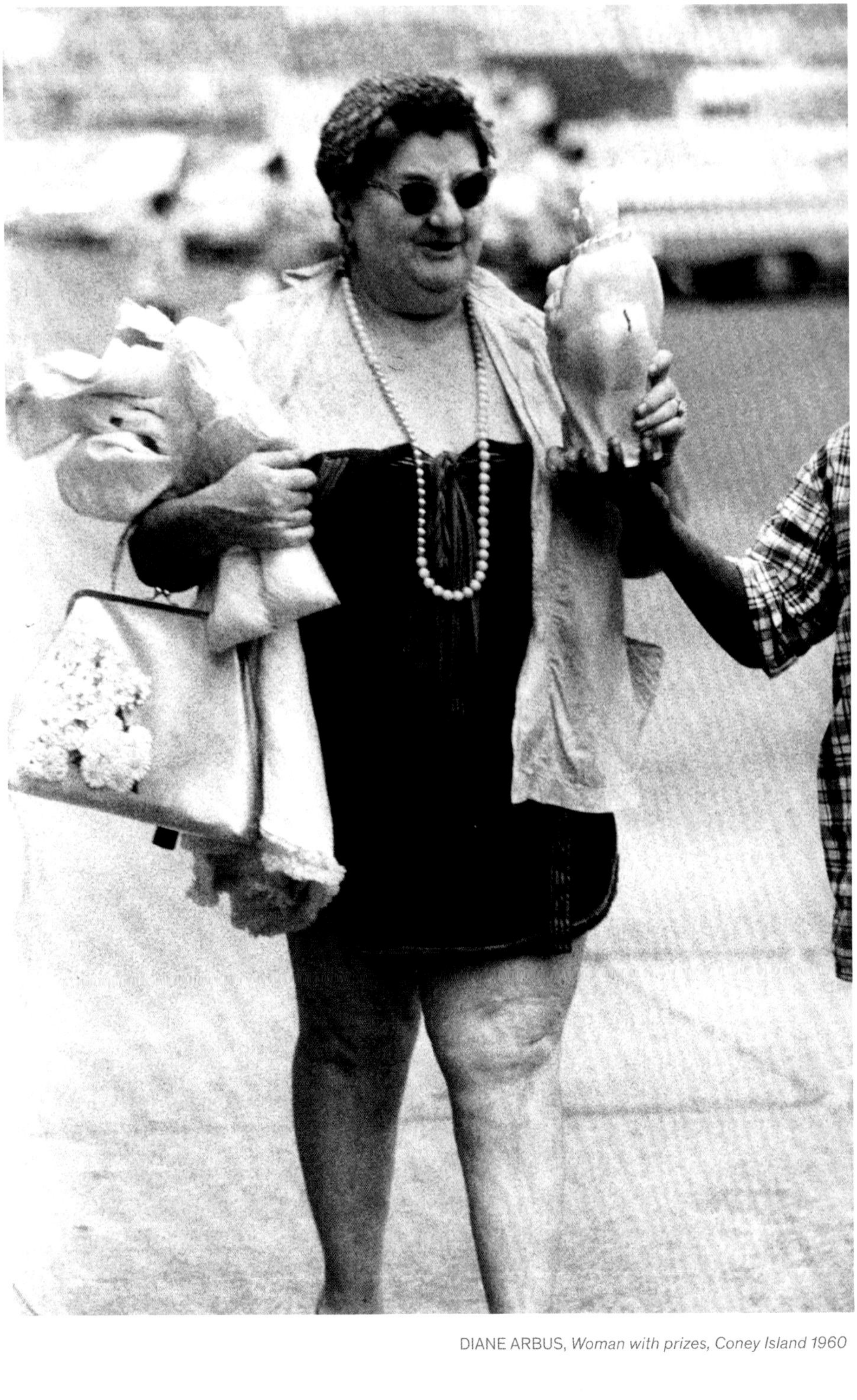

DIANE ARBUS, *Woman with prizes, Coney Island 1960*

The End of Nature?
Spring 2026

Columns

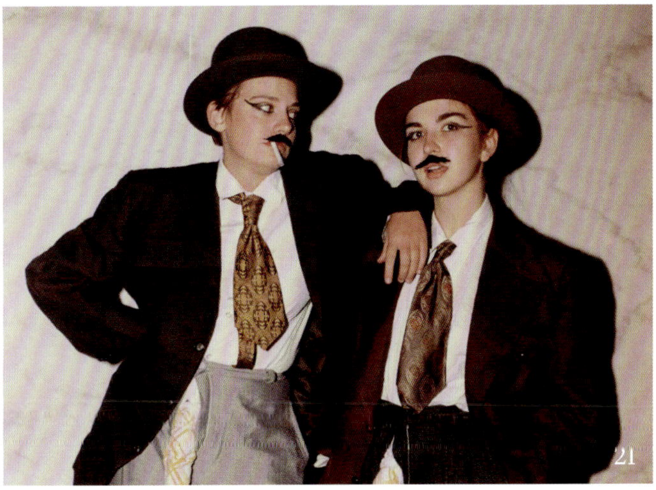
21

Features

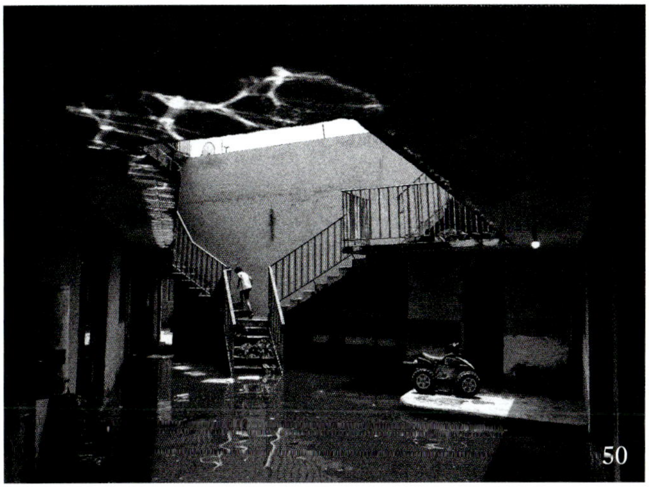
50

Features

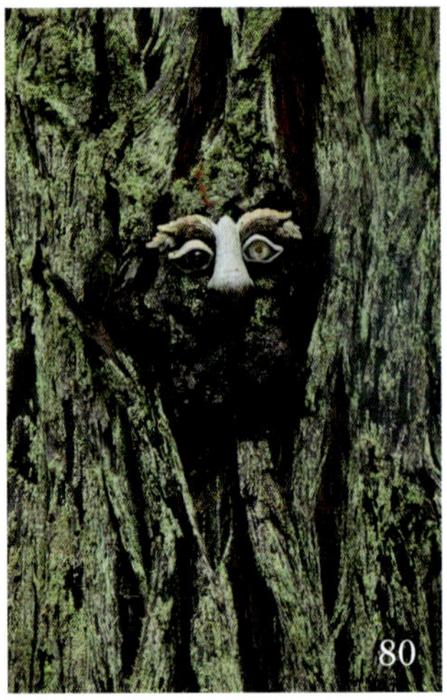

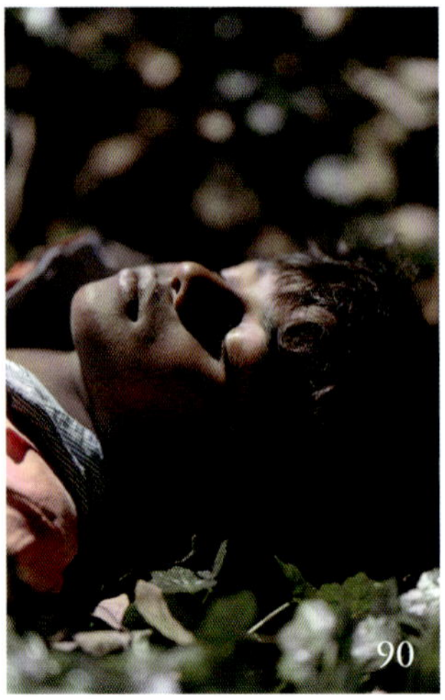

The PhotoBook Review

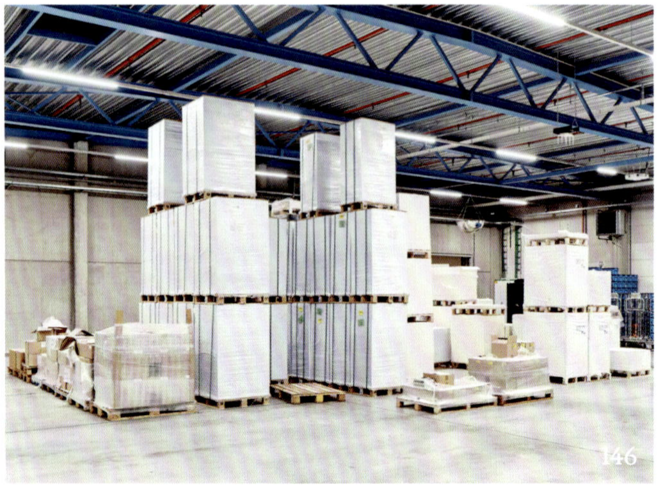

Front cover:
Hashem Shakeri, from the series *The Kahur Does Not Fall Unless the Earth Wills It*, Balochistan, Iran, 2018–ongoing
Supported by Magnum Foundation
(See page 62)

Subscribe to *Aperture* and read more at aperture.org.

Aperture is a nonprofit publisher dedicated to creating insight, community, and understanding through photography. Established in 1952 to advance "creative thinking, significantly expressed in words and photographs," Aperture champions photography's vital role in nurturing curiosity and encouraging a more just, tolerant society.

Aperture (ISSN 0003-6420) is published quarterly, in spring, summer, fall, and winter, at 380 Columbus Avenue, New York, NY 10024. Subscriptions are $75/year. For delivery in Canada, add $20; for other countries, add $35. Single copies may be purchased for $24.95. To subscribe or buy single copies, visit aperture.org. Periodicals postage paid at New York and additional mailing offices. POSTMASTER: Send address changes to Aperture, PO Box 3000, Denville, NJ 07834. For customer service, please call 866-457-4603 (US and Canada) or email custsvc_aperture@fulcoinc.com. Newsstand distribution in the US is handled by CMG. For international distribution, contact Central Books, centralbooks.com. Other inquiries, email orders@aperture.org or call 212-505-5555.

Credits for "Timeline," pp. 24–25: Carte-de-visite: Courtesy Eric Robbins; Muray: Courtesy Nickolas Muray Photo Archives and the George Eastman Museum; Hocus Focus gum: Courtesy the collection of Barbara Levine and Paige Ramey/Project B; Collier: © the artist and courtesy the San Francisco Museum of Modern Art, Anton Kern Gallery, New York, Galerie Neu, Berlin, Gladstone Gallery, Brussels, and The Modern Institute/Toby Webster Ltd., Glasgow; Taggart: © the artist

Credits for "Curriculum," pp. 28–29: Ito: *Exterior-in*, 1970, © Estate of Miyoko Ito and courtesy Karen Lennox Gallery, Chicago, and Matthew Marks Gallery, New York; Anger: Jimmy DeSana, *Kenneth Anger*, 1980, © and courtesy the Jimmy DeSana Trust, and P·P·O·W, New York; *My Own Private Idaho*: © Fine Line and courtesy Photofest; Adams: © the artist and courtesy Fraenkel Gallery, San Francisco; P-Orridge: *Madwoman Poor Trait #5*, 2019, photograph by Laure Leber, courtesy the artists and New Discretions, New York

Library of Congress Catalog Card No: 58-30845.

Support has been provided by members of Aperture's Magazine Council: Jon Stryker and Slobodan Randjelović, Susan and Thomas Dunn, Kate Cordsen and Denis O'Leary, and Michael W. Sonnenfeldt, MUUS Collection.

ISBN 978-1-59711-601-5

Printed in Turkey by Ofset Yapimevi

OFSET
YAPIMEVİ

Statement of Ownership, Management, and Circulation (Required by 39 U.S.C. 3685). 1. Publication Title: Aperture; 2. Publication no.: 687250; 3. Filing Date: September 30, 2025 4. Issue Frequency: Quarterly; 5. No. of Issues Published Annually: 4; 6. Annual Subscription Price: $75; 7. Complete Mailing Address of Known Office of Publication: Aperture, 548 West 28th Street, 4th Floor, New York, NY 10001-5982; Contact Person: Mary Colman St. John; Telephone: 212-946-7113; 8. Complete Mailing Address of Headquarters or General Business Office of Publisher: Aperture, 548 West 28th Street, 4th Floor, New York, NY 10001-5982; 9. Full Names and Complete Mailing Addresses of Publisher, Editor, and Managing Editor: Publisher: Sarah Meister, Aperture, 548 West 28th Street, 4th Floor, New York, NY 10001-5982; Editor: Michael Famighetti, Aperture, 548 West 28th Street, 4th Floor, New York, NY 10001-5982; Managing Editor: Zack Hatfield, Aperture, 548 West 28th Street, 4th Floor, New York, NY 10001-5982; 10. Owner: Aperture Foundation, Inc., 548 West 28th Street, 4th Fl., New York, NY 10001; 11. Known Bondholders, Mortgagees, and Other Security Holders Owning or Holding 1 Percent or More of Total Amount of Bonds, Mortgages, or Other Securities: None; 12. Tax Status: The purpose, function, and nonprofit status of this organization and the exempt status for federal income tax purposes: Has Not Changed During Preceding 12 Months; 13. Publication Title: Aperture; 14. Issue Date for Circulation Data Below: 06/11/2025; 15. Extent and Nature of Circulation (Average No. Copies Each Issue During Preceding 12 Months; No. Copies of Single Issue Published Nearest to Filing Date): a. Total Number of Copies (Net press run): 12,045; 12,635; b. Paid Circulation; (1) Mailed Outside-County Paid Subscriptions Stated on PS Form 3541: 5,520; 5,634; (2) Mailed In-County Paid Subscriptions Stated on PS Form 3541: 0; 0; (3) Paid Distribution Outside the Mails Including Sales Through Dealers and Carriers, Street Vendors, Counter Sales, and Other Paid Distribution Outside USPS: 3,014; 2,950; (4) Paid Distribution by Other Classes of Mail Through the USPS: 15; 15; c. Total Paid Distribution: 8,534; 8,584; d. Free or Nominal Rate Distribution: (1) Free or Nominal Rate Outside-County Copies included on PS Form 3541: 368; 312; (2) Free or Nominal Rate In-County Copies Included on PS From 3541: 0; 0; (3) Free or Nominal Rate Copies Mailed at Other Classes Through the USPS: 58; 47; (4) Free or Nominal Rate Distribution Outside the Mail: 0; 0; e. Total Free or Nominal Rate Distribution: 426; 359; f. Total Distribution: 8,960; 8943; g. Copies not Distributed: 3,085; 3,692; h. Total: 12,045; 12,635; i. Percent Paid 95.25%; 95.99%; 16. Electronic Copy Circulation, a. Paid Electronic Copies: 1,005; 993; b. Total Paid Print Copies + Paid Electronic Copies: 9,539; 9,577; c. Total Print Distribution + Paid Electronic Copies: 9,965; 9,936; d. Percent Paid (Both Print & Electronic Copies); 95.73%; 96.39%; I certify that 50% of all my distributed copies (Electronic & Print) are paid above a nominal price. 17. Publication of Statement of Ownership: Will be printed in the Spring 2026 issue of this publication. 18. I certify that all information furnished on this form is true and complete. I understand that anyone who furnishes false or misleading information on this form or who omits material or information requested on the form may be subject to criminal sanctions (including fines and imprisonment) and/or civil sanctions (including civil penalties). Signature and Title of Editor, Publisher, Business Manager, or Owner: Mary Colman St. John, Chief Financial Officer, 9/30/2025

aperture

The Magazine of Photography and Ideas

aperture.org

Contributors

IAN BOURLAND ("Beneath the Surface," page 72) is an associate professor of contemporary art history at Georgetown University and the author of *Bloodflowers: Rotimi Fani-Kayode, Photography, and the 1980s* (2019) and *Black & Gold: Transmutations of Metal and Modernity*, which was published in February. Previously, Bourland contributed an essay for *Aperture* on photographer Robert Frank's connections to music. Here, he illuminates how the histories of American image-making and natural resource extraction are deeply entwined in an essay prompted by the exhibition *Beneath the Surface: Mining and American Photography*, which opens this May at the National Gallery of Art in Washington, DC.

SEAN J PATRICK CARNEY ("Terra Infirma," page 126) is a writer, visual artist, and educator, and the founder of Social Malpractice Publishing, an independent distribution label for artists' books. He is the creator and host of the podcasts *Humor and the Abject*, about the intersection of contemporary art and comedy, and *Time Zero*, which explores political, environmental, and cultural legacies of the nuclear industries. In this issue, he writes on Victoria Sambunaris's photographs of the American West.

ELISA DÍAZ CASTELO ("Flood Zone," page 50) is a writer and translator based in Mexico City whose poetry books include *Principia* (2018) and *El reino de lo no lineal* (The kingdom of the nonlinear, 2020). In 2019, she was awarded the Fine Arts Prize for Literary Translation for her translation of Ocean Vuong's *Night Sky with Exit Wounds*. Her debut novel, *Malacría*, was published by Sexto Piso last year. In this issue, Díaz Castelo writes on César Rodríguez's photographs chronicling Mexico's coastal communities as they contend with climate change.

EVA DÍAZ ("The Far Side of the Earth," page 112) is a critic and a professor of contemporary art history at Pratt Institute. Her first book, *The Experimenters: Chance and Design at Black Mountain College* (2015), traces the legacy of this small school in mid-century North Carolina that changed the course of art history. A Getty Scholar from 2023 to 2024, Díaz is currently researching her next book, about nonvisual art experiences. For *Aperture*, Díaz has previously covered ecofeminism and interviewed the celebrated documentary filmmaker Matt Wolf about his film *Spaceship Earth* (2020). Her new book is *After Spaceship Earth: Art, Techno-utopia, and Other Science Fictions* (2025). In this issue, she explores the unfulfilled promise of astronaut William Anders's *Earthrise* image.

PICO IYER ("Alight," page 100) has elevated the genre of cross-cultural writing across a career spanning eighty countries, seventeen books translated into twenty-three languages, and countless essays. His most recent book, the best-selling *Aflame: Learning from Silence* (2025), is about monasticism, wildfires, and sitting still. A regular contributor to *Aperture* over the years, he has written on the work of Robert Adams, Tom Sandberg, and Balarama Heller. In these pages, Iyer introduces a portfolio of previously unseen photographs made in Japan and Iceland by Rinko Kawauchi, whose book *Illuminance* was first published by Aperture in 2011.

AMITAVA KUMAR ("The Pregnant Tree," page 90) is the author of the novel *My Beloved Life* (2024) and thirteen other books of fiction and nonfiction, including *A Time Outside This Time* (2021) and *A Foreigner Carrying in the Crook of His Arm a Tiny Bomb* (2010), which explores intellectual and creative responses to the war on terror. A 2016 Guggenheim Fellow and visual diarist, Kumar teaches writing at Vassar College. Here, he writes on a series of photographs by Gayatri Ganju that tell the story of an Adivasi community's connection to a sacred, endangered forest in Tamil Nadu, India.

JEREMY MILLER ("Back to the Land," page 80) is a Bay Area–based writer and journalist. A contributor to *Harper's*, *The New Yorker*, *Outside*, and many other magazines, his subjects have included California's grizzly bears, the controversial practice of cloud seeding, and the "tectonic time bomb" of the Bay Area's Hayward Fault; for several years, he maintained an astronomy column in *Sierra* magazine. In his first piece for *Aperture*, he introduces a portfolio of Michael Schmelling's photographs documenting what remains of Northern California's utopian back-to-the-land movement of the 1960s and 1970s.

LYDIA MILLET ("Butterfly Effect," page 118) is a novelist based in the desert outside Tucson, Arizona. A Pulitzer Prize finalist, she is also the deputy creative director at the Center for Biological Diversity, where she has worked since 1999. In her environmental work and in her writing, Millet deals with extinction, climate change, and human-nonhuman relations. *Atavists* (2025), her twenty-first book, is a collection of interconnected short stories that follow bodybuilders, stalkers, professors, and worried parents living in the post-pandemic United States. In these pages, she writes on Lucas Foglia's series *Constant Bloom*, which traces the migration of painted lady butterflies across Europe, Africa, and the Middle East.

KAELEN WILSON-GOLDIE ("Dry Spells," page 62) is a Geneva-based critic and the author of the books *Etel Adnan* (2018) and *Beautiful, Gruesome, and True: Artists at Work in the Face of War* (2022). Wilson-Goldie last wrote for *Aperture* on the work of the French Algerian photographer Karim Kal. Here, she considers the ongoing work of Hashem Shakeri, who captures the stark beauty and environmental degradation of Iran's rural southeastern provinces.

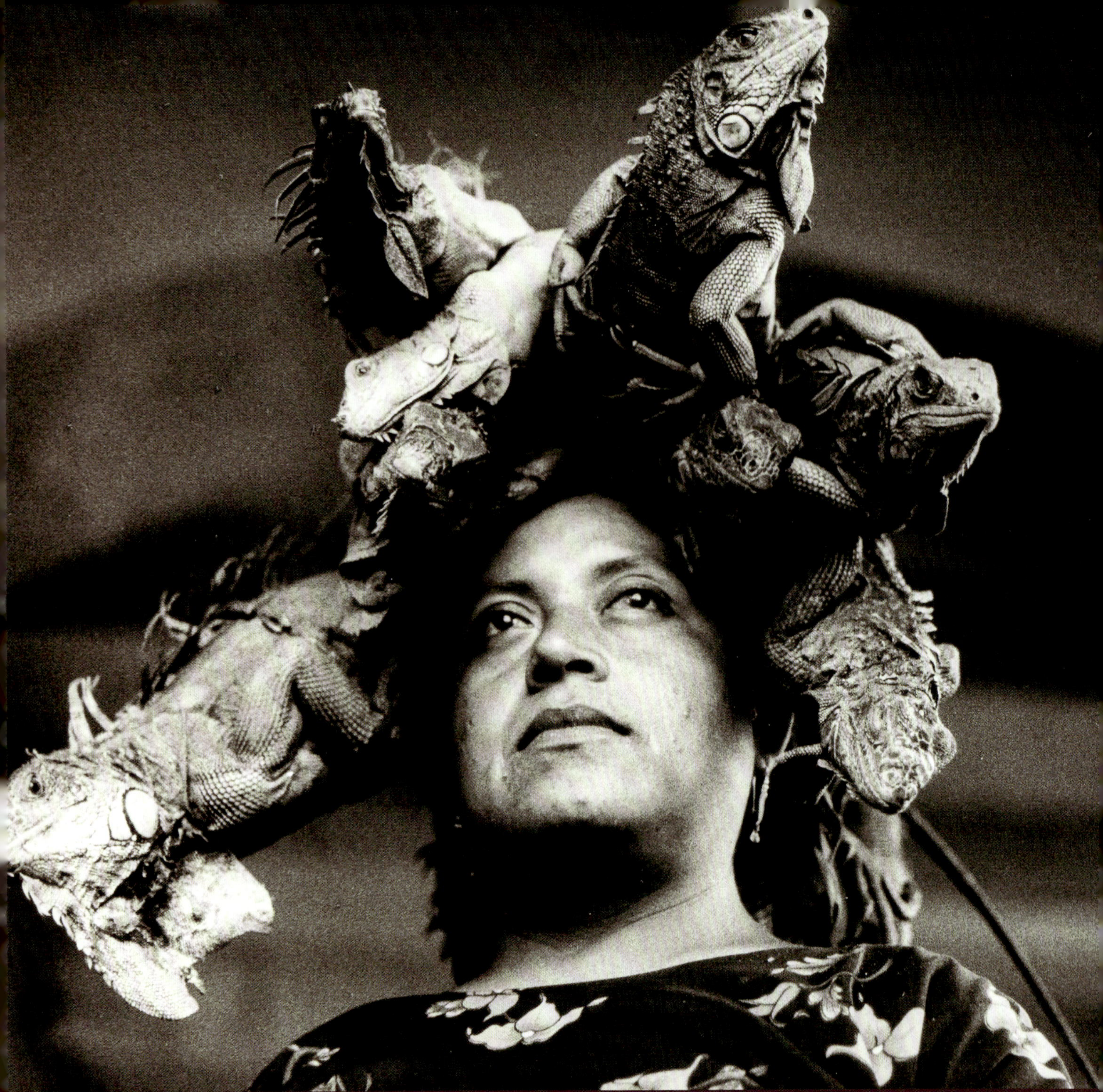

Agenda
Exhibitions to See

Catherine Opie

Catherine Opie rose to eminence in the 1990s as the court portraitist to Los Angeles's leather-dyke scene during the height of the culture wars. Since then, she has continued to photograph her queer circle of friends and intimates while documenting other subcultures: surfers, protestors, football players, ice fishermen, Boy Scouts. Opie's first retrospective in the United Kingdom explores this expansive, conceptually charged body of portraiture and how it makes visible the countenance of American democracy itself.

Catherine Opie: To Be Seen at the National Portrait Gallery, London, March 5–May 31, 2026

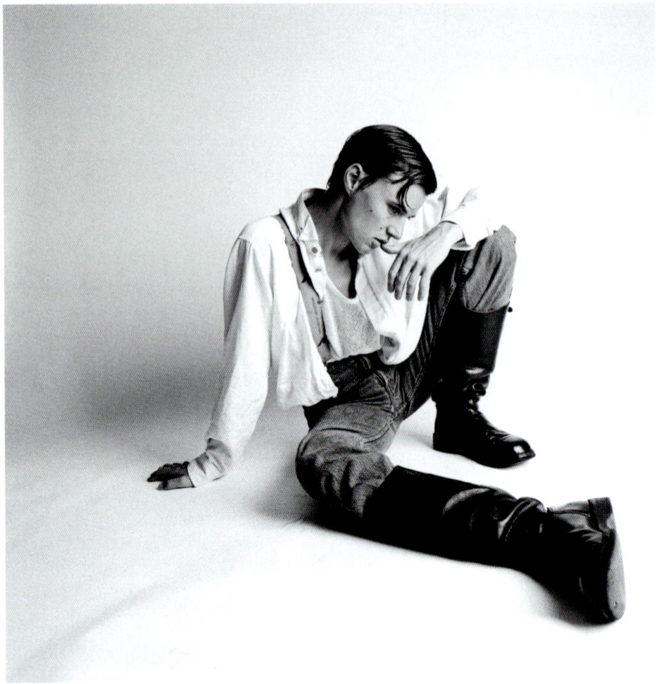

Catherine Opie, *Angela (boots)*, 1992
© the artist

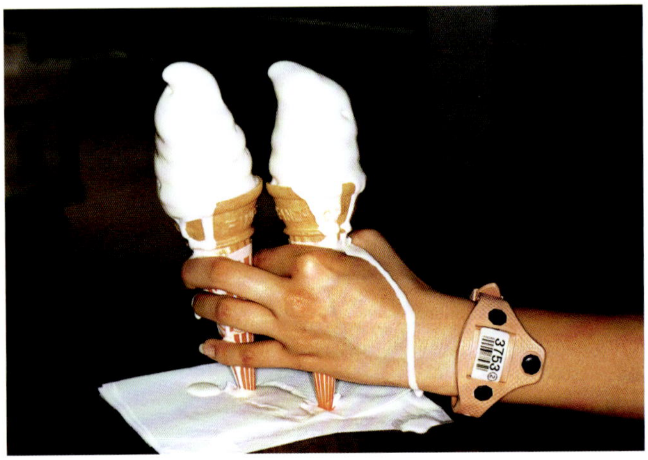

Martin Parr, Tokyo, Japan, 1998
© the artist/Magnum Photos

Martin Parr

"I respect what you're doing, but I think you're from a different planet," Henri Cartier-Bresson once told Martin Parr. With his lurid flash and ultrasaturated palette, the British photographer might seem like an emissary from outer space, sent to give earthlings a surreal reality check. A current exhibition in Paris frames his work against the backdrop of climate change—a ripe theme for Parr, whose tragicomic pictures, far from shallow satire, have always spoken deeply to how we want to see the world.

Martin Parr: Global Warning at Jeu de Paume, Paris, January 30–May 24, 2026

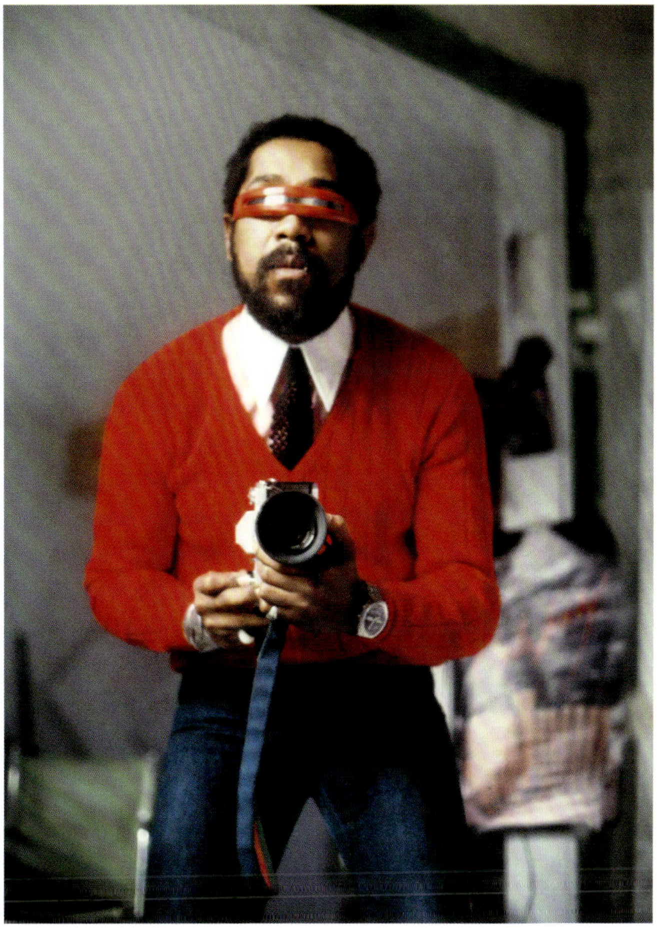

Barkley L. Hendricks, *Self-Portrait with Red Sweater*, 1980

Photography and the Black Arts Movement

Flourishing in the 1960s and 1970s, the Black Arts movement formed a revolutionary cultural front against the marginalization of Black life and art in the United States. This substantial show, curated by Philip Brookman and Deborah Willis, is the first to historicize the role of photography in what is often called the Second Renaissance, whose image makers—among them Barkley L. Hendricks with his pioneering portraiture that venerated everyday Black people—advanced a new visual language of self-representation and community building.

Photography and the Black Arts Movement, 1955–1985 at the Getty Center, Los Angeles, February 24–June 14, 2026

Deborah Turbeville

Alongside Guy Bourdin and Helmut Newton, Deborah Turbeville brought an edgy theatricality to fashion photography beginning in the 1970s. She rejected the glossy sex appeal that motivated commercial photoshoots by xeroxing, cutting, blurring, scratching, and pinning prints together to conjure otherworldly narratives. This exhibition concentrates on Turbeville's personal experiments with photo collage, a means through which she heightened the distinct air of unreality that distinguishes her work, in which the forces of fashion and fiction coalesce.

Deborah Turbeville: Photocollage at Moderna Museet, Malmö, May 2–September 27, 2026

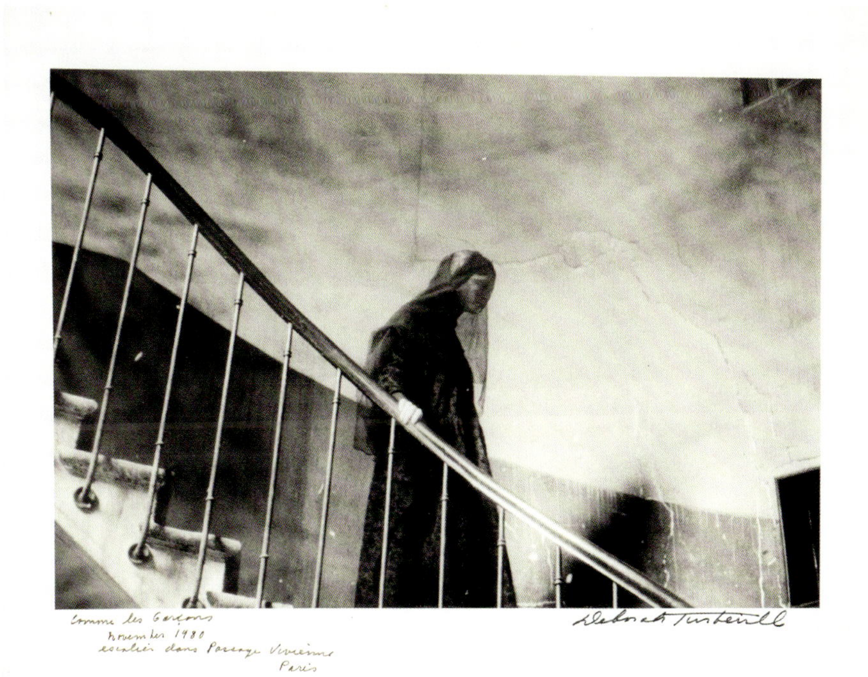

Deborah Turbeville, *Comme des Garçons, Escalier dans Passage Vivienne, Paris, France, November 1980*, from the series *Comme des Garçons*

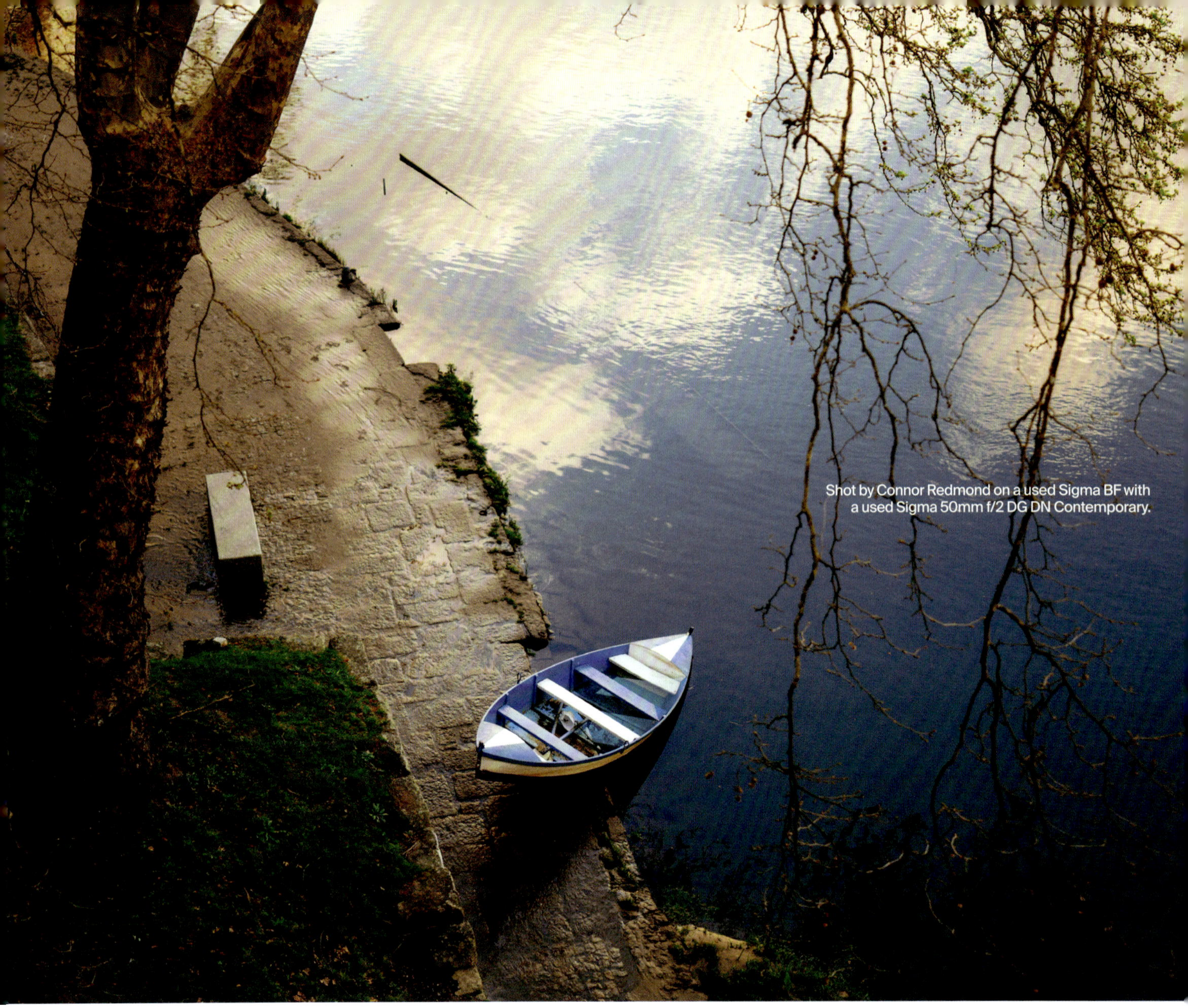

Studio Visit

For decades, Louis Mendes and his press camera have been a staple of New York street life.

Tanisha C. Ford

It is the second day of fall, and the steps of the Metropolitan Museum of Art are alive with the layered rhythms of New York. A performance artist slathered in white paint moves slowly across the plaza as a saxophonist bends a bluesy note nearby. Anti-Trump protesters chant along Fifth Avenue. Painters hawk canvases from folding tables, tourists pose for pictures, and fashionistas stage their own impromptu photoshoots on the museum's iconic steps.

Into this scene steps Louis Mendes, eighty-five years old and impeccably dressed in a beige suit, oxblood turtleneck, and brimmed hat. Around his shoulder, a massive vintage Speed Graphic press camera fitted with old-style flash bulbs, a relic from a bygone era. In one sense, Mendes is just another participant in this street-side economy, offering his wares to passersby. Yet he also stands apart. A New York fixture since 1959, he has mastered what he calls the place "where commerce meets art." Mendes no longer hawks his services as he once did, when he would call out to strangers, "You could get a picture right away! Take a look

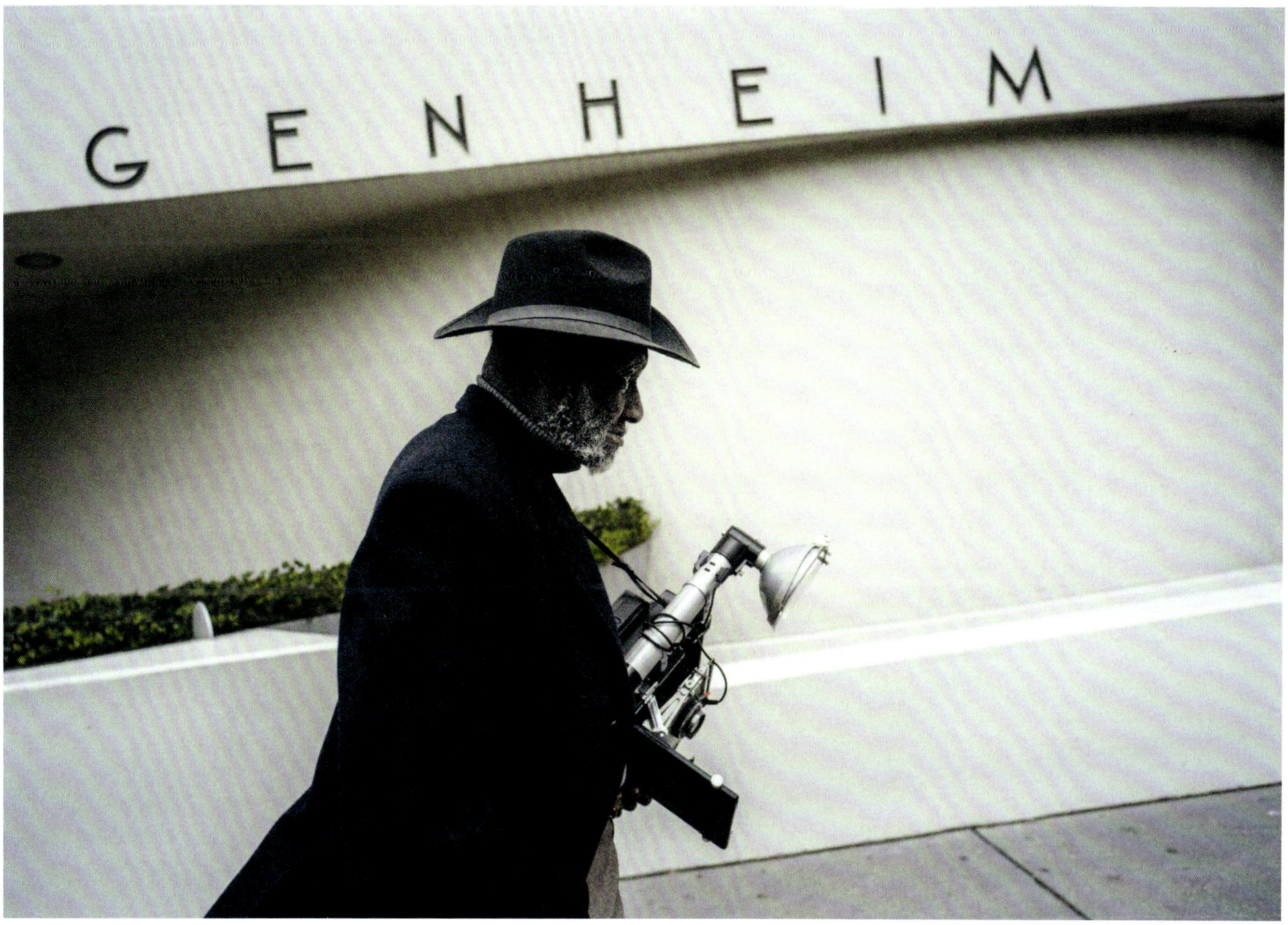

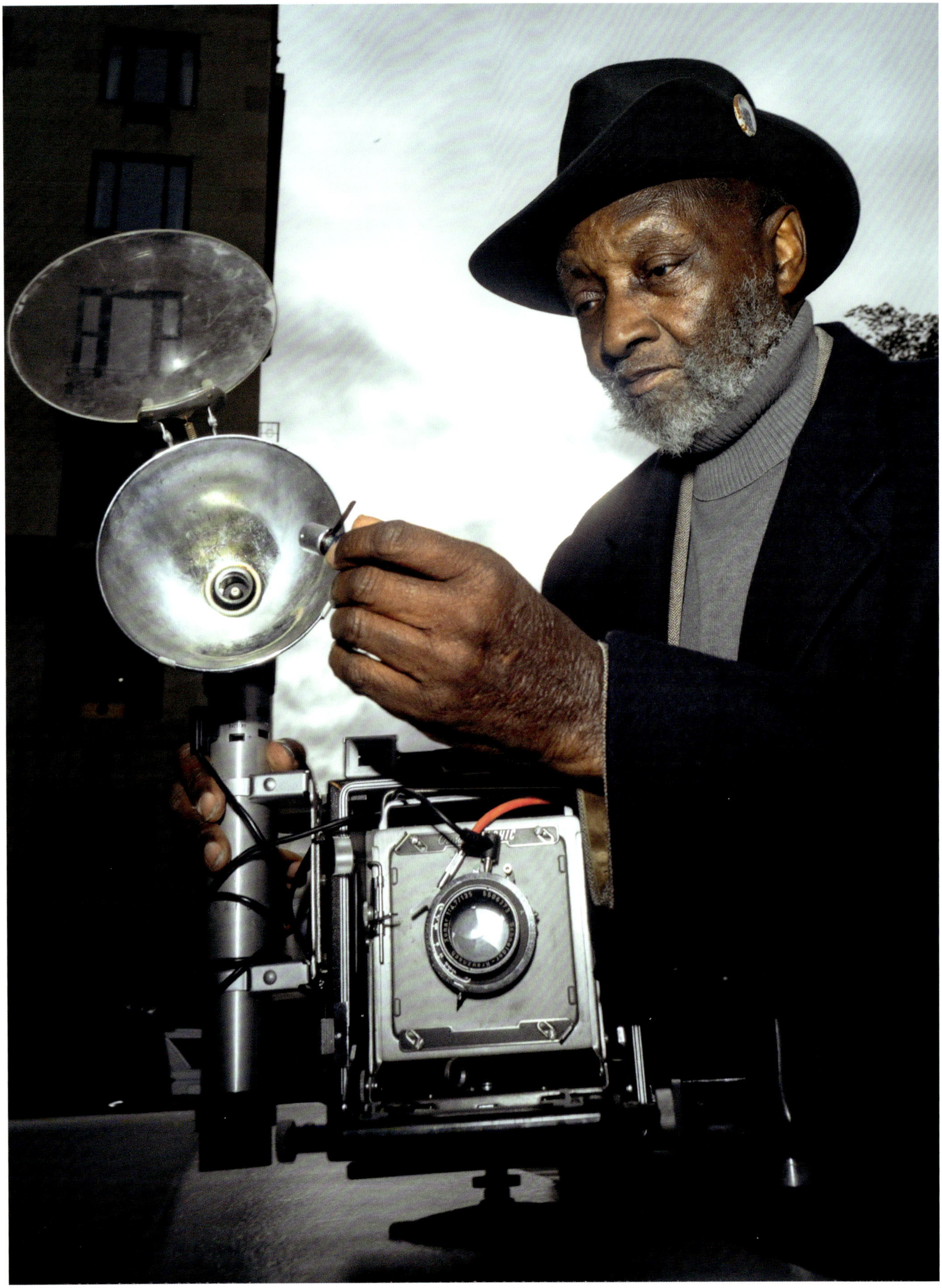

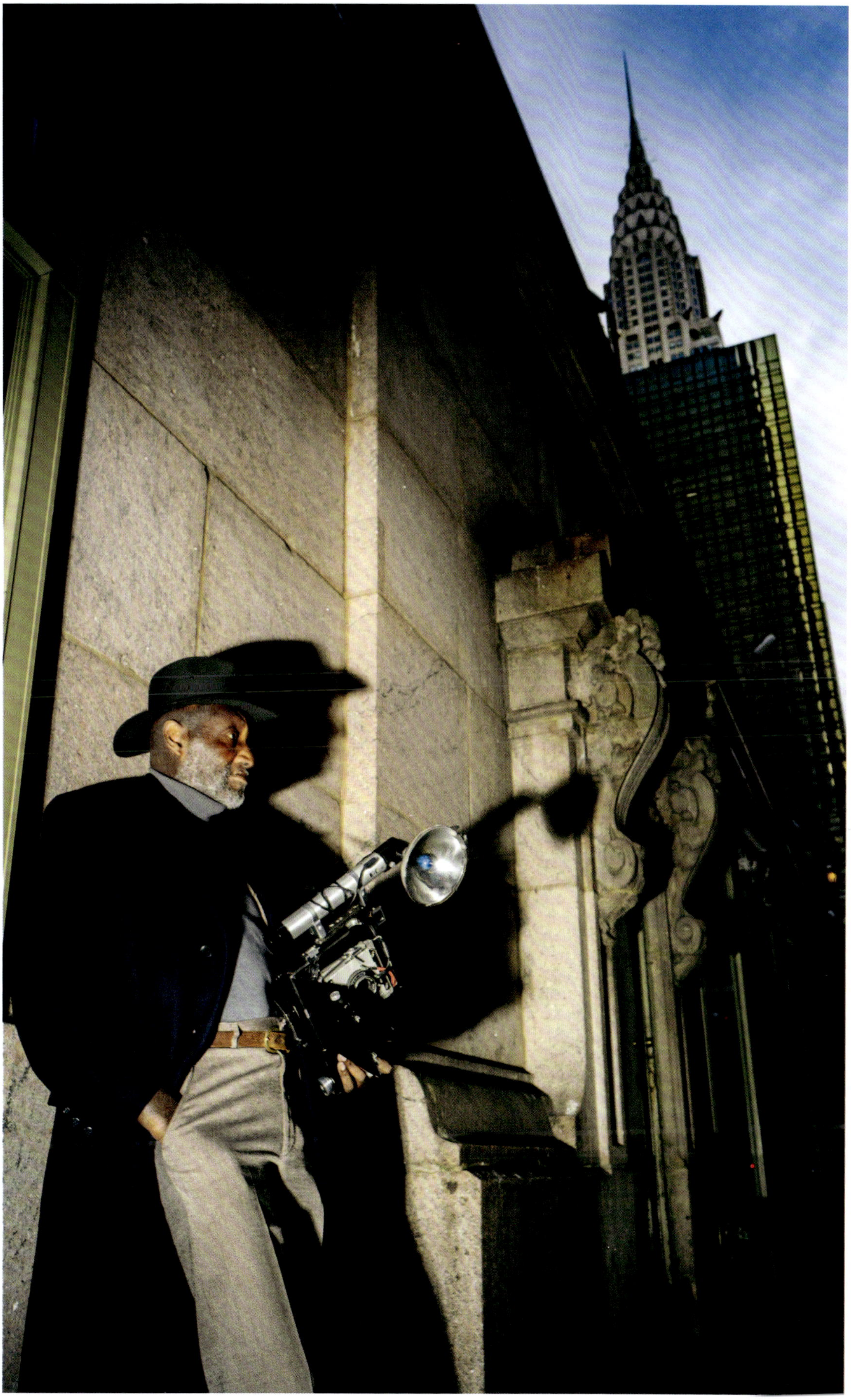

Previous spread and this page: Louis Mendes in New York, October 2025

at what I could do of you!" Now, his very presence is his sales pitch.

Curiosity draws people toward him. Many ask about the old camera. "Google me," he tells a woman who stops to chat. When she does, she smiles and says, "It's an honor to meet you." Others want to photograph him, and he strikes a subtle pose while keeping his eyes peeled on the crowds. "It happens every day," Mendes said. "And I capitalize on it as much as I can." He often proposes a trade to the curious person who thinks their quick snap has gone unnoticed: "I let you take a photograph of me, now let me take one of you."

This afternoon, a middle-aged Black man with a camera around his neck approaches to shake Mendes's hand. He tells him he grew up in New York and remembers seeing him in action decades ago. After a brief exchange, the man disappears into the crowd.

Such encounters point to a long, storied career. Mendes was born in Jamaica, Queens, in 1940. He started taking photographs in 1954, when his older sister, the family photographer, handed him the camera so she could be included in a portrait. "A week later, I got the results back, and I liked what I did," he recalled. "That's when the bug hit me." By 1959, he had begun photographing parties and weddings. That same year, he bought the camera he still uses. One night, he was working a party at the famed Audubon Ballroom, in Harlem. "This camera can make a living for you if you use it that way," a man told him. Mendes took the advice to heart: "I've been using it that way ever since."

As Mendes learned the trade, he made the street his studio. Those early years taught him the physical and creative demands of the job. "You try to do both day and night, you kill yourself," he said. "A little day, and a little night, and you got the week done." The street itself is both teacher and collaborator. "The street is always difficult," Mendes told me. "There are so many different people, constantly interacting. You learn more, and you do more."

Mendes once used Polaroid film but now works with Fujifilm Instax Wide. His archive includes decades of test shots and outtakes. But most often, the client leaves with the only copy of the photograph. "I have the memory and the money," he said. Occasionally, those memories return. A photograph he took

Terri Hyacinth holds her portrait by Louis Mendes in Grand Central Terminal
Photographs by Sinna Nasseri for *Aperture*

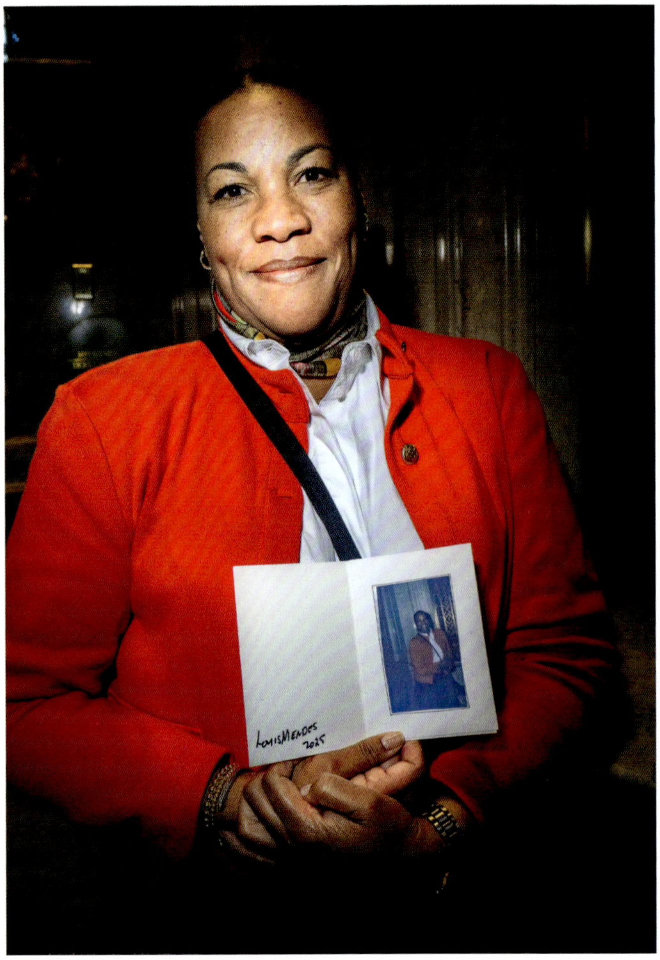

Mendes no longer hawks his services as he once did. Now, his very presence is his sales pitch.

of Gordon Parks and gave away resurfaced years later, and others reappear online when clients tag him on Instagram. These moments show what Mendes's practice is about: a simple commercial transaction that becomes a shared imprint, the material trace of a fleeting connection.

Mendes's work has evolved in step with the city itself. He photographed through the pandemic, even when Times Square was nearly empty. He has adapted to an increasingly cashless society. Yet the core of his work remains unchanged. His compositions are consistent, and his focus has always been on people, capturing something essential about the humanity of everyday life. "I photograph everywhere I can," he said. "Every day, nine days a week."

Tanisha C. Ford is a writer, cultural critic, and professor of history at the Graduate Center, City University of New York.

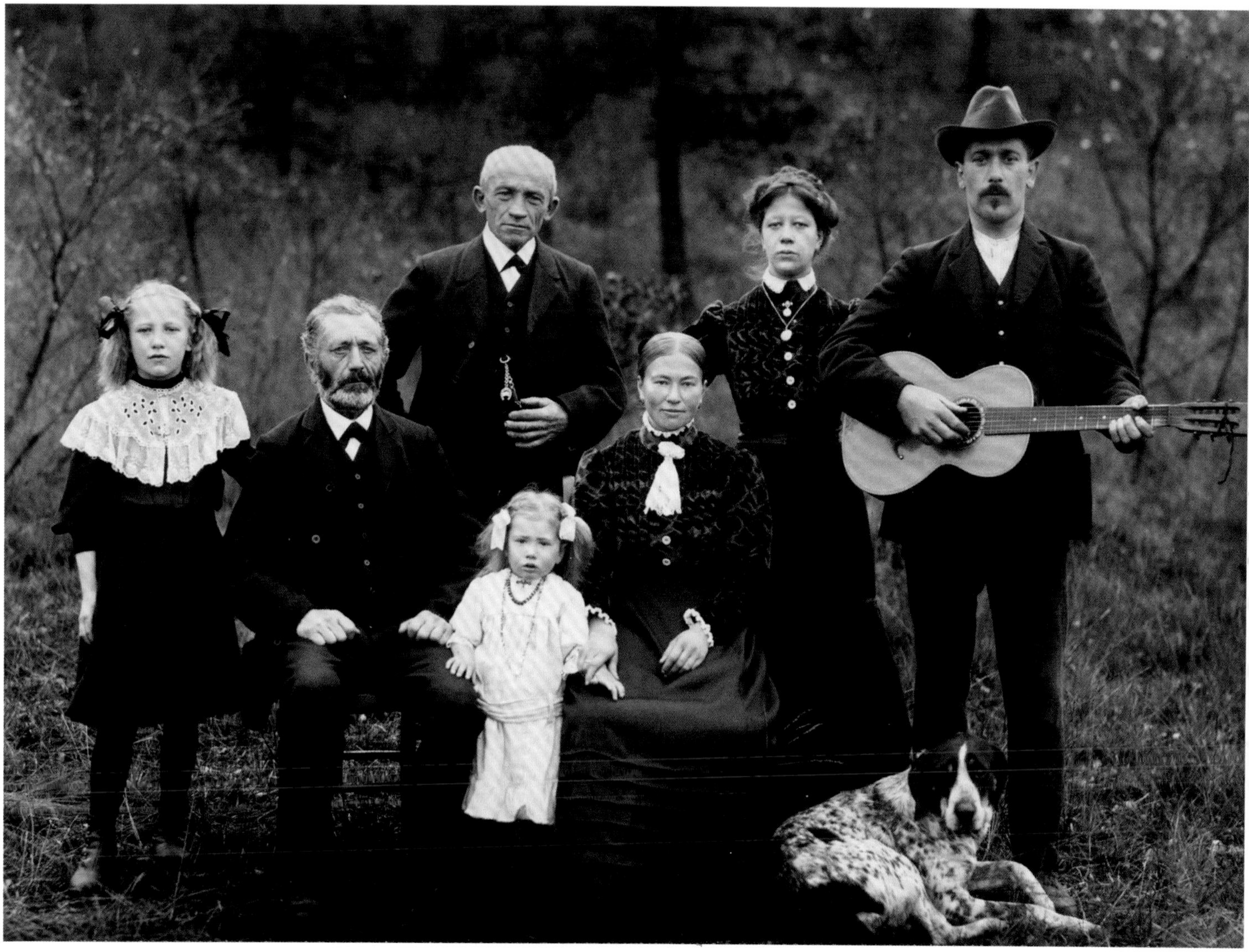

Backstory

Sophie Rivera brought sidelined New Yorkers into focus. A new show returns the favor.

Yxta Maya Murray

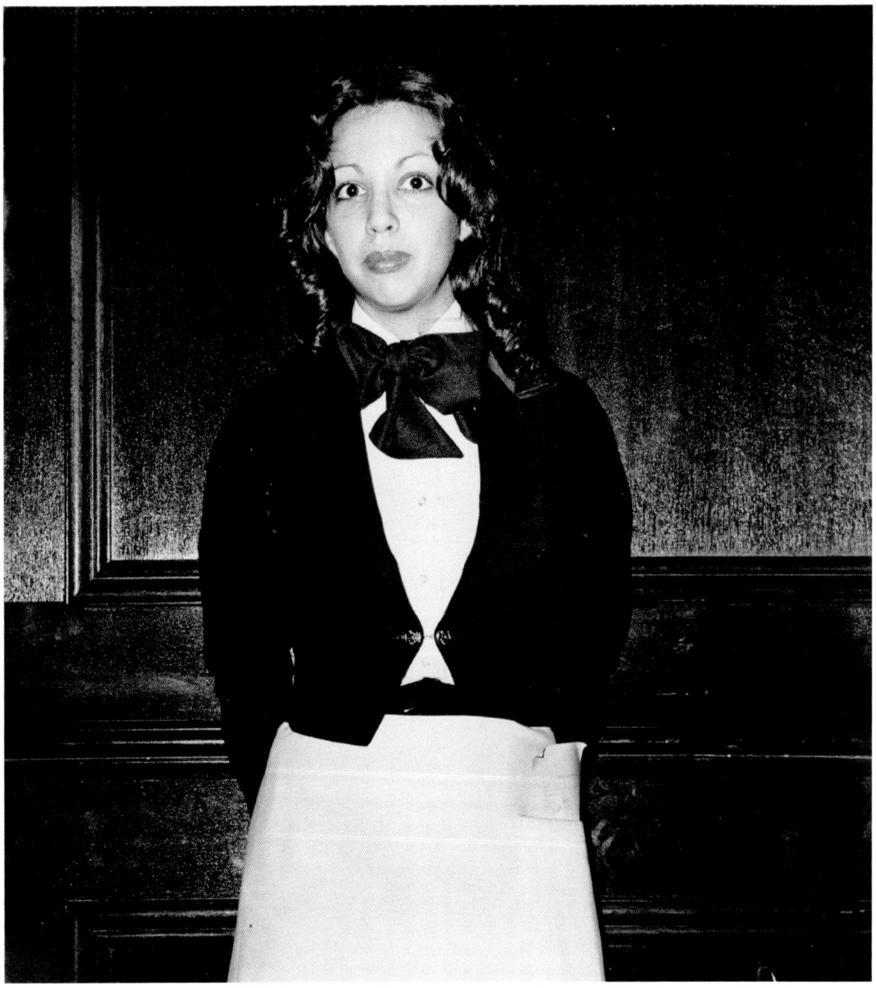

In 1978, the photographer Sophie Rivera had a style break—or, more precisely, a breakthrough. A former ballet dancer who pivoted to image-making in her thirties, she immediately demonstrated a talent for confronting society's ideals of the human body. Her first solo show, at the West Village's Third Eye Gallery, in 1973, featured male nudes in tender close-up. She followed this work with photographs of anatomically correct dolls and a series of "self-portraits" in the form of her own bloody tampons floating in a toilet bowl. In 1978, though, she shifted to a more classical, yet arguably even more vulnerable, kind of body-conscious image-making. Rivera, who was born in New York but was of Puerto Rican descent, ventured out from her studio to ask passersby in Morningside Heights whether they were Latino. If they answered yes, she asked if they'd like to have their photograph taken. She then proceeded to make portraits showing Nuyoricans from the thighs up and positioned in the middle of the frame. She printed the portraits at massive scale. The resulting body of images, known as the Latino Portraits (1978–79), is a thrilling and subtle exploration of Latinx subjectivity.

Visitors to the exhibition *Sophie Rivera: Double Exposures*, on view from April to August this year at El Museo del Barrio, in Manhattan, will have the chance to stand in the presence of these anonymous icons and also witness Rivera's progression as a politically engaged artist. Rivera "was very much a participant in different activist circles, mainly through the arts, and always through her lens-based work," noted Susanna Temkin, the show's curator. "She was very savvy and aware of the kind of intersectional identity that she embodied. And the Latino Portraits series was a crux for her development."

Rivera, who died at eighty-two in 2021, founded the Sophie Rivera Gallery, located in Washington Heights, in 1975. She also wrote and edited for feminist newspapers and journals and had an active practice of photographing political protests and marches. Her commitment to fighting for subordinated peoples' liberty shines through in the first of Rivera's *Latino Portraits*. Here, we encounter an alert young woman with shining ringlets and expertly tweezed eyebrows, her lips slicked with a luscious application of gloss. Clad in a natty, nip-waisted black jacket and an enormous black taffeta pussy bow, as well as a large white apron,

Previous page:
Untitled, 1978–79, from the series Latino Portraits

This page:
Untitled, 1986–87

Rivera possessed a flair for intimating the complex inner lives of working-class people.

she poses against the dark wood-paneled walls of her restaurant, perhaps between shifts. To achieve the radiant halations around her subjects in this series, Rivera used an actual spotlight.

It's worth noting that she began her Latino Portraits during a charged moment in Puerto Rico's history: On July 25, 1978, Constitution Day, police murdered the independence activists Carlos Soto Arriví and Arnaldo Darío Rosado in an ambush that the government later covered up, resulting in a scandal that rocked the island and its diaspora. It's likely no coincidence that Rivera was making these monuments to Puerto Ricans and Latinos when their values, politics, and bodies were under attack.

In the mid-1980s, she shifted from the anti-imperial messaging of Latino portraiture to rendering lively, joyous images of folks dressed up for Halloween.

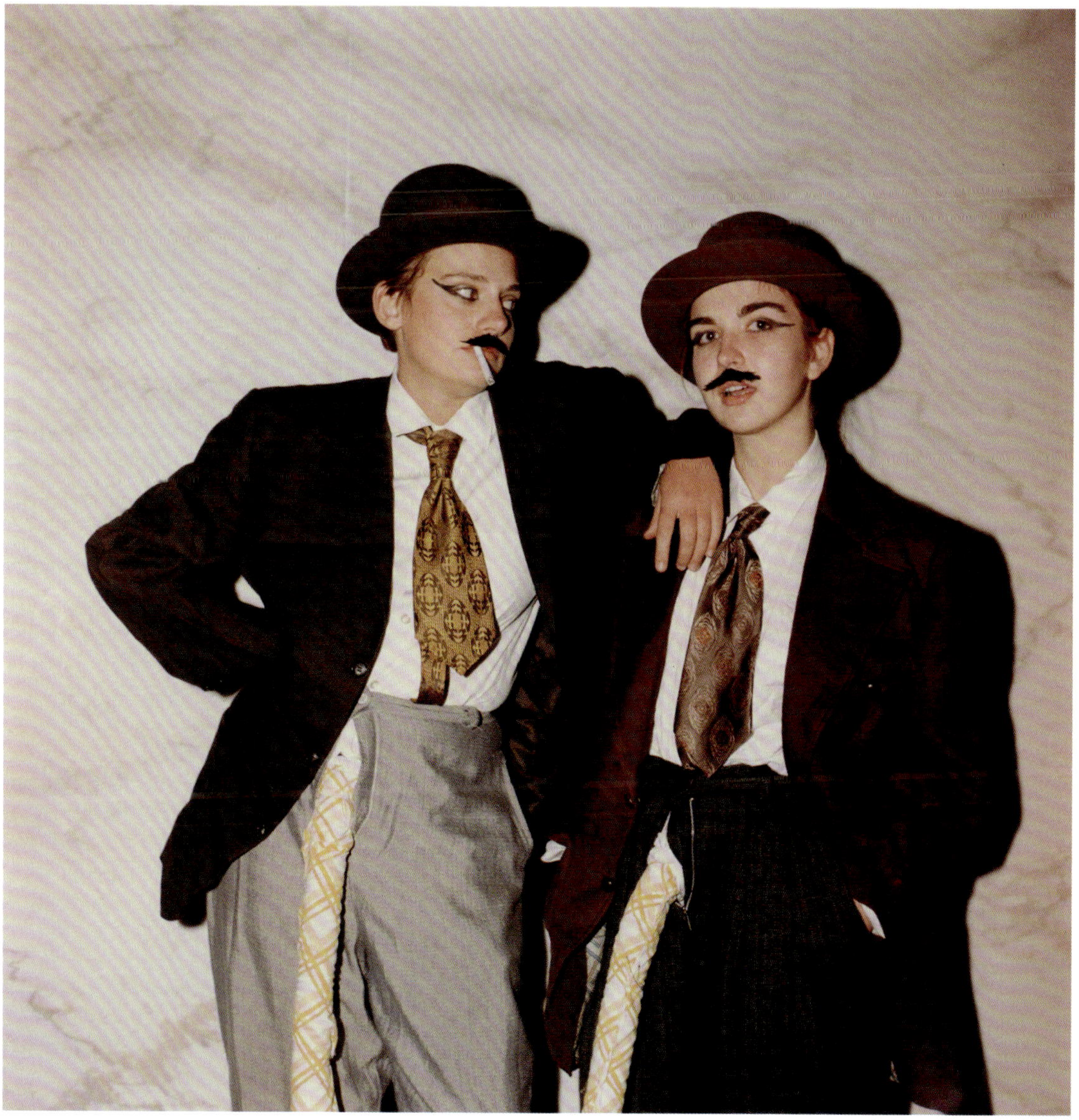

Waiter at Nedick's,
ca. 1970s–80s

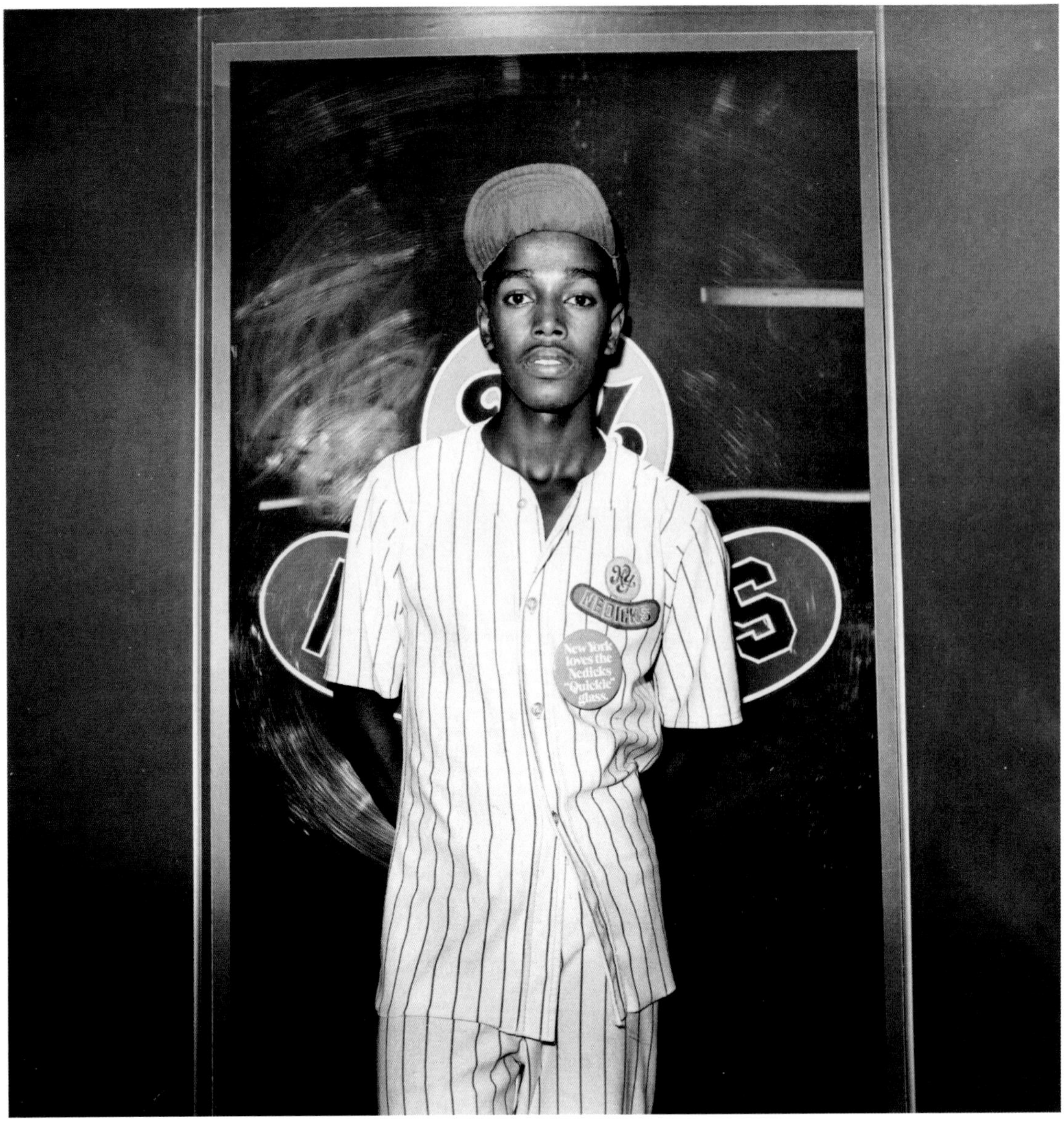

A sassy, decidedly queer image of two youngsters duded up in bowler hats, jackets, and ties, looking something like James Cagney, shows the playful side of Rivera's portraiture. In an undated photograph from another series, a Black man wears a striped Nedick's uniform (Nedick's was a food chain known for its orange drink and hot dogs), his lips slightly parted. The shades of nuance in his facial expression—a little guarded, yet serenely open—are a credit to Rivera's flair for intimating the complex inner lives of working-class people.

Much about Rivera's own life and work remains a mystery. Temkin hopes that the *Double Exposures* show, which coincides with Rivera's first monograph, published by Aperture, will encourage more scholarship, rather than serve as a final word. "She has a bit of slyness," Temkin said. "She has a very loving and sensual and sexual gaze, and you see that in the intimacy she establishes with the people she meets. Who is Sophie Rivera? In a way, I'm not even sure that this exhibition is going to answer that question."

Yxta Maya Murray is a novelist, law professor, and art critic based in Los Angeles.

Timeline
Photography & Magic

Colorful auras, headless figures, ghosts caught on camera: Photographers have long been drawn to the macabre and the occult. The press in 1839 called daguerreotypes "magic mirrors" and said that photographs appeared "as if by magic." After all, the medium developed during a time when stage magicians packed theaters and spiritualists, many of them women, promised contact with the dead. Ever since, photographers have sought to not just document the world but evoke a sense of wonder and spectacle that we continue to call magic.
—**Shana Lopes**

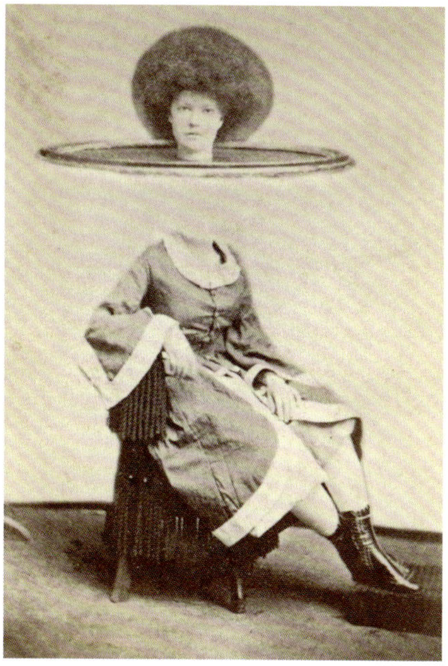

Among the strangest novelties of Victorian photography were disembodied heads—displayed on platters, tucked under arms, even juggled. By the 1870s, faux decapitations had become a popular amusement, captured in cartes-de-visite like this one.

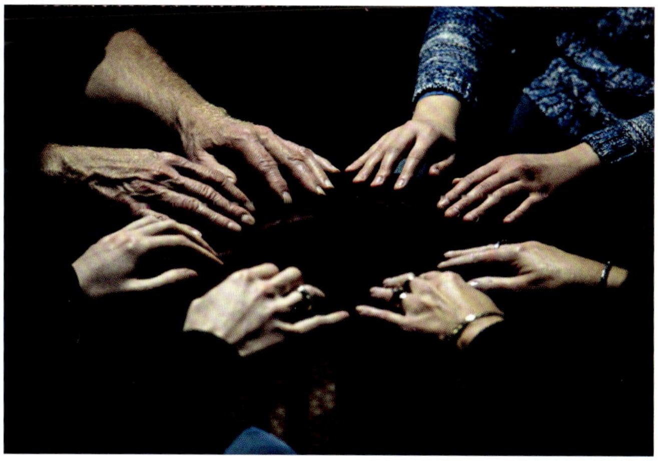

Shannon Taggart's long-term project *Séance* (2001–ongoing) centers on Lily Dale, New York, a small lakeside hamlet recognized as the world's largest spiritualist community. In this photograph of a table-tipping session, hands converge in darkness, echoing the intimate gestures of nineteenth-century séance circles. Such rituals often resurface in periods of collective loss, when grief sends people to mediums in search of communion with those who have passed.

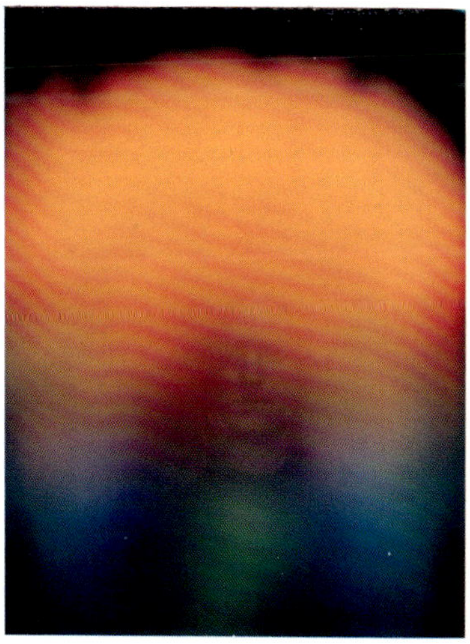

Between 2003 and 2004, Anne Collier brought various friends and fellow artists to a psychic shop in Oakland, California, to sit for what became more than forty aura portraits. Made with a modified Polaroid camera connected to hand sensors, these images claimed to reveal the sitter's energy as a cloud of surrounding color fields. Collier herself appears here in a self-portrait.

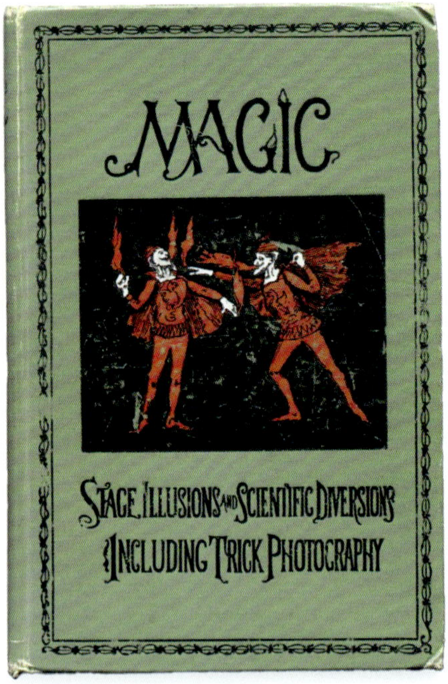

When Albert A. Hopkins published *Magic* in 1897, he entered a territory few had written about: the intersection of stage illusions and trick photography. Drawing on trade secrets extracted from prominent magicians, Hopkins described spirit photographs, multiple exposures, and optical curiosities alongside classic conjuring tricks. The volume reflected a key moment when photography, science, and theater overlapped under the guise of magic, and it quickly became a handbook for amateur magicians.

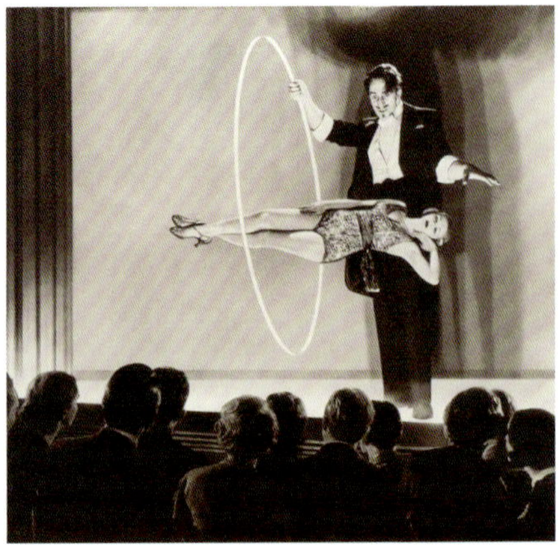

During the Great Depression, when people craved inspiration and escape, Camel cigarettes turned to magic to sell its product. The photographer Nickolas Muray staged dramatic illusions such as levitation and sawing acts for a national ad campaign that paired spectacle with the promise of pleasure.

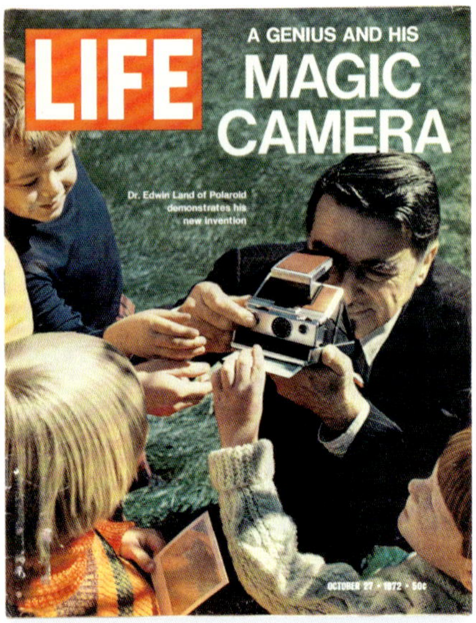

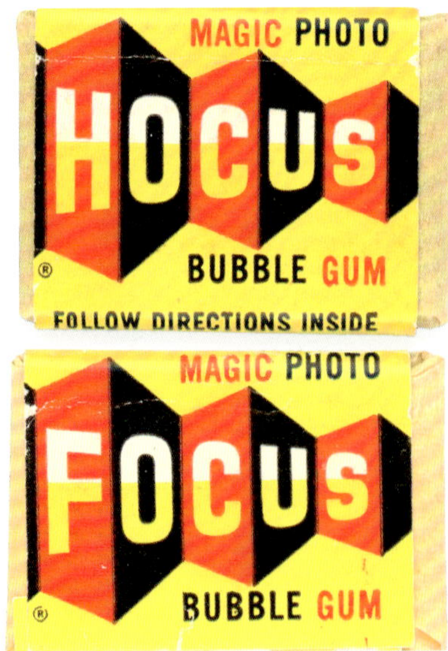

When Polaroid released the SX-70 in 1972, *Life* hailed it as "the latest piece of wizardry." Push a button, and in seconds the camera ejects a blank card that slowly transforms into a color photograph right before your eyes. For $180 (that's $1,395 today), consumers could own "the most complicated simple camera ever." Combining mirrors, electronics, and new film chemistry, the SX-70 turned instantaneity itself into what felt like a magic trick.

"Look, kids!! Magic pictures!!" So promised the tagline for penny packs of Hocus Focus bubble gum in the late 1940s. Each one contained a tiny card that looked blank until dipped in water and rubbed with the wrapper. In less than a minute, sports heroes, Hollywood actors, or Western gunslingers magically appeared. For a dime, children could order an album to hold all 126 photographs in the series.

See page 8 for image credits.

Shana Lopes is an assistant curator of photography at the San Francisco Museum of Modern Art.

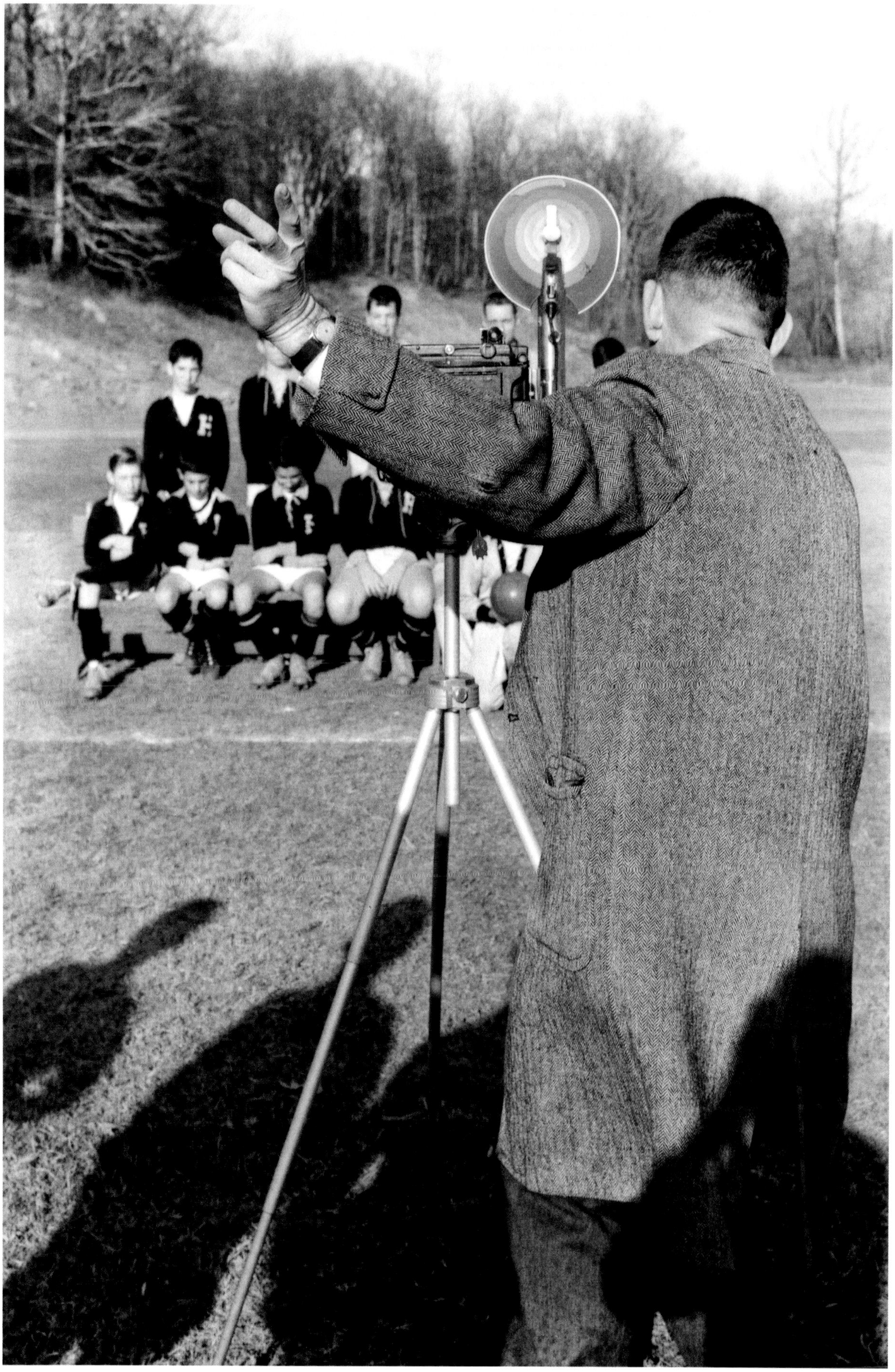

Notebook

A legendary photographer rediscovers one of his first pictures —and finds a world of its own.

Stephen Shore

This is a photograph of William Dexter, headmaster of the Lower School at Hackley, a boarding school in the Lower Hudson Valley that my parents banished me to when I was eleven. He's making a group portrait of the soccer team. Mr. D., as we called him, had an apartment at the end of my hall, where he had a darkroom. He knew of and encouraged my interest in photography and let me work in his darkroom. Up until then, I had only used my converted bathroom for processing and printing.

I made this picture in the autumn of 1960, when I was twelve, or perhaps had just turned thirteen. I took it with my new Nikon F. For the previous four years, I had been using a Ricoh 35 but had wanted a more sophisticated camera with interchangeable lenses. In January of 1960, my father made a deal with me—he'd buy me the Nikon I so wanted if I would get straight A's at school. So, for that spring semester, I studied diligently. This may have been the only semester in my educational career that I did so.

I recently published a book of photographs I made between 1960 and 1965, *Early Work*. And of the early work, this picture is the earliest. While I remember the events of my life that led to this photograph, and I know well the prints I had made of it, which I've kept in a box for decades, I have absolutely no memory of taking the picture. So, in a sense, I come to it as an observer, as I might view the work of a student of mine. The visual thinking that goes into making a photograph embeds itself in the image. It is there to be read. What I see in this picture is that its photographer, let's call him Steve, was paying attention to his lens's depth of field. Steve has chosen to put the soccer team a little out of focus, but still readable. This sets the stage for the picture while drawing the viewer's attention to the photographer in the picture, where the focus lies, just as his raised hand is directing the attention of the team.

I see Steve thinking about framing. The space he gave between the photographer and the frame seems carefully attended to. There is a sense of formal poise. The structure seems felt.

And it feels like autumn: the soccer team, the topcoat, the thinness of the light, the shortening days, and the lengthening shadows drawing the viewer into the picture and implying the invisible spectators witnessing this scene. And then there's Steve's shadow, camera held to his face, falling on the back of the photographer's herringbone topcoat. Twelve-year-old Steve certainly would not have known the word *metacognition* (the word wasn't even coined until more than ten years later), but he took a picture of a photographer taking a picture of a photographer taking a picture.

And I see something else. I see in this image an understanding of the gap, the lacuna, between the world of our experience and the world bounded by the four edges of a photograph. I see an understanding that a photograph's world needs to be complete in itself, separated to a large extent from its context. A world of silent description—description without explanation.

This writing began by giving the narrative context, the backstory, of this photograph. This story is relevant to me and to my memories and feelings, but the image needs to exist divorced from this context. When I wrote that I felt "banished" by my parents, you, perhaps, experienced a chain of associate thoughts. This image needs to exist divorced from this emotional context as well.

There is also a more significant, more all-encompassing context that is separate from the image. It's the world of our experience, three-dimensional, flowing in time.

Garry Winogrand wrote: "A still photograph is the illusion of a literal description of how a camera saw a piece of time and space." And what a camera sees is two-dimensional, bounded in space and bounded in time.

An aspect of the meaning of a photograph resides in the gap between our experience and how a camera sees—the image's silence. Advanced photographers understand this. They understand that while a photograph has its roots in the world in front of the camera, the picture they are making is a transformation of that world through the specific mechanisms of photography. They understand that they are creating something rather than reproducing something.

A photographer who doesn't grasp this, who hasn't internalized how a camera sees, produces what I think of as an illustration. They are hoping to illustrate, in a sense reproduce in attenuated form, the scene they see. They don't understand the lacuna.

The lacuna is the fundamental disconnect between continuous reality and photography's inherent constraints. Photography necessarily fragments: It isolates a rectangle from infinite space, flattens dimensional depth into a plane, prioritizes a single plane of focus, and freezes flowing time into a moment. These aren't technical limitations to overcome—they're the medium's defining characteristics. The photograph's meaning expands precisely because its temporal and spatial boundaries contract.

Because of the lacuna, a photograph can be alive and suggestive rather than closed and explained—simultaneously specific and universal, historical and timeless.

Stephen Shore, *Tarrytown, New York*, 1960
© the artist and courtesy 303 Gallery, New York

Stephen Shore is a photographer and the director of the photography program at Bard College.

Curriculum
David Benjamin Sherry

David Benjamin Sherry is best known for his vivid monochrome landscapes, each one a hallucinatory color field and environmentalist warning sign. A self-styled "nostalgic futurist," the Santa Fe–based artist builds on traditions of picturing the American West but adds a queer and sometimes sci-fi twist. A devotee of analog processes, he's hauled his 8-by-10-inch camera everywhere from Zabriskie Point to the melting ice sheets of Antarctica.

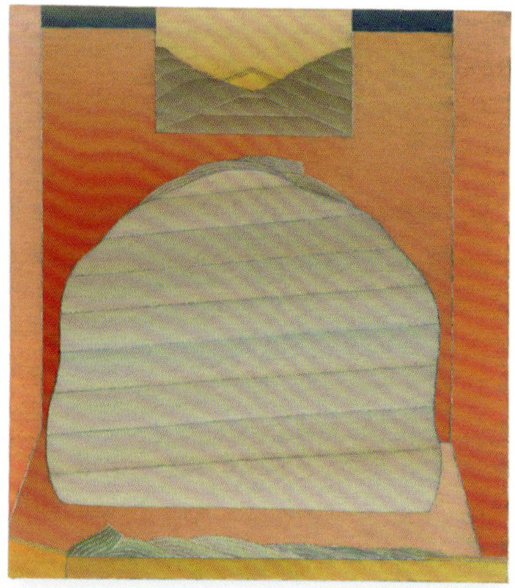

MIYOKO ITO
My first encounter with this late artist's canvases was at Matthew Marks Gallery in New York, in 2023. I had what felt like an out-of-body experience: tears, joy, laughter, nostalgia, sadness, and wonder all within the span of an hour. I left the gallery, only to return twenty minutes later to experience it again. The monograph *Miyoko Ito: Heart of Hearts* (2023) is the next best thing to seeing her paintings in person; I consult it daily for inspiration.

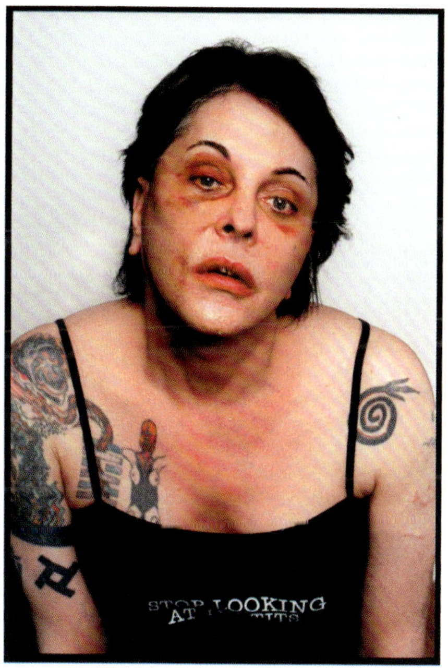

GENESIS P-ORRIDGE
Genesis P-Orridge's output alone is astonishing: more than one hundred albums with Psychic TV, nine with Throbbing Gristle, and countless artworks and writings. Every so often, I come across a track that resonates more deeply than it did twenty years ago. For instance, the cover of "Good Vibrations" recently played on repeat for a week in my studio, and I think I finally channeled its message. I met P-Orridge once and had the chance to tell h/er how profoundly s/he influenced my life and work. I'll never forget the look in h/er eyes. P-Orridge endures as a guiding spirit of perpetual transformation.

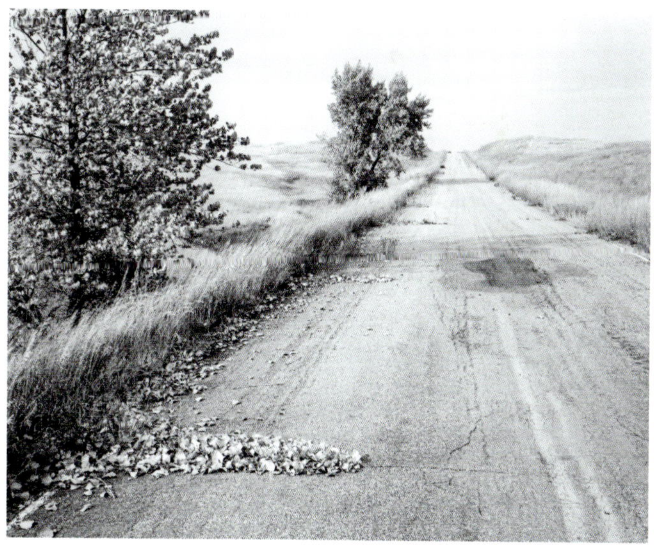

ROBERT ADAMS
If I could own one piece of art, it would be Robert Adams's *Nebraska State Highway 2, Box Butte County, Nebraska* (1978). Adams continually provides me with insights about light, loneliness, wonder, beauty, destruction, and our complex relationship with the American landscape. His books sit at my bedside and serve as my bibles. His photography is meditative—the quietness and subtlety are exactly what we all need more of in this moment.

See page 8 for image credits.

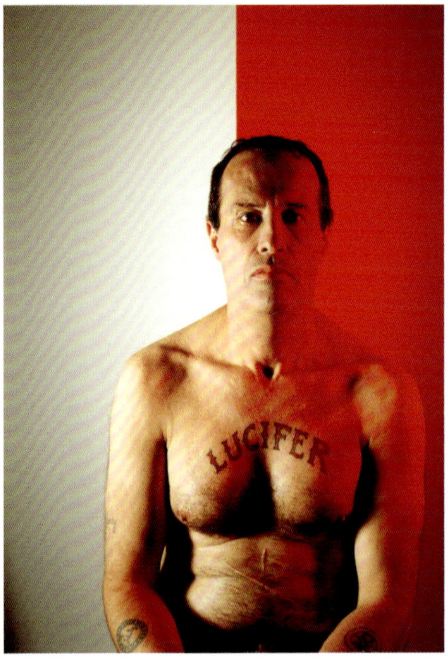

KENNETH ANGER
I don't know who I'd be without Kenneth Anger's work. I believe his films raise the dead and induce the viewer into an altered state—there's a transmittal of energy imprinted onto the celluloid. He broke ground using analog technologies, something I've always aspired to do. The films' subliminal undertones and "magick" have strongly shaped my world. Anger taught me about queer mysticism—his films embody it at their core.

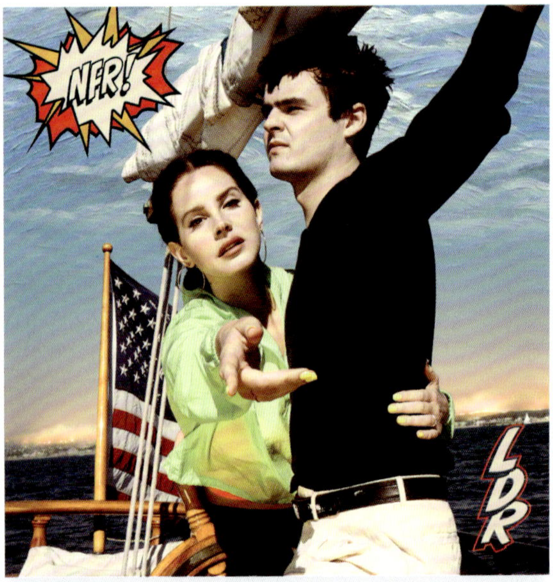

LANA DEL REY
I've been a Lanatic since the very beginning—and I finally have this in print! Lana Del Rey creates an auditory space unlike anyone else today. It's dark, elegant, wistful, smart, campy, and, at its best, feels like a morphine drip with the curtains drawn and the lights low.

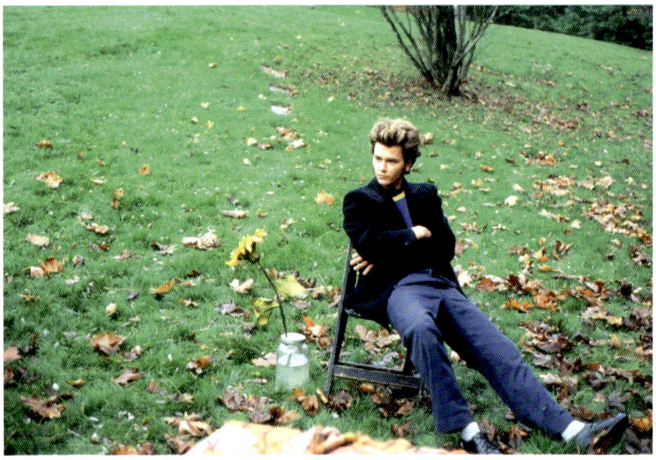

MY OWN PRIVATE IDAHO, 1991
Gus Van Sant's story of unrequited love between two beautiful (and stylish) male hustlers drifting through space and time under the spell of narcolepsy is my idea of heaven. Add a touch of Shakespeare, stunning cinematography, and on-camera interviews with real Portland street kids—what more could you want?

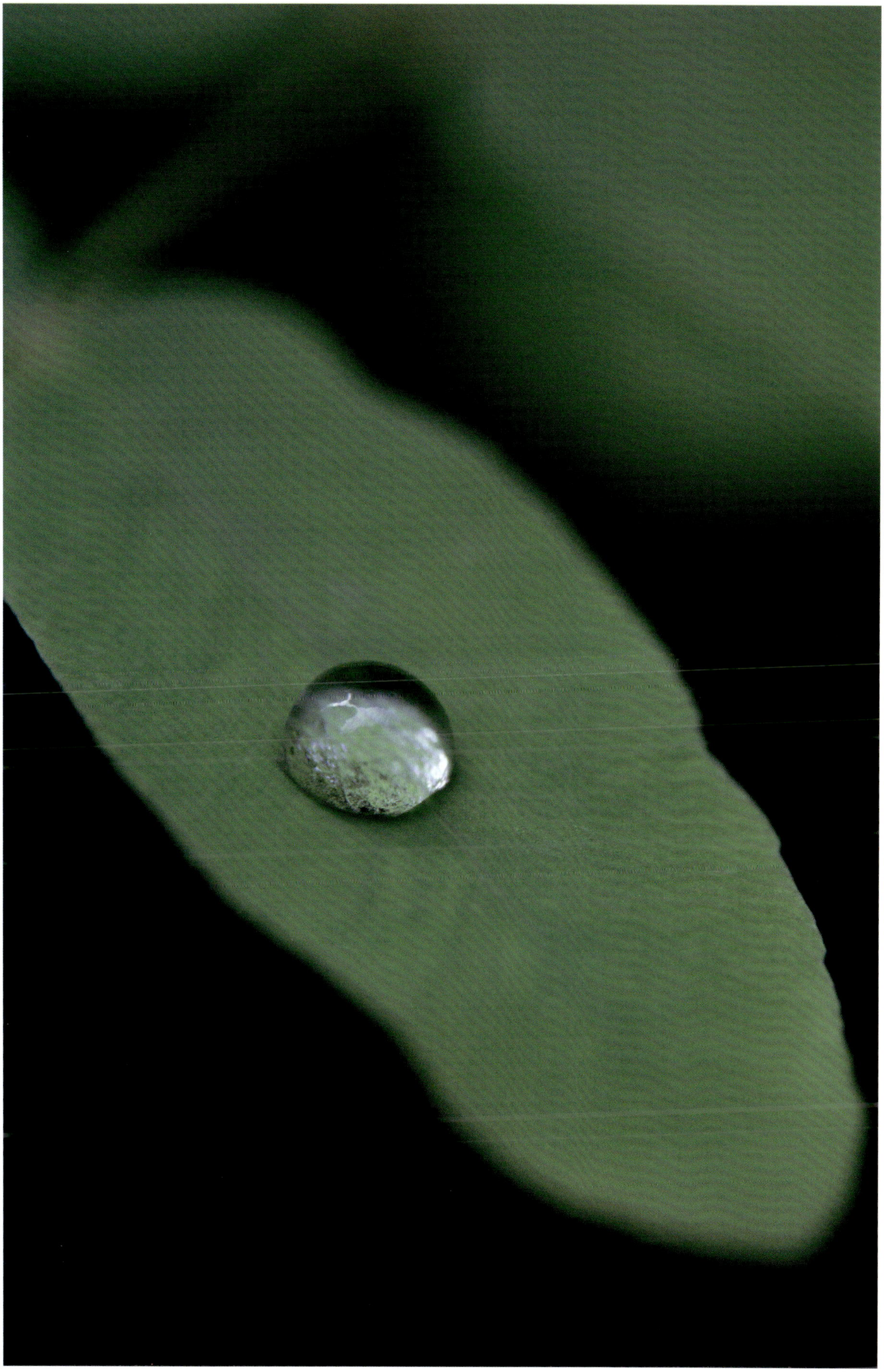

Rinko Kawauchi, *Untitled*, 2020, from the series *M/E*
Courtesy the artist
(See page 100)

The End of Nature?

"Nature, we believe, takes forever," wrote Bill McKibben in *The End of Nature*, the 1989 manifesto that rang the alarm on global warming. "Since even a million years is utterly unfathomable, the message is: Nothing happens quickly." McKibben's book made the case that, at least since the Industrial Revolution, humans had fundamentally altered their relationship to the environment. He argued that climate change had begun to shatter a collective illusion that nature was something separate from our species, and to diminish our false sense of permanency around the natural world.

Things are happening quickly. The science of global warming has since become mainstream, even as it is discredited and obfuscated by powerful interests. But the oceans rise, storm clouds gather, seasons blur. Strange weather and related cataclysms arrive with numbing regularity. Scrolling through social media during peak hurricane or wildfire activity becomes a form of voyeuristic disaster tourism.

The urge to turn the camera on nature is as old as photography itself. Anna Atkins created the first book of photographs, cyanotypes of botanical specimens, in 1843. And across its evolution, the medium itself has relied on resources and metals extracted from the earth. Photographers have long celebrated nature, elevating it to the sublime, often portraying it as a realm of spiritual or aesthetic contemplation detached from people. In 1968, the *Earthrise* image went viral before that concept existed, revealing both the isolation of our planet and its stark vulnerability. More recently, image makers have turned the degradation of nature into large-scale spectacles to shock and awe viewers from their complacency.

Almost four decades after McKibben made his plea, how might photographers address our ecological emergency? The artists in this issue work from the assumption that we are part of nature, belonging to something vast. They document endangered forests, chronicle bygone utopias and vanishing oases, and trace the entwined odysseys of butterflies and migrants. Along the shores of coastal Mexico, fishing towns exist at the mercy of the tides that give and take life with equal measure. There, a photographer embraces light leaks and imperfections that erode and distort the pictures—but somehow this helps us to see, and feel, the stakes.

The End of Nature claimed not that nature was literally ending but that its meanings were changing. With that in mind, this issue tries to picture how the world's deep, ancient rhythms have begun to shift under the weight of a climate we've inadvertently reshaped. As McKibben wrote, "The rain will still fall and the sun shine, though differently than before."

Tree of Life MITCH EPSTEIN

A photographer's journey to document the majesty of ancient forests hidden throughout the United States—before they disappear completely.

Dan Beachy-Quick

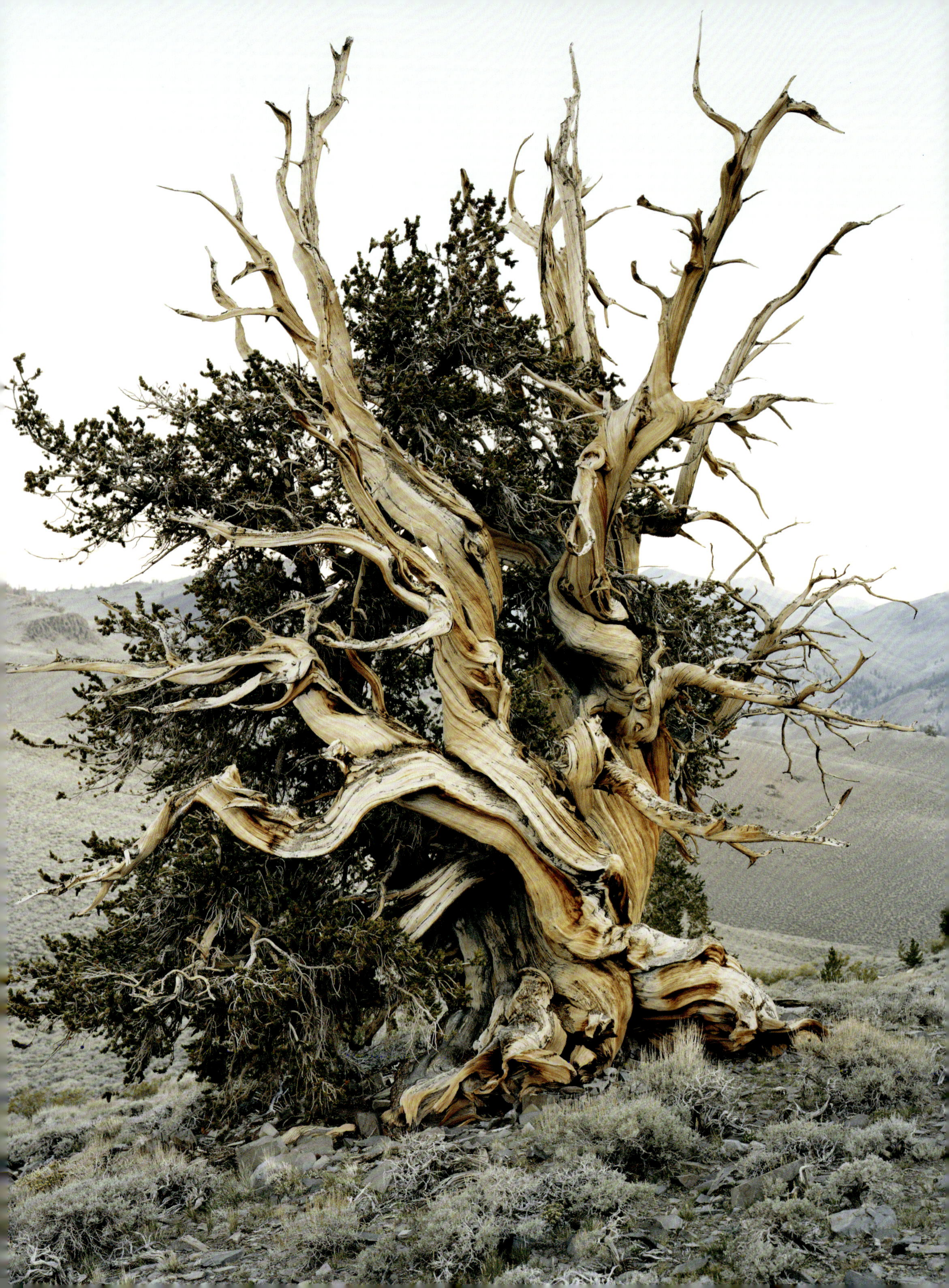

Page 33: *Ancient Bristlecone Pine Forest, California*, 2022; this page: *Ancient Bristlecone Pine Forest, California III*, 2023; opposite: *Sequoia National Park, California*, 2022

These images offer a complicated consolation to the ecological tragedies Epstein has spent his career recording.

OUR CHILDHOOD HAUNTS LATER HAUNT US. MITCH Epstein, as an adolescent bristling at suburbia's confines and the strictures of his boarding school, sought refuge in the Berkshire woods, in Western Massachusetts, getting high and getting lost in the forest of his childhood. Such wandering seeks no destination or arrival, nor is it exactly an escape. The hope is for a proper bewilderment that undoes the awful straight lines of familial and social pressures, those stifling forces of sturdy expectation. The woods are a space of initiation, redolent in the American imagination, where Henry David Thoreau built his cabin to live life more deliberately. Those early days in the woods, Epstein's induction into the wild care the forest provides, imprinted in him the fate of an inevitable return, no longer a teenager fleeing the limits of his world but the grown man returning as an artist who has learned to do this hardest thing: to see.

Epstein has recently been photographing old-growth trees around the United States, the latest extension of his decades-long preoccupation with an altered American landscape. There has been an evolution of life and learning to arrive at his current way of seeing. Like other photographers of his generation, Epstein took workshops with Garry Winogrand, the celebrated street photographer. "He taught through silences," Epstein remembered. "He refused to reassure you. He wanted you to think for yourself, see for yourself. He never talked about meaning. It was enough for him to say, 'There is nothing as mysterious as a fact clearly described.'" Leica point-and-shoot in hand, framing the world in order to ponder it. Being in the world proved the proper education, more so than art school. The 1980s

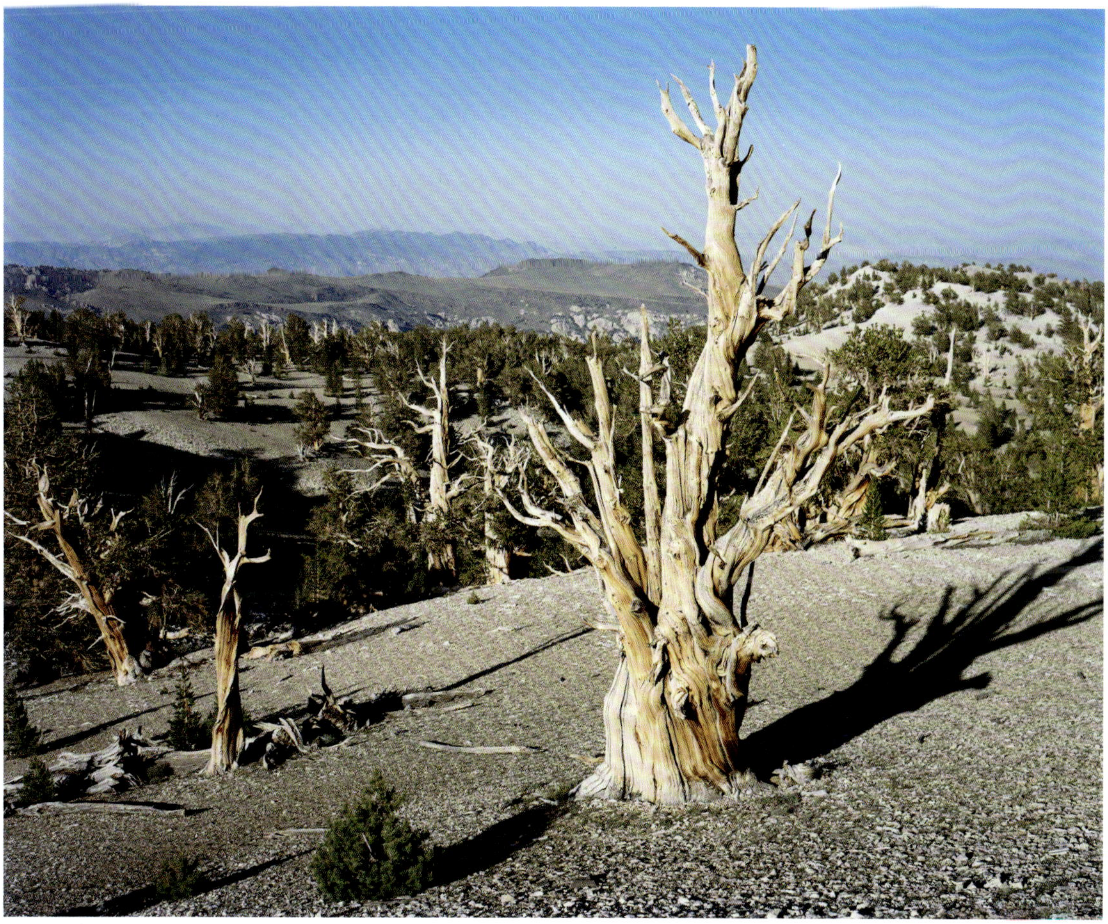

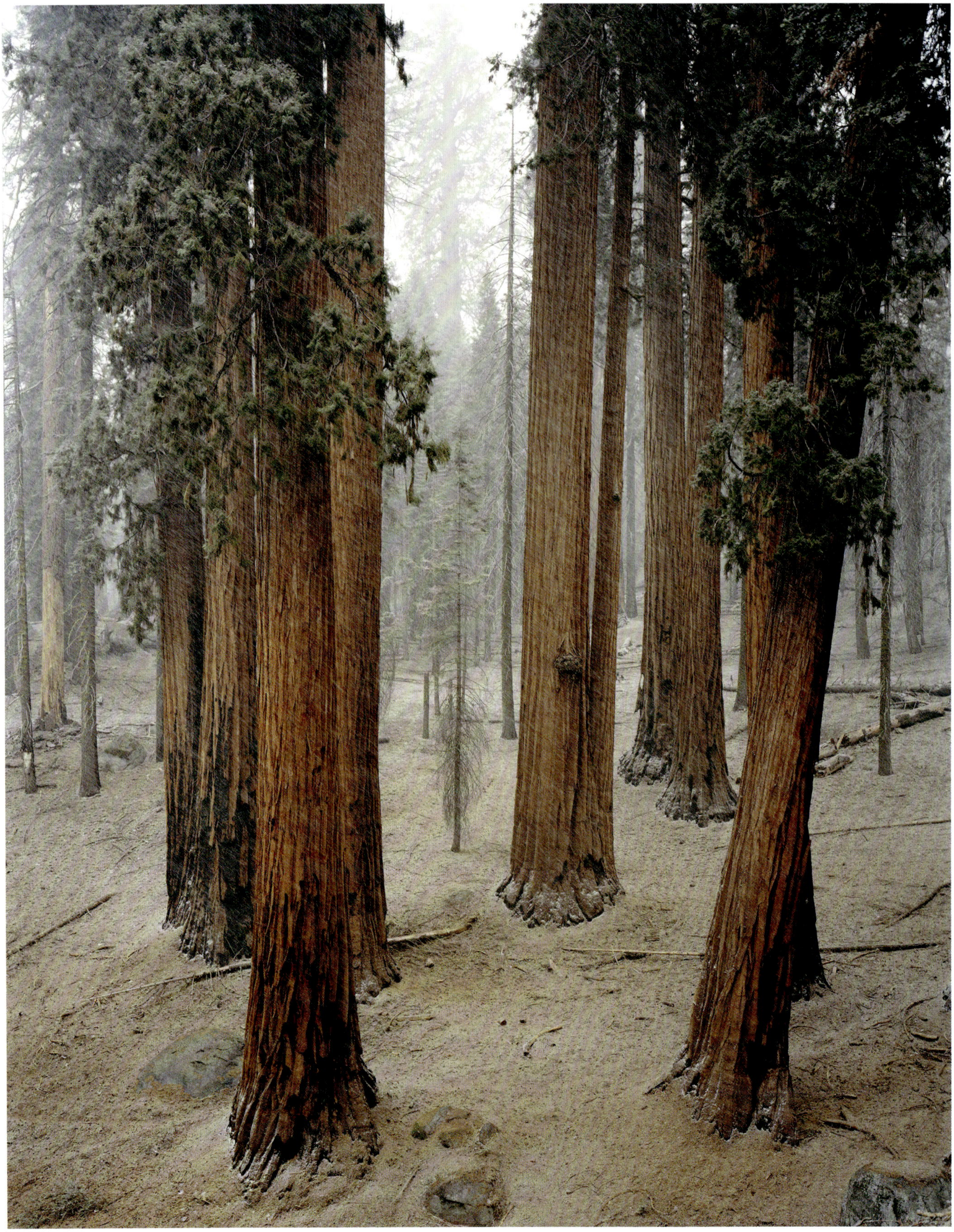

took Epstein back and forth to India. In the 1990s, he traveled to Vietnam to reckon with the ongoing reverberations of US political history. He would return to the United States with new eyes, a stranger's eyes, and an understanding of the camera as an ethical tool.

Strange eyes see in strange ways. In 2003, an assignment from *The New York Times* sent him to Cheshire, Ohio, a town in the death grip of the American Electric Power company. The assignment turned into years of investigation—crisscrossing the country, making photographs, using a large-format camera—that questioned the American dream, primarily in terms of the huge amounts of fossil fuel it took for the dream to come true.

Better than a dream come true is waking up from the dream—tuned to a different harmony, awake to the *fact clearly described*. This would culminate in the project *American Power* (2003–9), which pictures oil fields in Texas, where derricks tower in the shadows of wind turbines, and the Alaska Pipeline, where tourists exit buses to touch the nation's metal artery. In the paranoia of post-9/11 America, taking photographs of a coal plant beneath the dark hood of a camera whose accordion lens stretched out toward the smokestack brought attention from police and FBI agents. The scrutiny shifted his work to direct activism. He produced billboards with photographs documenting the environmental cost of our lust after power and comfort, juxtaposing pictures with quotes from the poets, thinkers, and activists who have sought to shake us from our slumbers.

Thoreau wrote in *Walden*: "To be awake is to be alive. I have never yet met a man who was quite awake." We spend most of our lives wiping away the sleep from our eyes, adjusting our vision to the daylight that shows us a miraculous world of so many troubles the glare nearly blinds even as it astounds. Artists give us the waking eyes we need to see, and Epstein, now in his seventies, has spent a lifetime with a camera tracing the ways in which a picture's composition might usher us into ethical realization: "Just as form and content are inextricably linked in photography," he said, "so is aesthetic judgment inextricably tied to moral clarity in our complex world." In the pandemic lockdown, when life quieted into the local, he learned that Massachusetts still contained pockets of old-growth forest, ancient woods Epstein assumed had long been logged away.

"I was particularly awed by the eastern white pines, most of which were not technically old growth but still significant for their stature and history, given that most white pines in New England were cut for sailing masts, first for the British navy and then the American navy and shipping industry," Epstein said. Those same trees, significant to many Indigenous tribes, kept a living root in Epstein's mind, helping him imagine the old-growth forests of precolonial Massachusetts. Not only the pines took hold. "I was also struck by sugar maples," he said, "which have enchanted me since childhood for their sweet syrup and expressive form." The woods tell the story of economy's hubris, the majesty of a white pine turned into martial masts. Long a collaborator by nature, Epstein contacted the old-growth ecologist and author Robert Leverett, who, with his wife, Monica, took Epstein—tripod and camera lugged along—up the Mohawk Trail to encounter the ancients.

Serendipity turned into patient years hiking into deep woods, climbing up to alpine heights in California. Bristlecone pines grow near tree lines, and lungs gasp thin oxygen to reach them, heartbeat so loud it deafens the ears. But it's a height from which one can take in the vista of a world, of a life. Take the

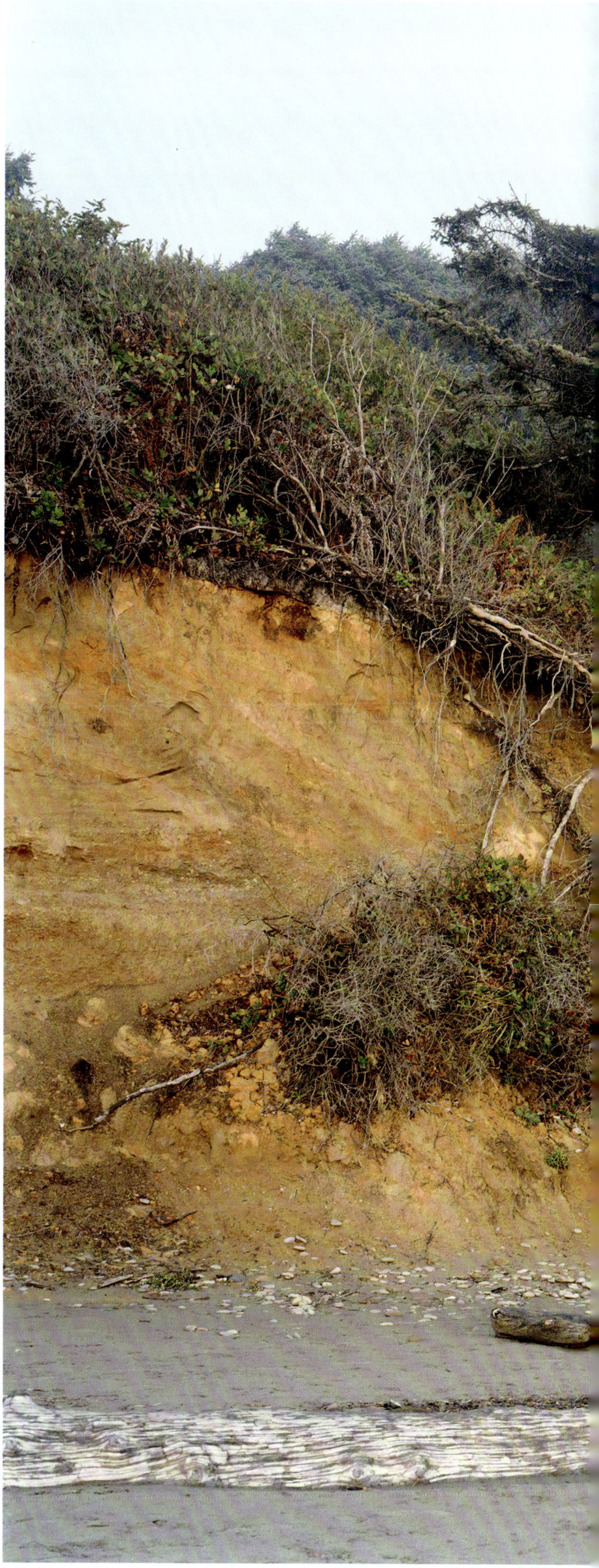

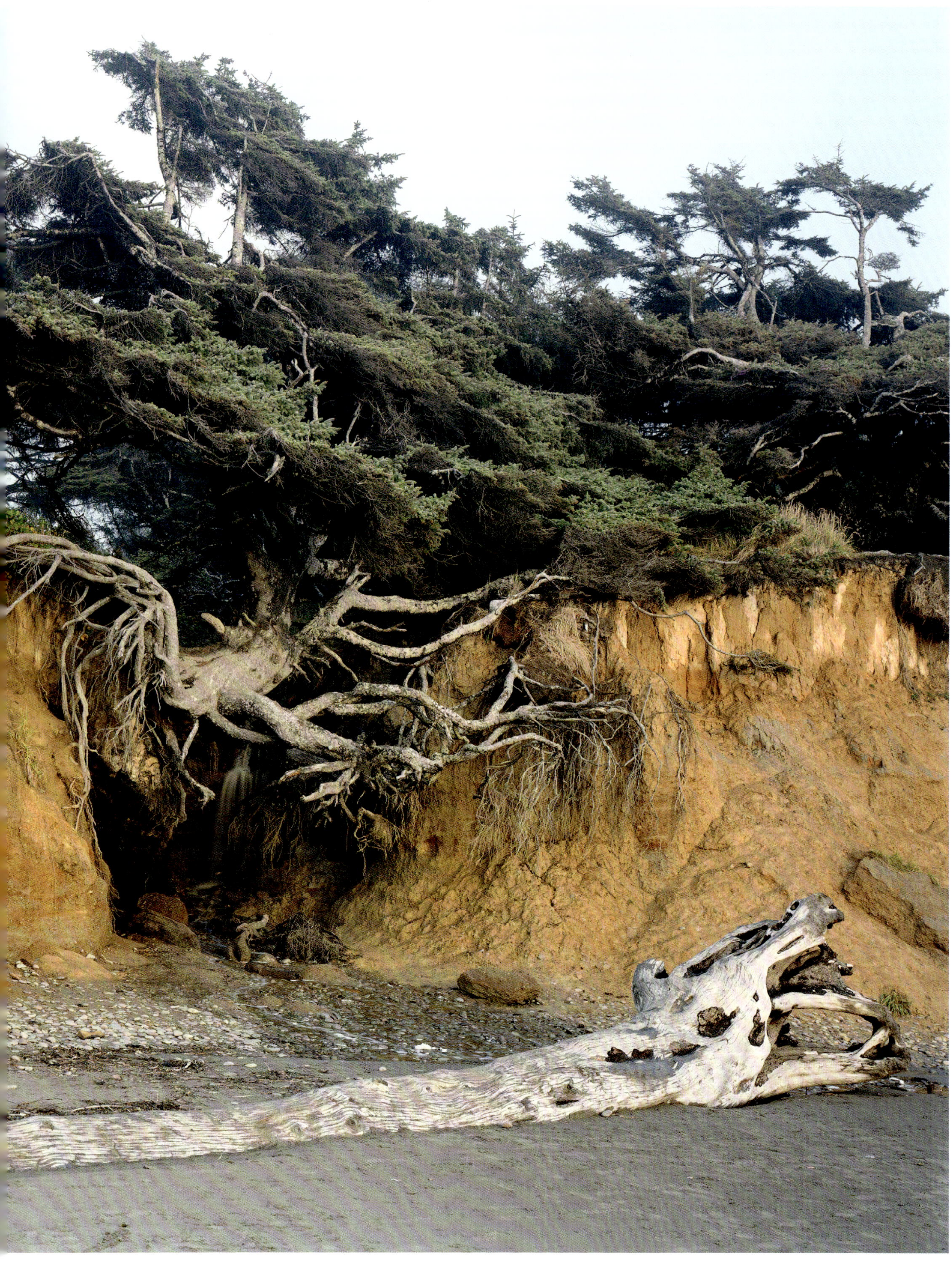

Previous spread:
Sitka Spruce (Tree of Life), Olympic National Park, Washington, 2021

This page:
Sitka Spruce, Hoh Rain Forest, Olympic National Park, Washington, 2017

Opposite:
Hoh Rain Forest, Olympic National Park, Washington III, 2017
Courtesy Steidl Publishers and Yancey Richardson Gallery, New York

Epstein has long traced the ways in which a picture's composition might usher us into ethical realization.

photograph of the singular bristlecone pine caught in first light, dead branches torquing upward in a gesture painfully human, desperate prayer or helpless plea, though the tree isn't dead at all—the green needles' dark nimbus promises that the sap which has flowed in the tree for as long as five centuries will still flow now. Here is a tree that could have been a sapling, or could have been two thousand years old, when the ancient Greek philosopher Thales claimed that "life and death are one." The tree seems proof of the paradox. This tree, and the other bristlecones Epstein photographed, exists in time at such a scale it feels nearly cosmic and offers, if not a reprieve, then a complicated consolation to the ethical quandaries and ecological tragedies Epstein has spent much of his career recording, pondering. Here is a tree that grew a cone before a single iron rail ever vibrated with the steam engine thundering down it, reached skyward long before a plane's contrail marred the blue with its straight line, a living proof of a *before* that can almost make you believe in an *after*.

The 8-by-10-inch camera Epstein uses allows him to angle the lens. The image he sees on the ground glass arrives as our vision does—though our mind corrects the bafflement—upside down, a disorientation that attunes him to the formal revelation of the tree he's observing. The results, printed at a size (58 by 72

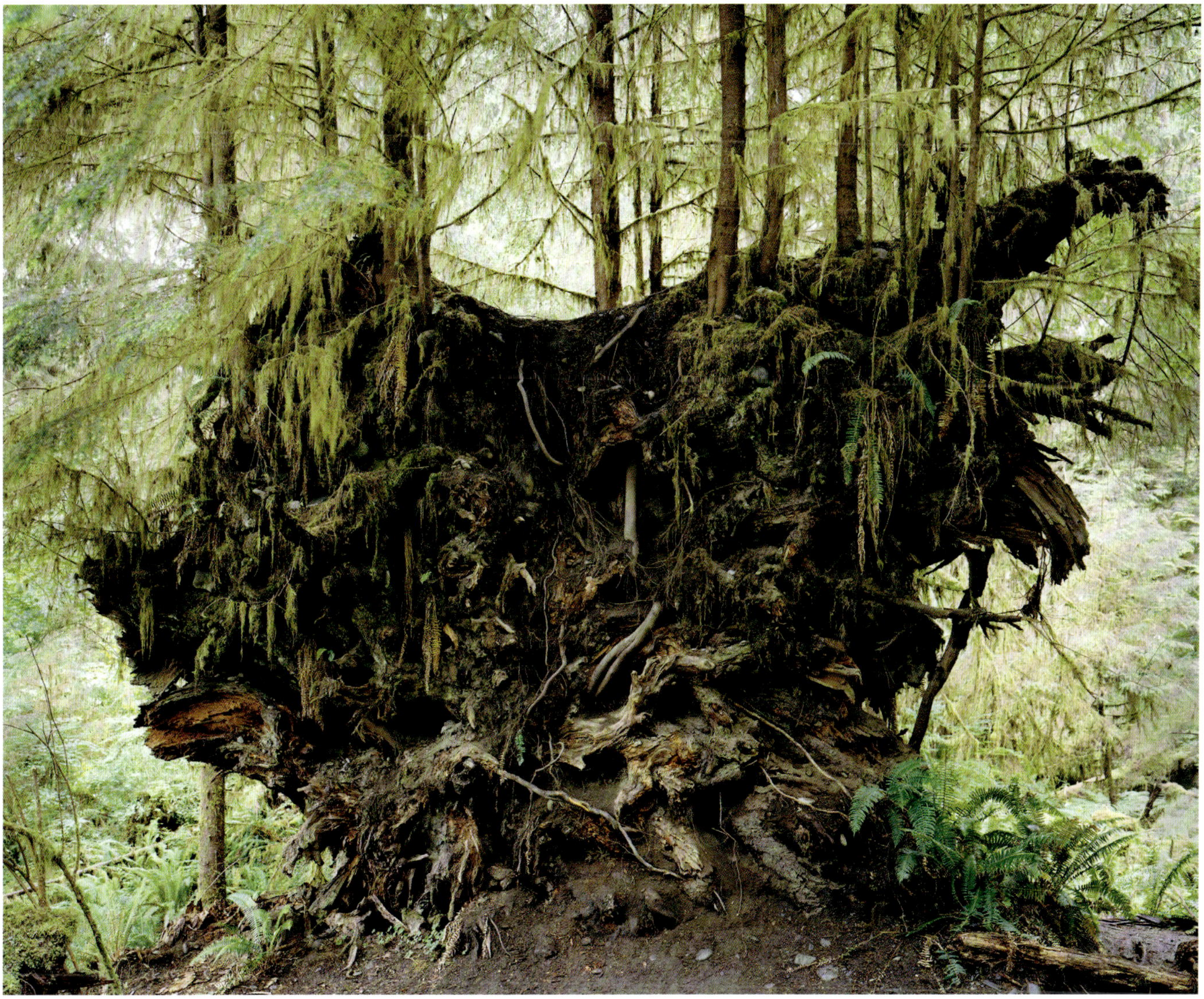

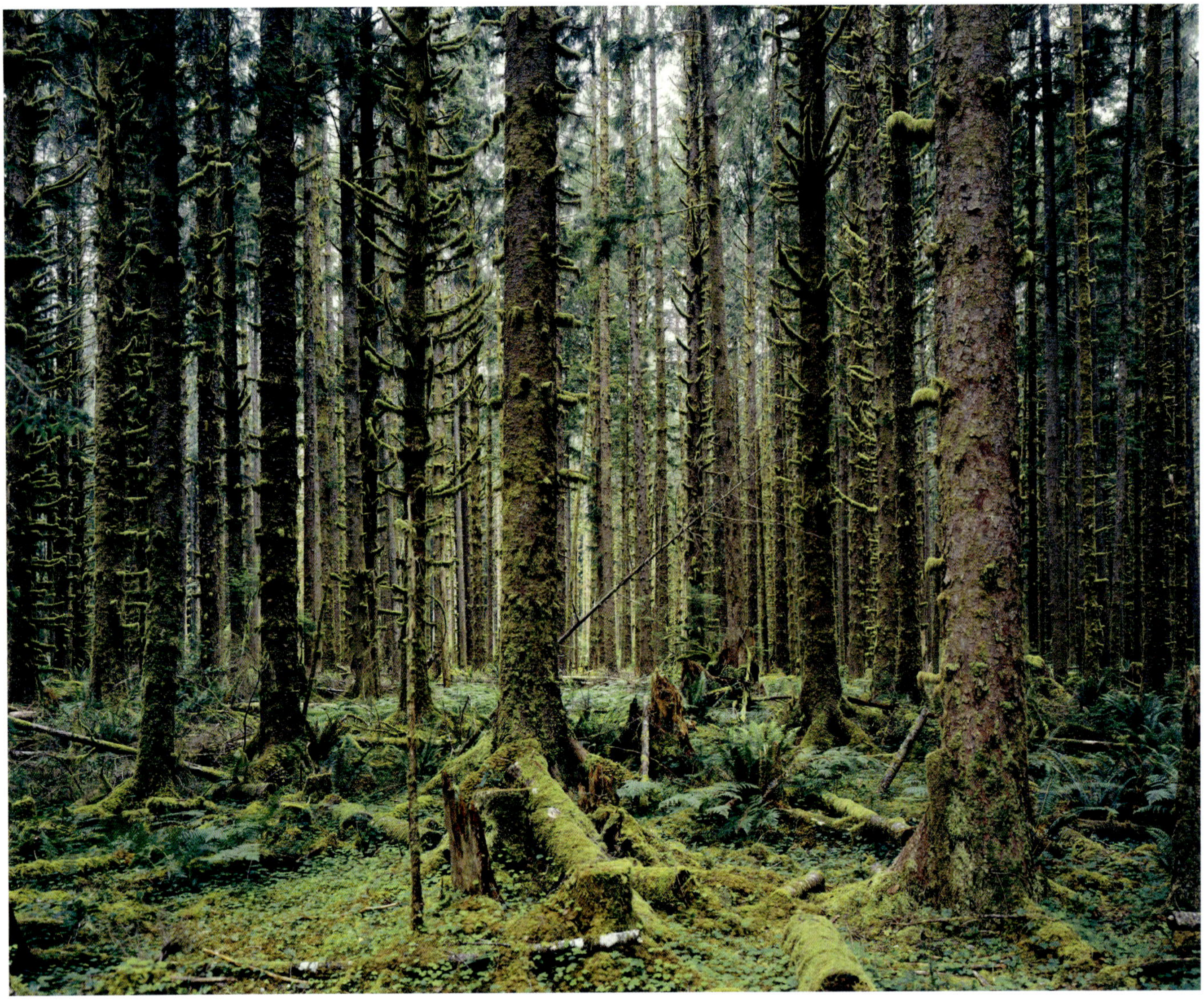

inches) that mimics our own stepping into the wilderness, feel part Taoist meditation, part cosmic iteration. As Epstein said, "The picture is more made than taken."

The statement might help us understand what we're looking at, more collaboration than instantaneous document. A trust that the tree speaks to a shared condition—a world, vast time, our mutual mortality. Why must joy and sorrow, hope and fear, so intermingle that we cannot tell one from the other? Epstein's photograph of a Sitka spruce bridging a runoff arroyo feels not an answer but a description of the problem—one crosses the gap, and thrives, if one can. To flourish above the abyss. Another photograph offers itself as demonstration of the same principle—an old-growth tree uprooted, the maze of the root system revealed, a death, yes, but a death that convinces life to begin again. Epstein has made himself an initiate to such mysteries, and so invites us to join the ancient cult. It's in every photograph here. The sudden snow squall in the sequoia copse, the elder trees standing like *The Burghers of Calais*, and a sapling nearly hidden by the mist, growing up in their midst, the sacred in-between. The girth of the burls exceeding the limits of the trunk, as if life makes one command: exuberance. The ferns among the Sitka, insisting that the oldest time still chants its now, now, now.

The ecological urgency here speaks quietly to us, as perhaps true emergency must—when we ourselves are the threat we must confront. Epstein offers us a subtle reminder of our own bewildered nature, driven toward the beauty of the earth that our own desire endangers. Here in this world, where Eros is cosmic law, dawn light behind the tree turns the sky into a blank page, and the bristlecone pine—half dead, half alive—is a figure of us all.

Dan Beachy-Quick is a poet, essayist, and translator.

M'hammed Kilito
Oases

I was eighteen years old when the desert first revealed its paradox to me. Driving toward the Sahara dunes in Morocco, I saw the endless beige monotony interrupted by a streak of green, a river of date palms stretching thirty miles along the road through the Ziz Valley. This was Tafilalt, one of the world's largest oases. Through the car window, I saw a miracle, an island of life defying the logic of the sand.

But miracles, I eventually learned, are fragile. Two decades later, in 2019, I returned to find the palm grove scarred by fire, a symptom of the rising heat and structural drought plaguing the region. Where I had once seen a haven, I now saw charred trunks and people rebuilding with what little they had. That image stripped away the romantic myth of the oasis, revealing its desperate reality. It was the catalyst for *Kafila* ("caravan" in Arabic), my ongoing project documenting oases across Morocco, Tunisia, Egypt, and Saudi Arabia.

I often ask myself how we should view these ecosystems today. Historically, they were destinations, vital anchors where trade flourished and civilizations took root. Today, they are uncertain sites of transition. I have come to view oases less as refuges and more as surviving landscapes and points of departure for those forced to leave, as the twin forces of accelerating climate change and destructive human activity systematically dismantle these ancient sanctuaries that sustained communities and cultures for thousands of years.

Tunisia's Chenini oasis, one of the rare places where the oasis meets the sea and the mountains the desert, should be a paradise. Instead, in one of my photographs, the horizon is broken. Fishermen cast their nets, dwarfed by the smoking chimneys of the Groupe Chimique Tunisien. Installed in the 1970s, this phosphate complex drains the aquifer and poisons both air and sea.

The human cost is etched into the posture of an elder I photographed in the scrubland in Gabès-Chenini. Dressed in a formal suit and a traditional red chechia, he maintains a dignified pose, yet he stands on ground rendered toxic by pollution. Despite this, resistance takes root. The Association de Sauvegarde de l'Oasis de Chenini has worked for decades to preserve the land. Inspired by the agroecology pioneer Pierre Rabhi, who worked with farmers in the 1990s, the community is turning to traditional wisdom to heal the soil, proving that working with nature is the only viable defense against its collapse.

I traveled to Egypt's Siwa oasis looking for solutions to salinization, but found another beleaguered landscape. In a closed basin below sea level, trapped water has turned the soil into a sterile, salt-white crust; the oasis is drowning in saltwater. One photograph focuses on a rusted sign reading "Mountain of the Dead." While it marks a sprawling system of ancient tombs—a testament to Siwa's Pharaonic and Amazigh heritage—the sign feels like a dark prophecy for the land itself.

To visualize this tension, I photographed a driver crossing the salt lake in a tuk-tuk. Wrapped in a traditional white thoub and turban, he looks straight ahead, but the rising brine surrounds him. It is a metaphor for the oasis inhabitants: navigating an uncertain future while the oasis is slowly submerged.

Ultimately, *Kafila* is not a eulogy. In the lush pockets that remain, we witness the persistent labor of care. The image of two farmers standing amid dense greenery reminds us that the oasis is an intentional act, a garden sustained by the precise balance of water, soil, and human effort. Relying on the endurance of these communities is no longer enough. Farmers may embody a model of coexistence with nature, but their efforts, along with those of researchers, residents, and local grassroots initiatives, cannot indefinitely resist the escalating industrial and climatic pressures surrounding them. Through the lives and words of those who dwell within them, these ecosystems make visible an undeniable truth that extends beyond the desert to the fate of the entire planet. Without a profound systemic reckoning and a genuine commitment from global leaders, the oases could disappear, and with them, we risk losing one of humanity's ideal models of sustainability.

M'hammed Kilito is a Moroccan photographer and National Geographic Explorer.

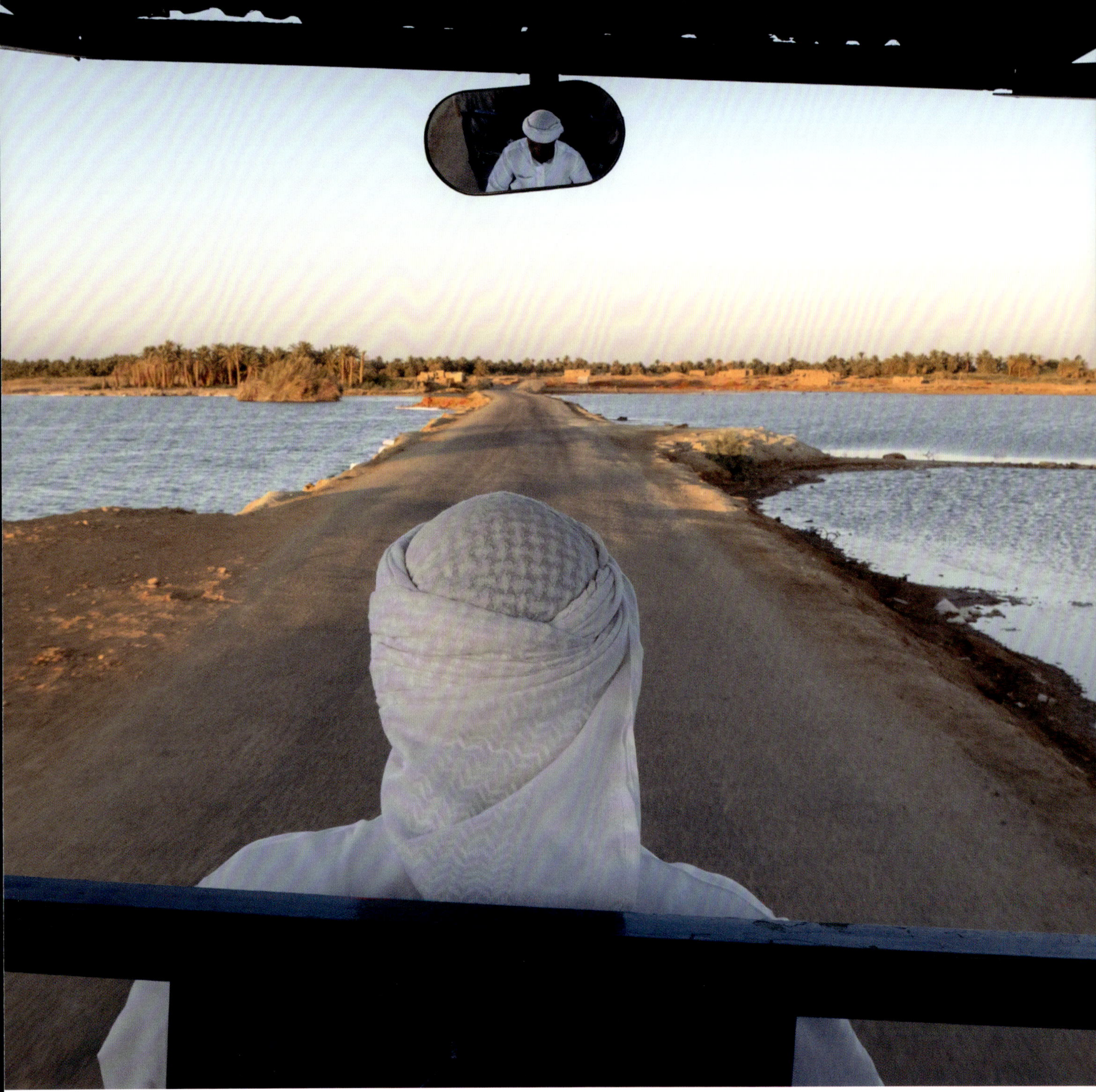

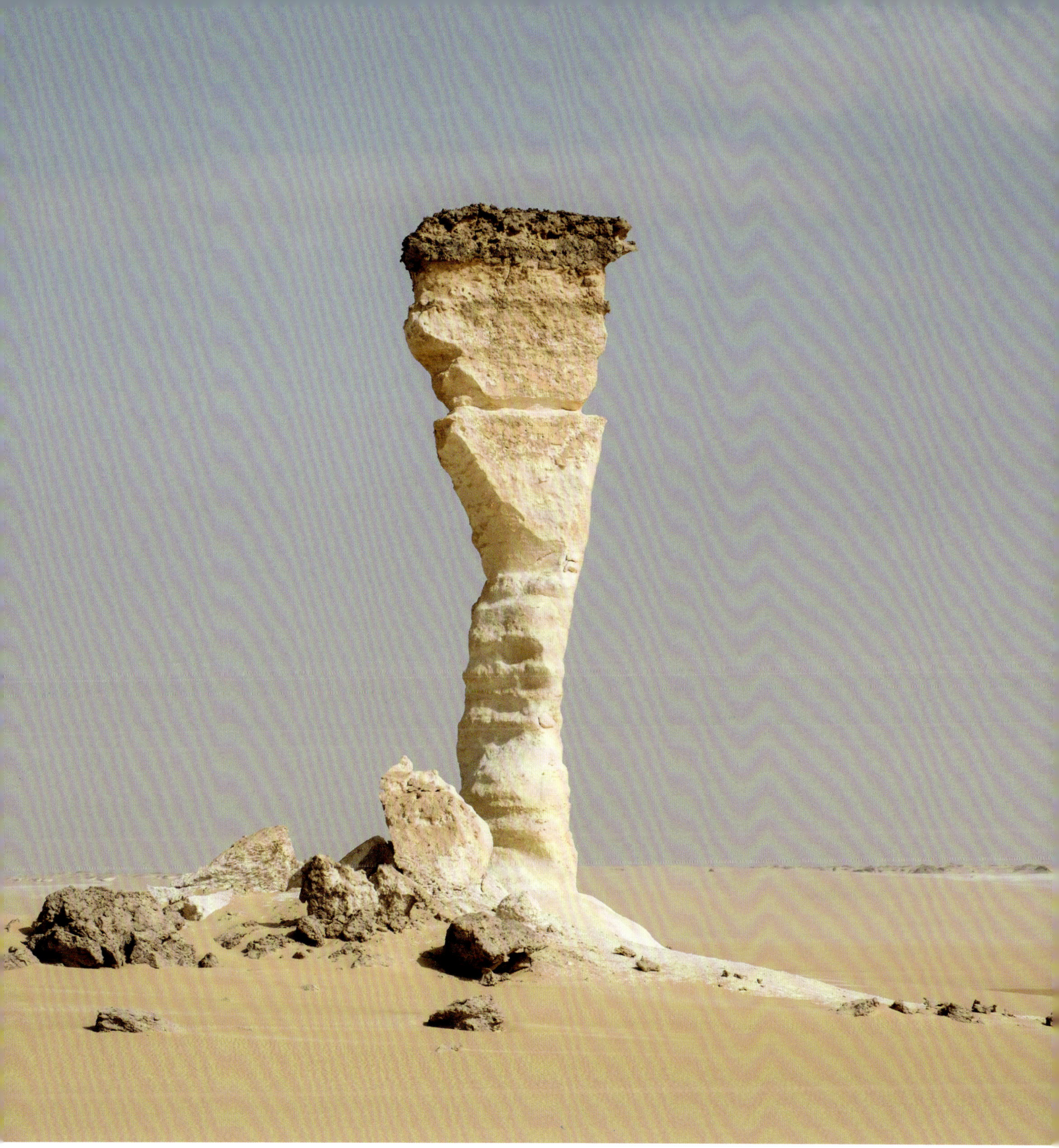

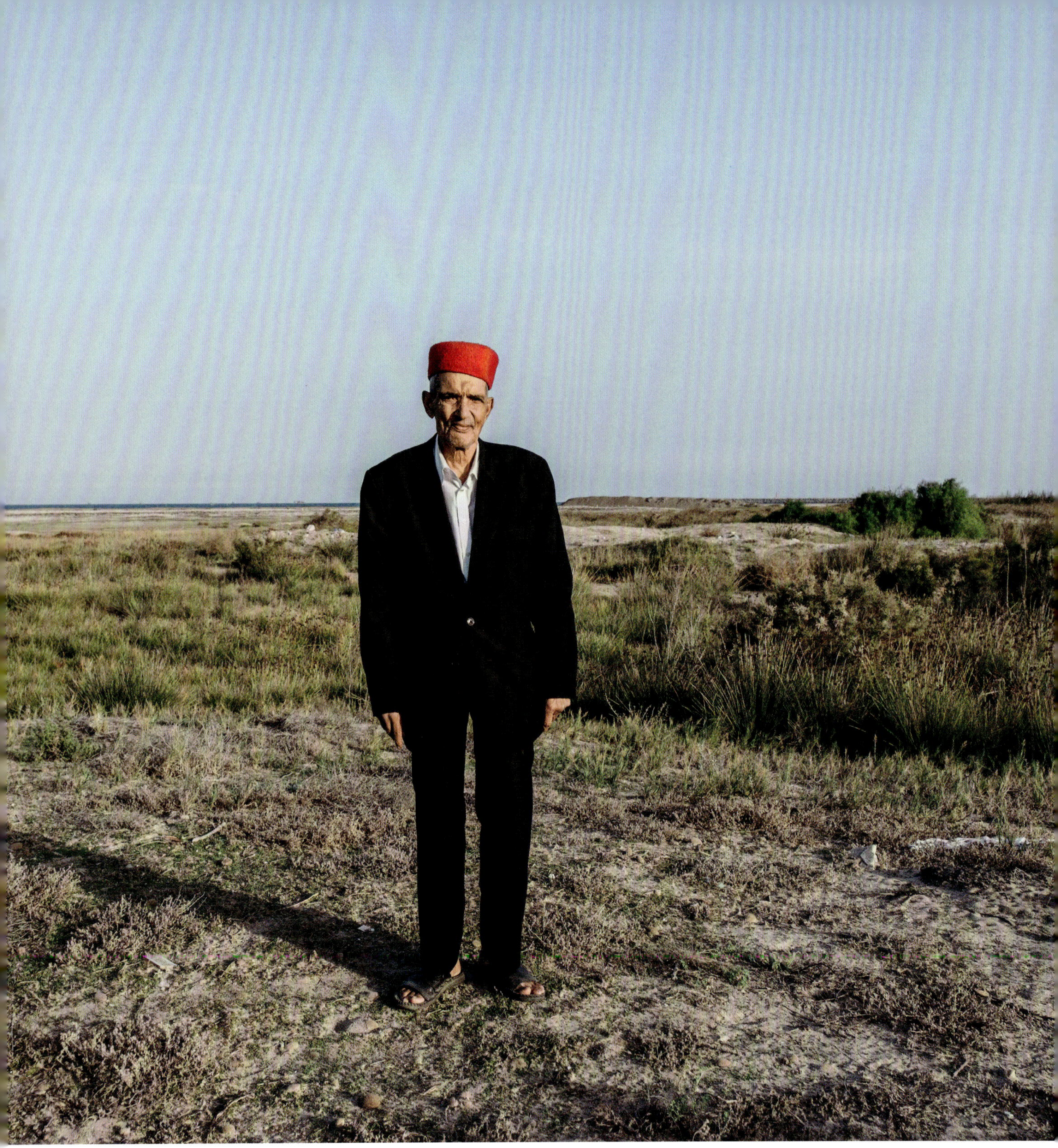

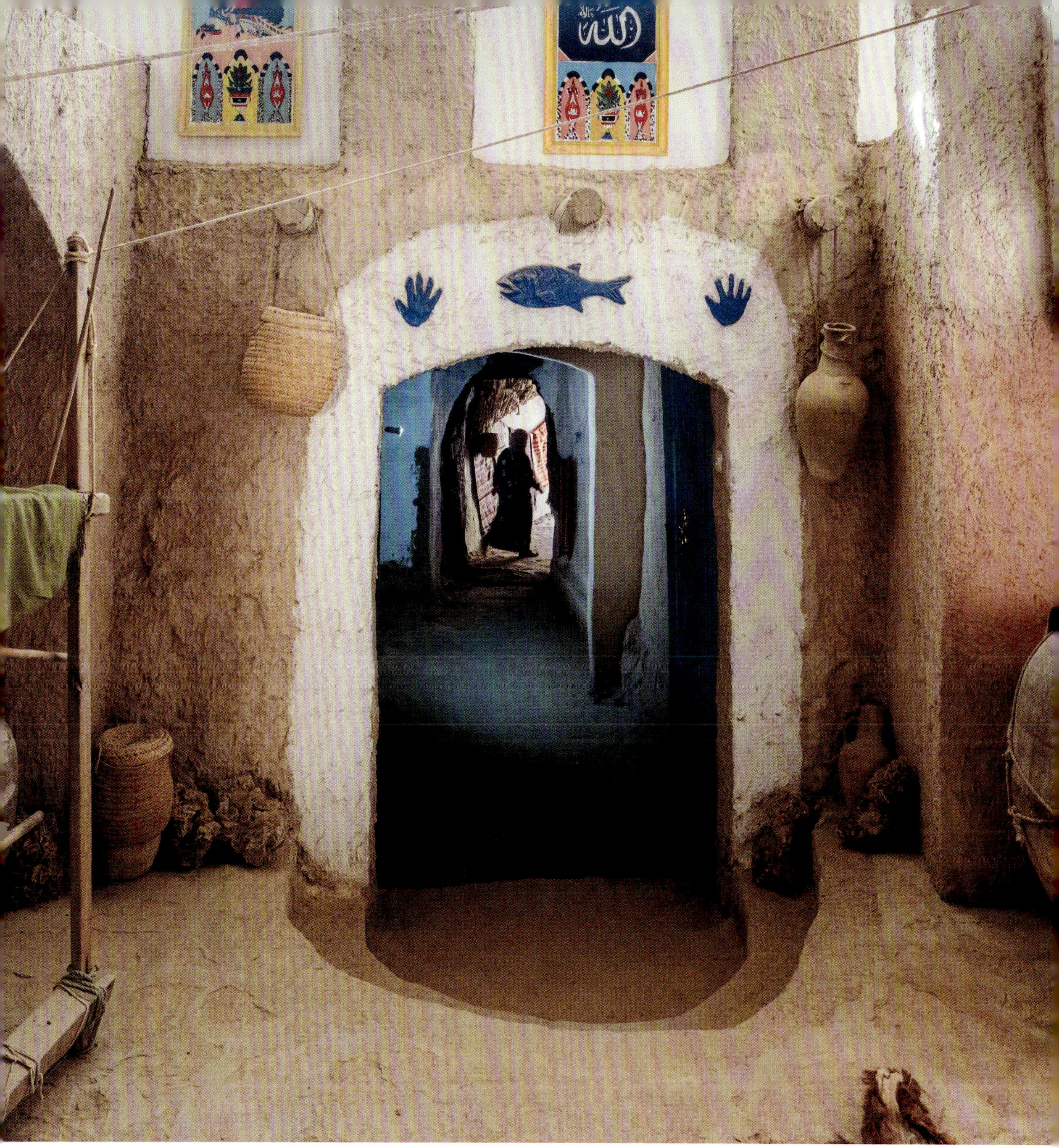

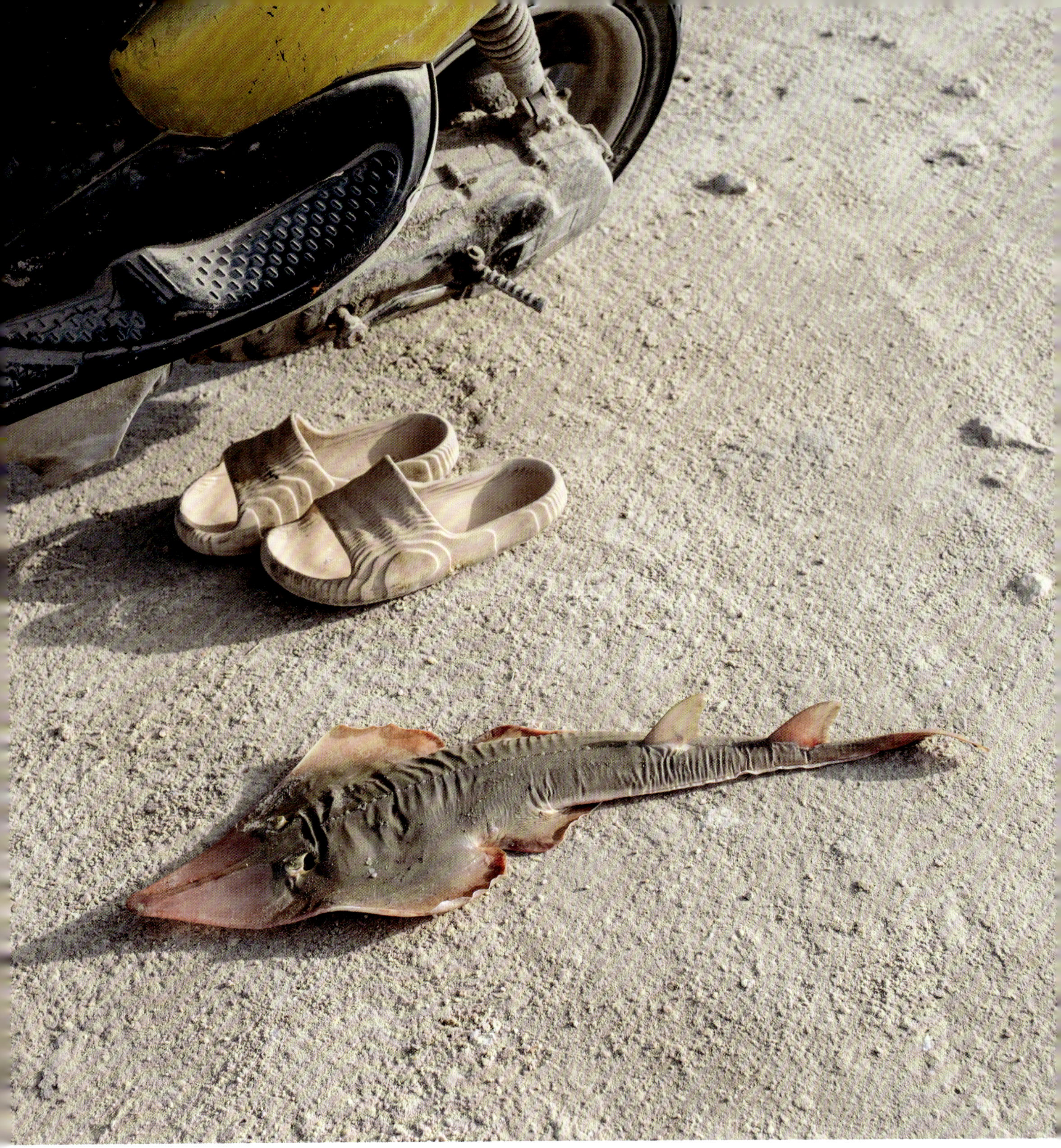

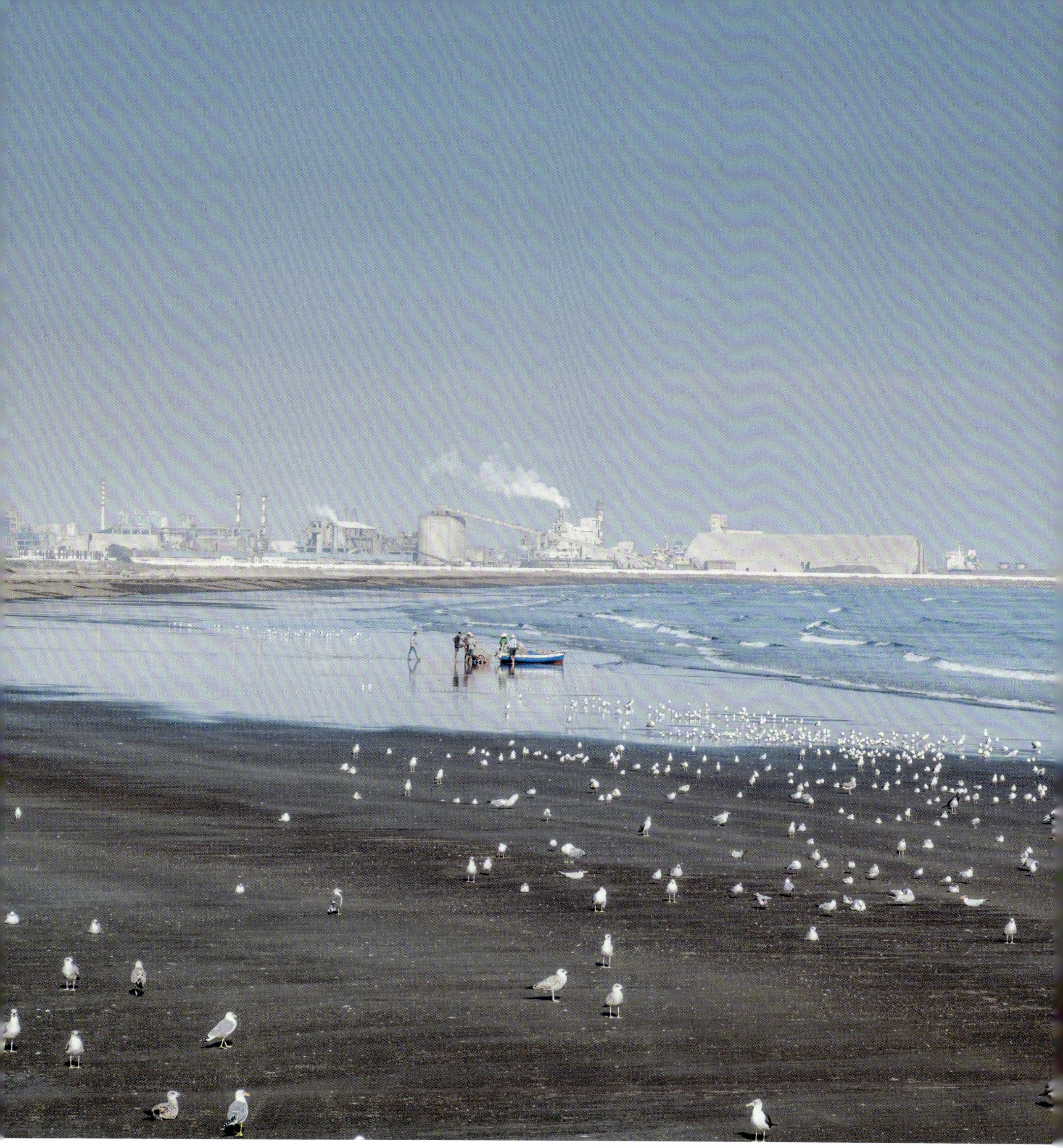

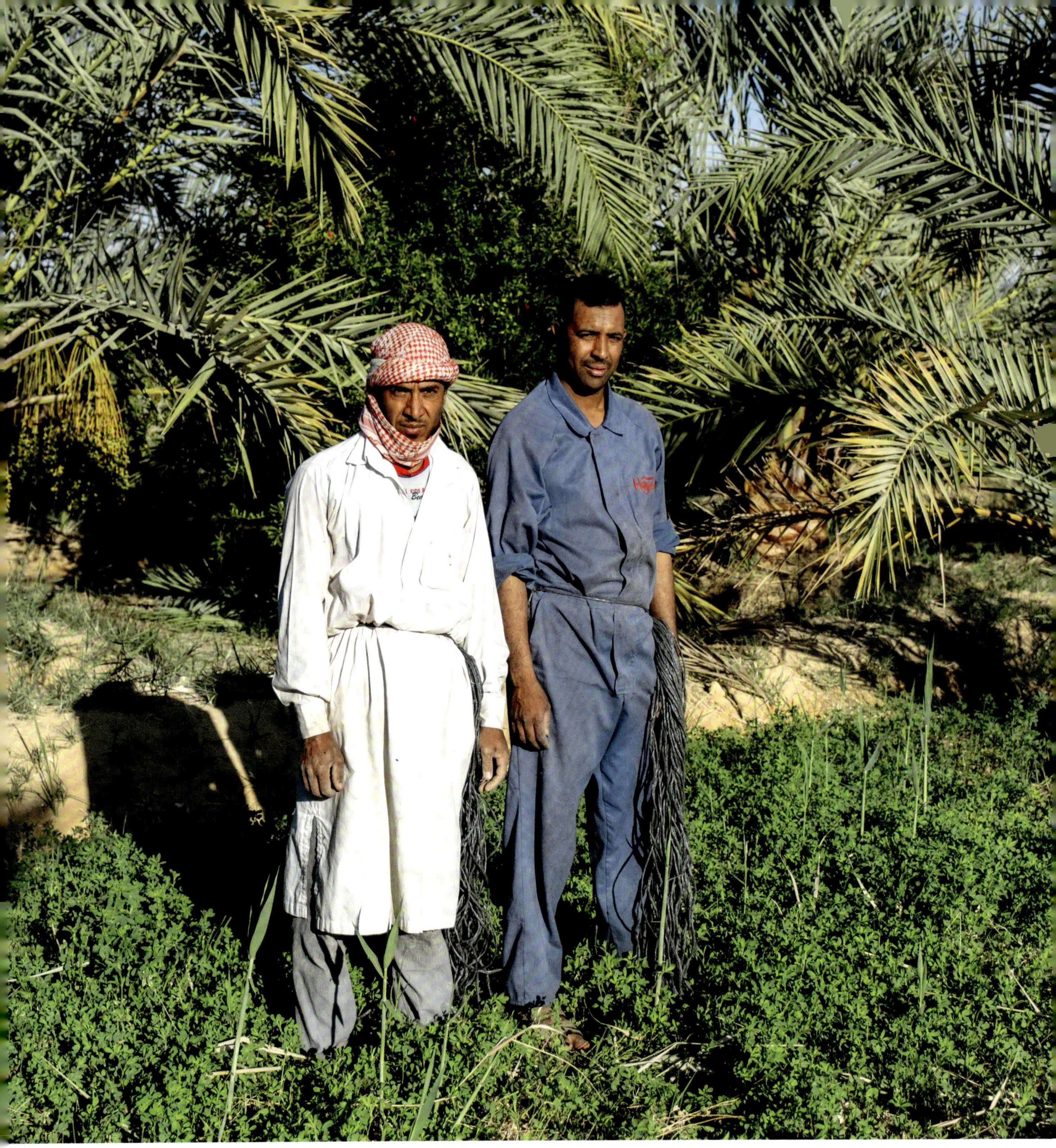

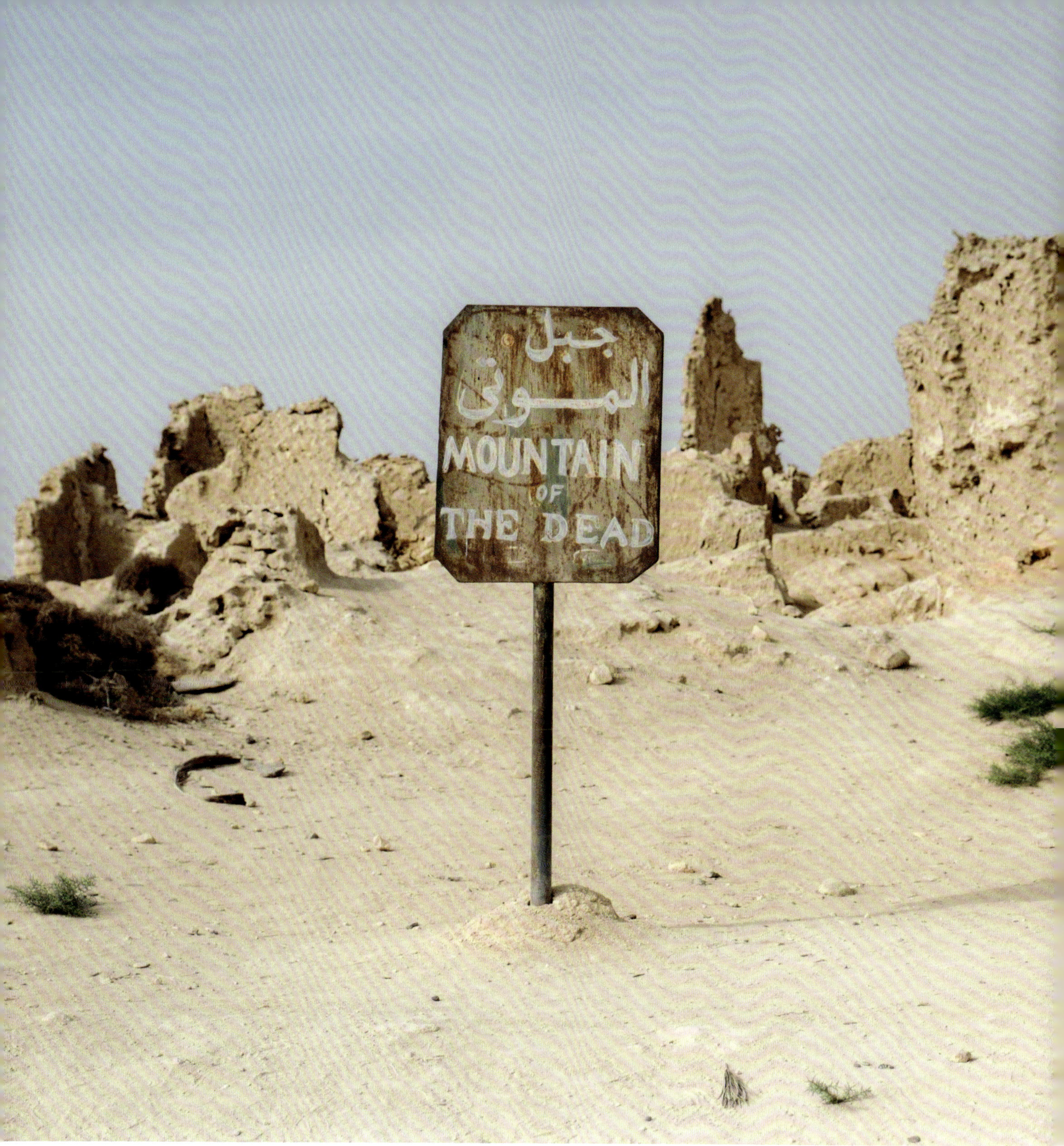
جبل
الموتى
MOUNTAIN
OF
THE DEAD

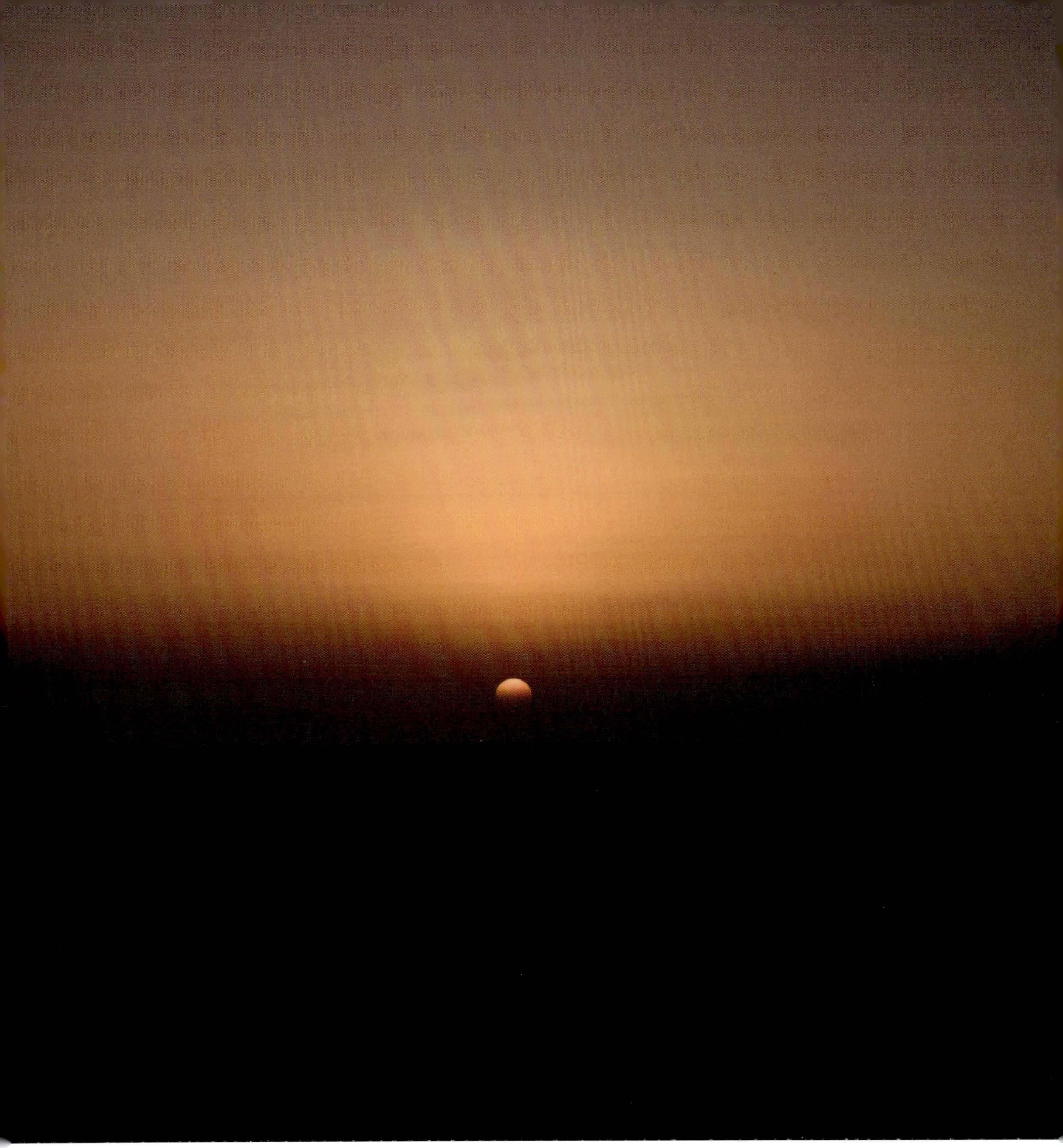

Pages 41–42, 47–49: Siwa Oases, Egypt, 2024; pp. 43–46: Chenini Oases, Tunisia, 2024; from the series *Kafila* (2019–ongoing)
Courtesy the artist and supported by the National Geographic Society

César Rodríguez
Flood Zone

Elisa Díaz Castelo

Almost nothing is visible. We're inside a house, it's true. We can tell by the walls, the decorations, the window, its translucent curtain. But a thick, external light renders much of the picture illegible. "Too much light," wrote Octavio Paz, "is like too much shadow: you cannot see." A vertical strip of it spills, searingly, onto a wall adorned with family photographs.

No one has a face in César Rodríguez's image of an expansive domestic interior. In its one unmarred fragment, a woman crosses the room, turning her back to us. She seems to be looking for something that has dropped to the floor. But there is no floor. The house is flooded, and the woman wades through the water as it devours her feet, rises above her ankles. She searches for something down in the shimmering liquid, or the water's gravity beckons to her, as it beckons to us. A flooded house. The stuff of dreams. But this is no dream.

The woman is named Elizabeth Cruz. The house belongs to her mother, Sofía, who lost almost everything in the 2024 floods that devastated the Valle de Chalco, on the outskirts of Mexico City. This municipality is built on the bed of what was once a lake. When anomalous summer rains overflowed the sewage system two years ago, the rain and wastewater rose over three feet high. Motorboats roamed the streets. Many families lost all they had.

Rodríguez has spent the last five years visiting communities affected by rising sea levels. He makes contact with their inhabitants and keeps in touch, chronicling their dispossession. The ongoing series, titled *Cuando hay luna llena, la marea sube* (When there is a full moon, the tide rises), began in 2021 as a commission from the Norwegian Red Cross, who sent him to document areas in the Mexican state of Tabasco that were suffering from coastal erosion. He visited Sánchez Magallanes, where he learned about the fishing village El Bosque. "I was told about a town that had completely disappeared," Rodríguez said. "I grabbed my things and went to see it." It's the first community in Mexico to be officially defined as displaced by climate change.

The primary victims of climate displacement in Mexico are, like in El Bosque, coastal, Indigenous, and rural populations already vulnerable to economic uncertainty and violence. As a result, their dislocation can be catastrophic. What's more, their inhabitants are often relocated far from their main source of sustenance, which is also the bedrock of their culture. "Their identity is the ocean," Rodríguez said of former El Bosque residents. "They're fisher people. If they ran out of food, all they had to do was go out to sea and catch something. Now they can't."

Water gives us life, but it can also turn against us. This ambivalence lends tension and drama to Rodríguez's work. There, we find landscapes ravaged by the lack of water (the scar the ocean leaves) or overwhelmed by its excess (the violence of water where it doesn't belong). "When it eats up houses, the ocean leaves nothing behind. Only water. Everything you can't see, the water ate it," he said. Sometimes, where an entire village once stood, just one or two houses remain.

Guadalupe Cobos and her husband live in one of those homes. "They and two or three others are the only people left in El Bosque. The other eighty or so families have been relocated," Rodríguez said. There's no water in Rodríguez's photograph of them, but its effects are visible: Erosion has worn away at the walls. And on the left side, through a window beyond the frame, light streams in with liquid insistence. Another form of light corrodes the lower edge of the picture, threatening to obscure the scene and erase the couple altogether.

Just as water destroys these people's homes, a ruthless, scorching light intrudes into their portraits. "I used an analog camera with lots of flaws, lots of openings for the light," Rodríguez said. "I lose control when I take photos with it. It seems to make its own decisions."

In these images, light decides to do as water does: It erodes. The information lost in the negatives reflects everything these families have lost. Light, which makes photography possible, can also disrupt it. In the same way, the ocean, which sustains these communities and allows them to exist, now threatens to destroy them.

Translated from the Spanish by Robin Myers.

Elisa Díaz Castelo is a poet and novelist based in Mexico City.

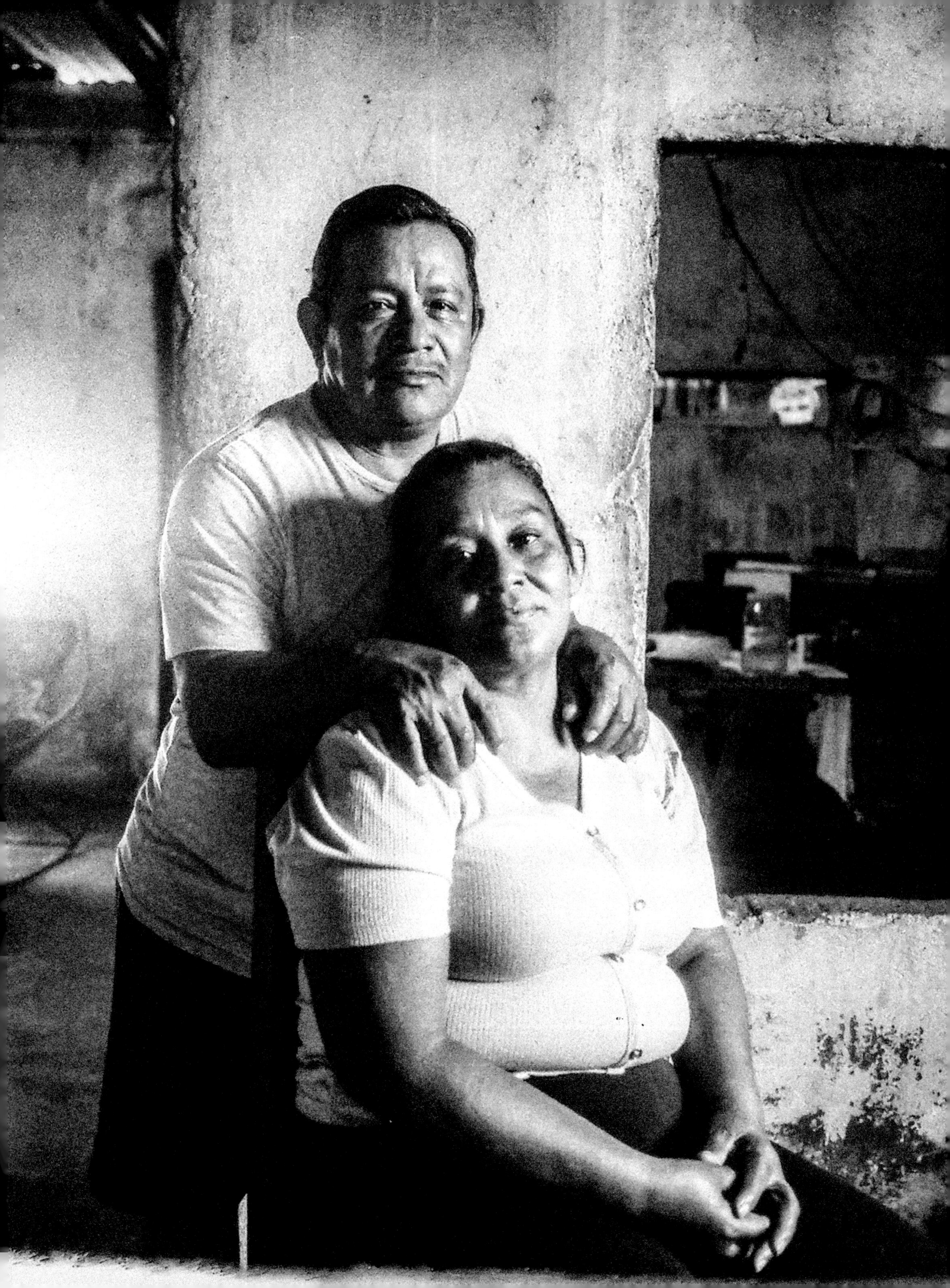

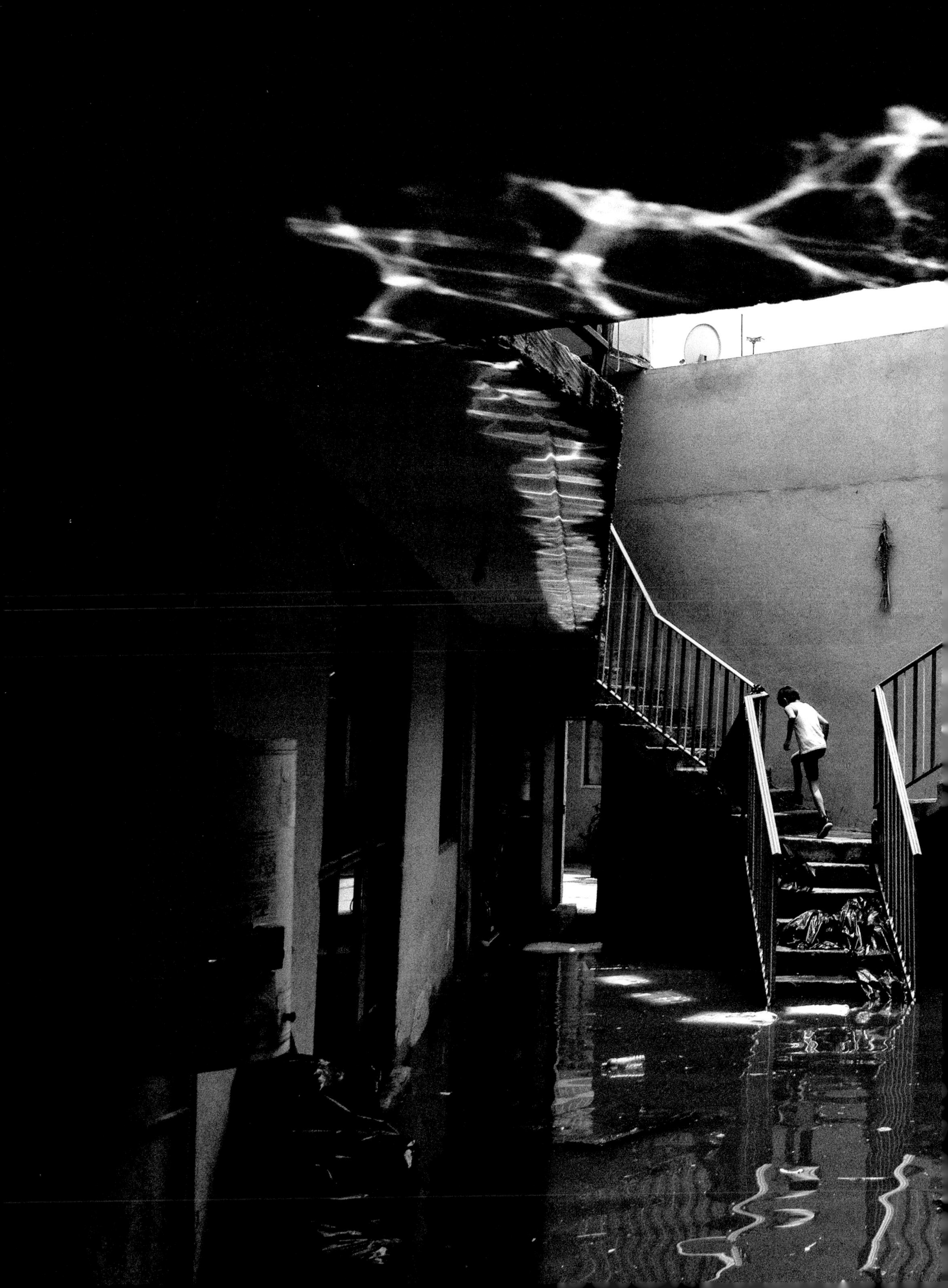

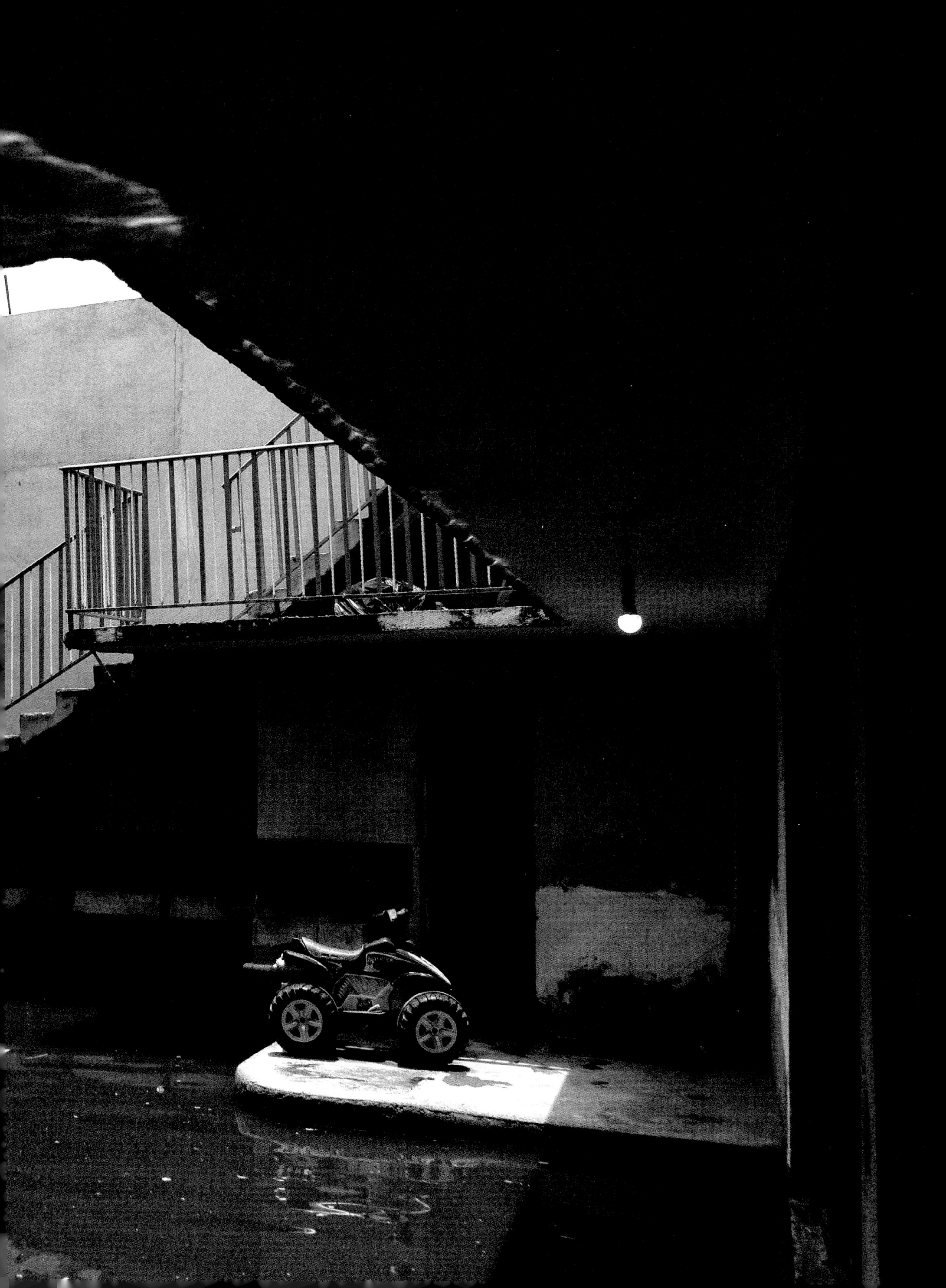

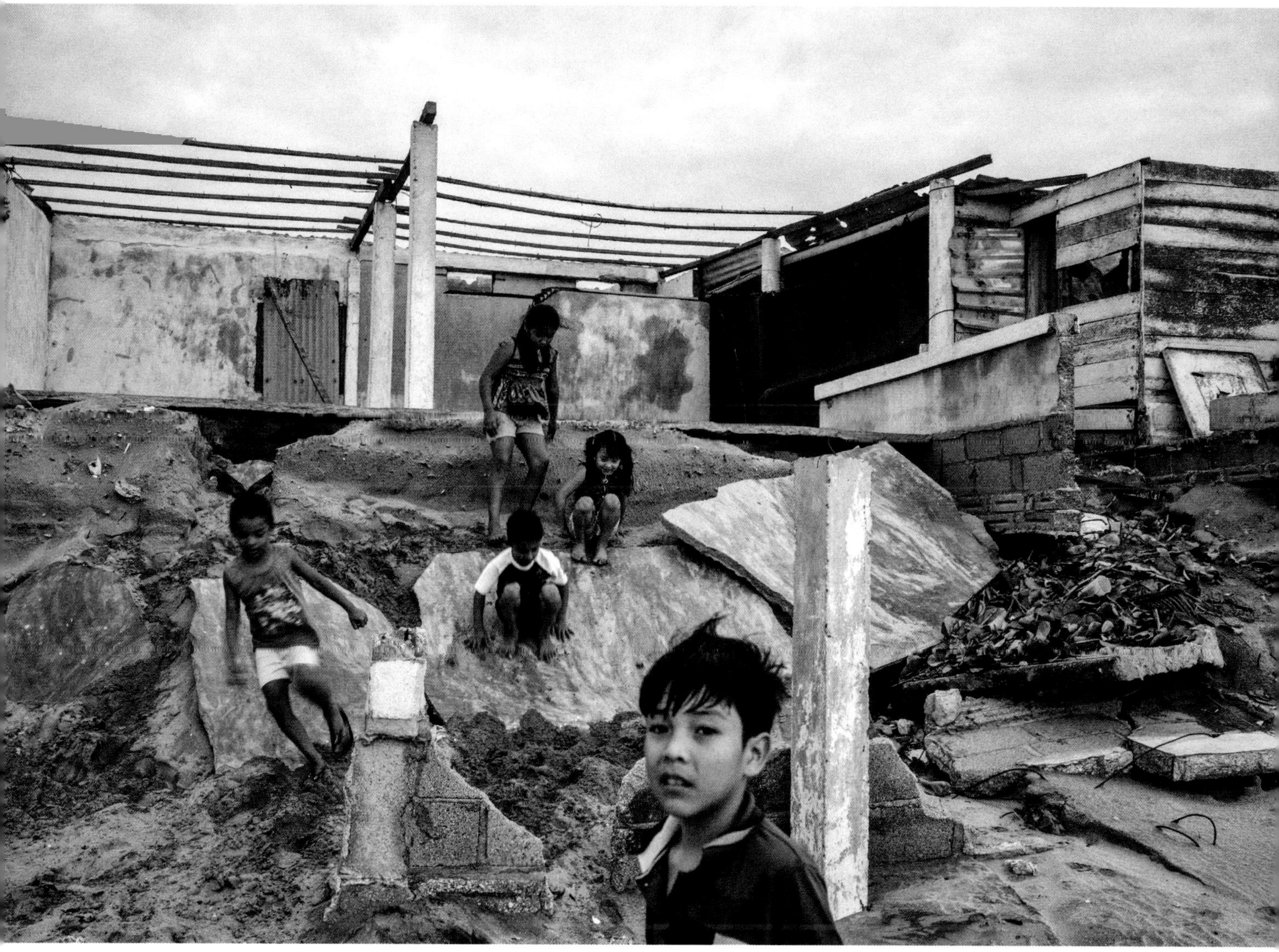

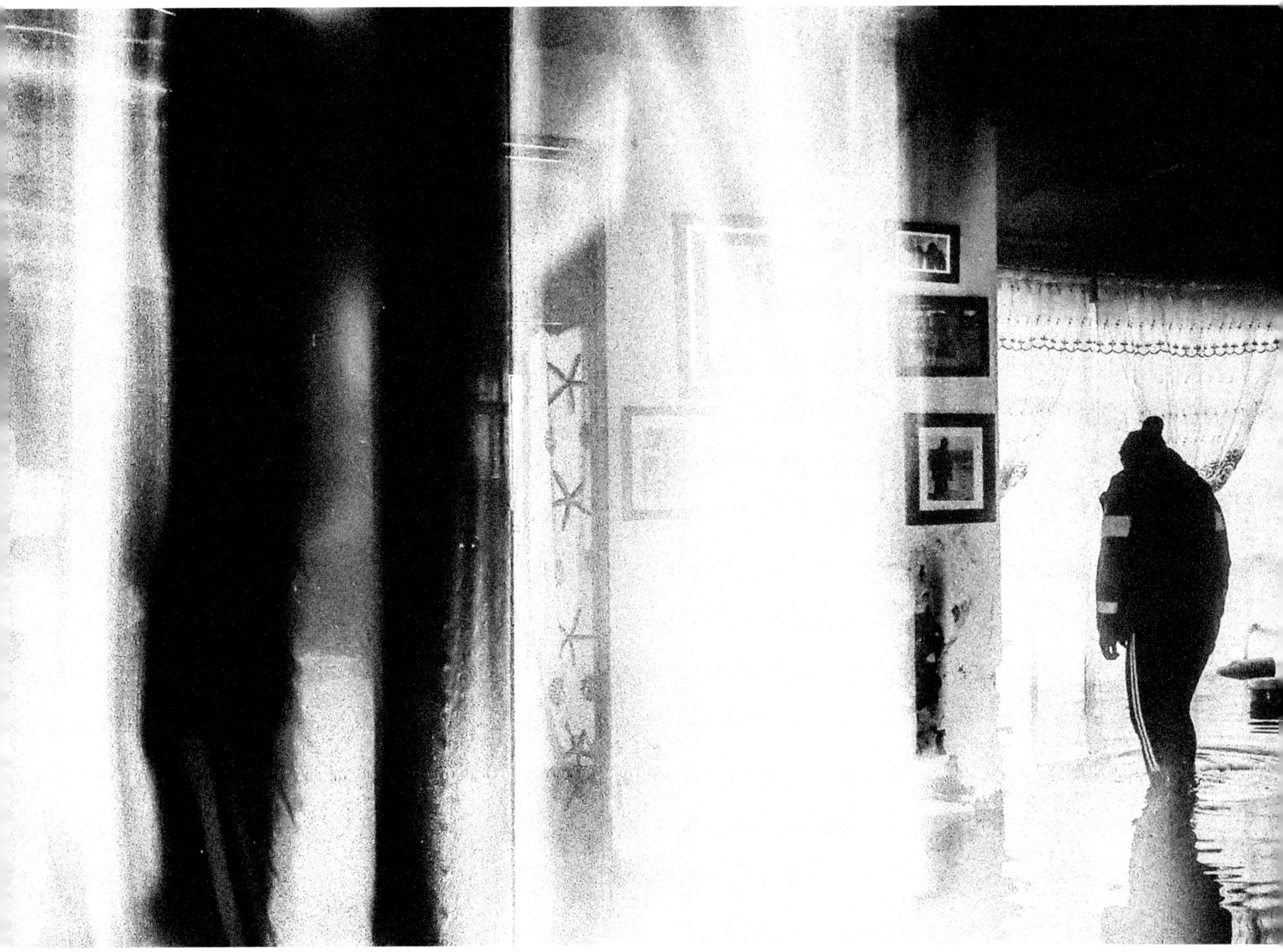

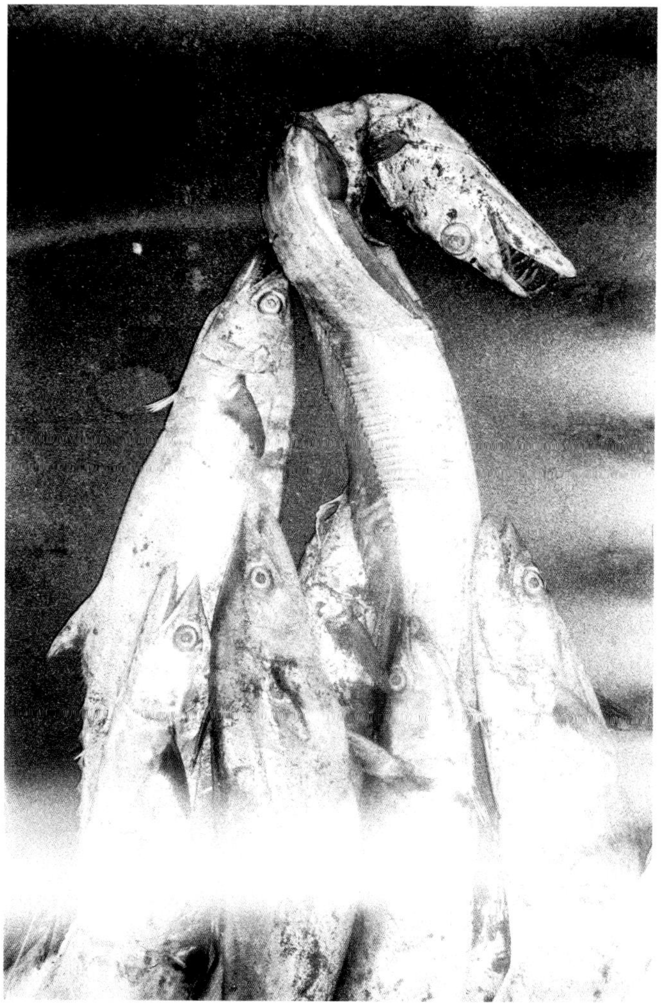

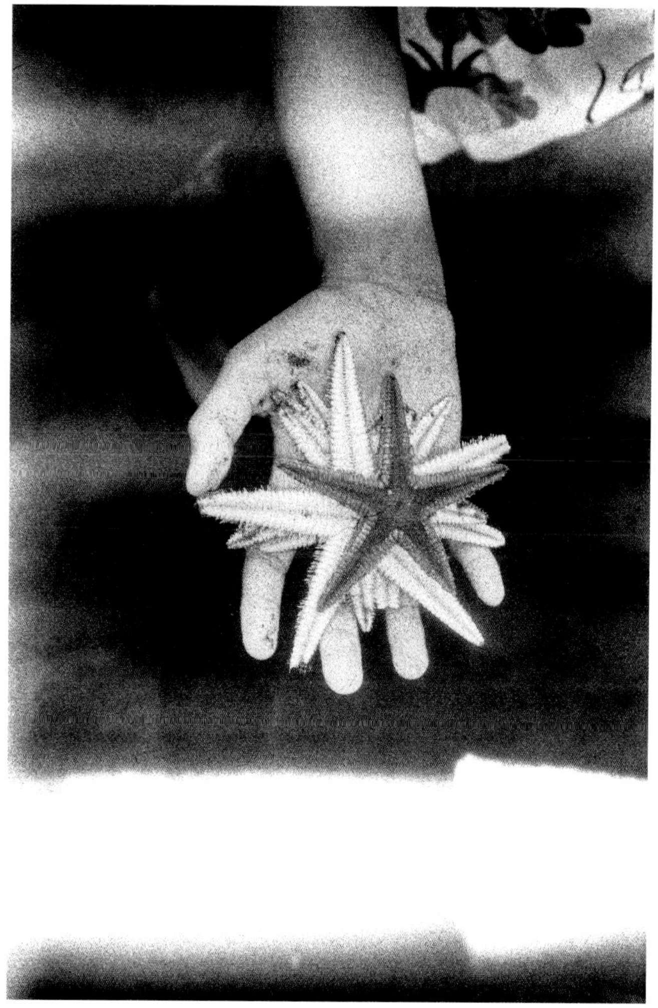

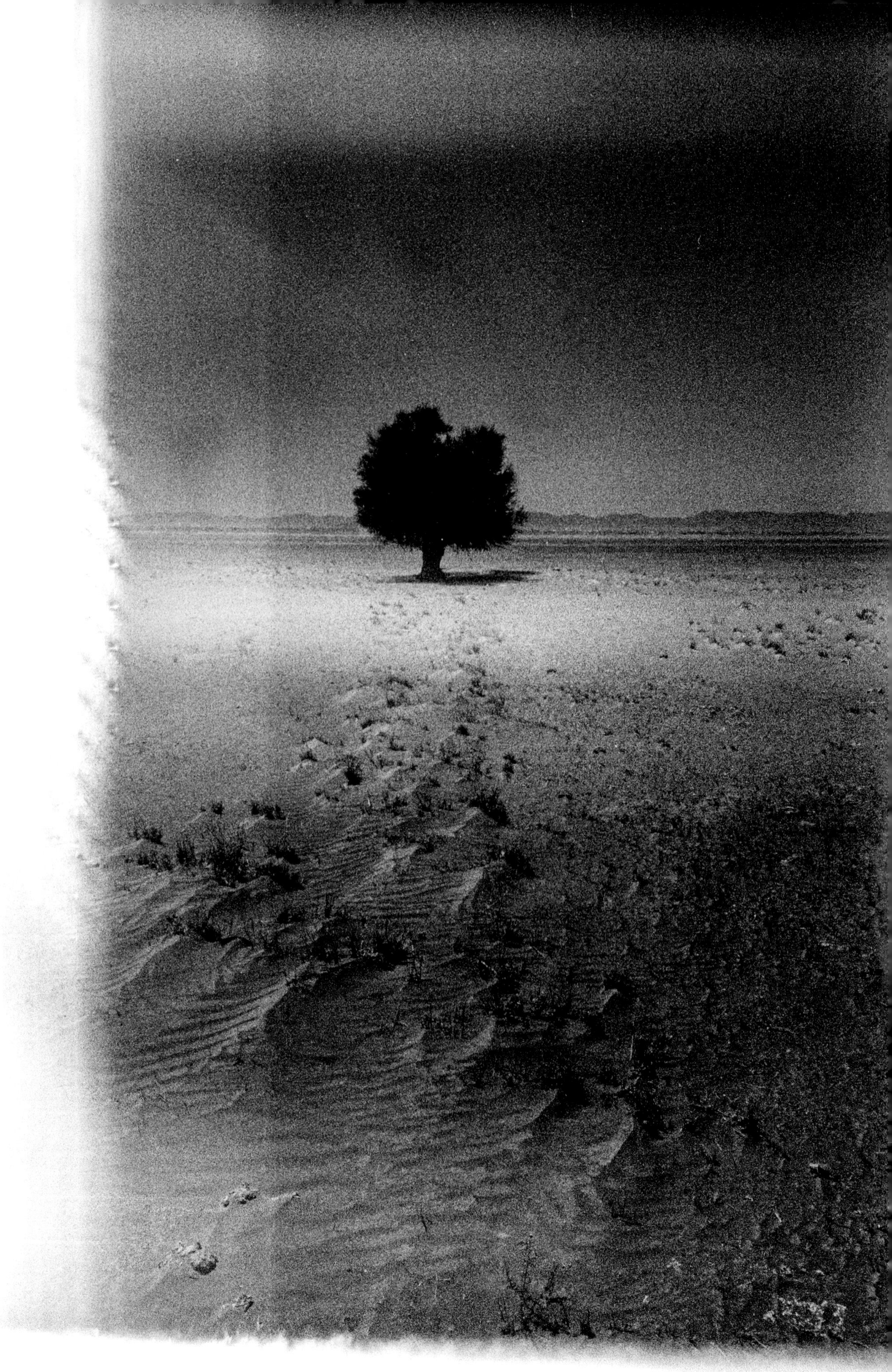

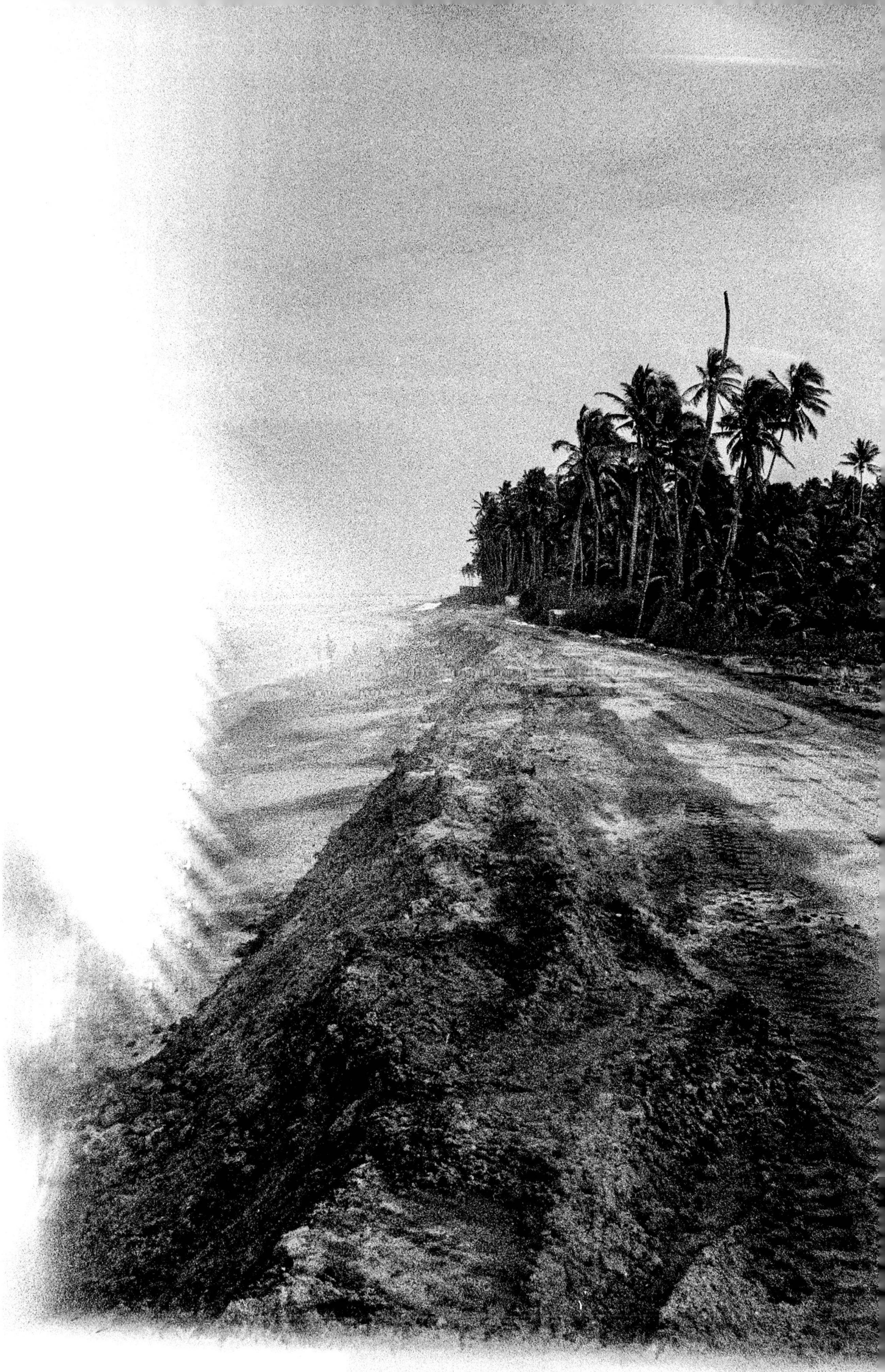

All photographs from the series *Cuando hay luna llena, la marea sube* (When there is a full moon, the tide rises), 2021–ongoing
Courtesy the artist

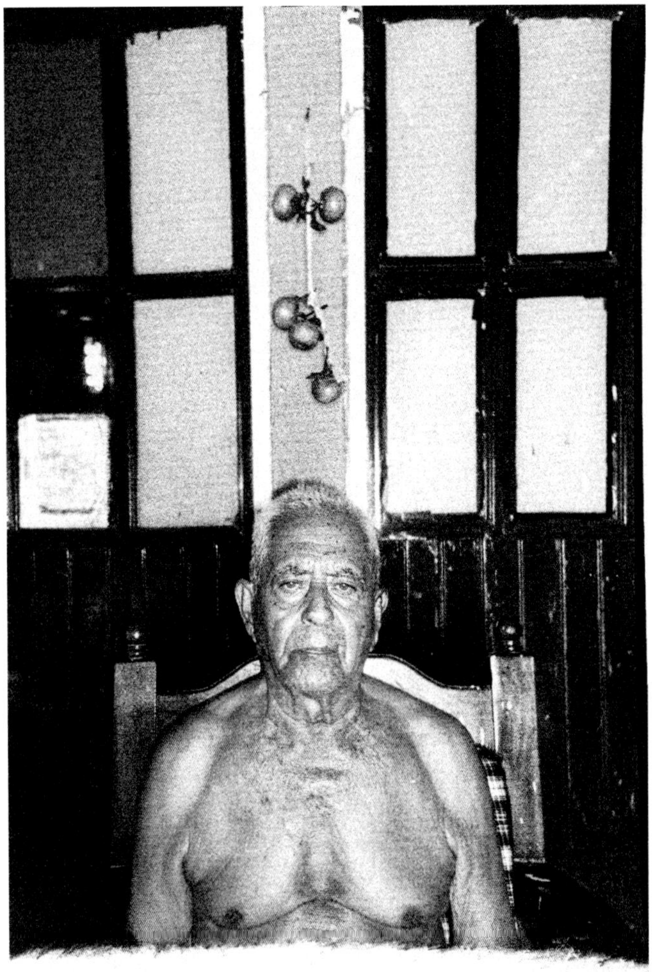

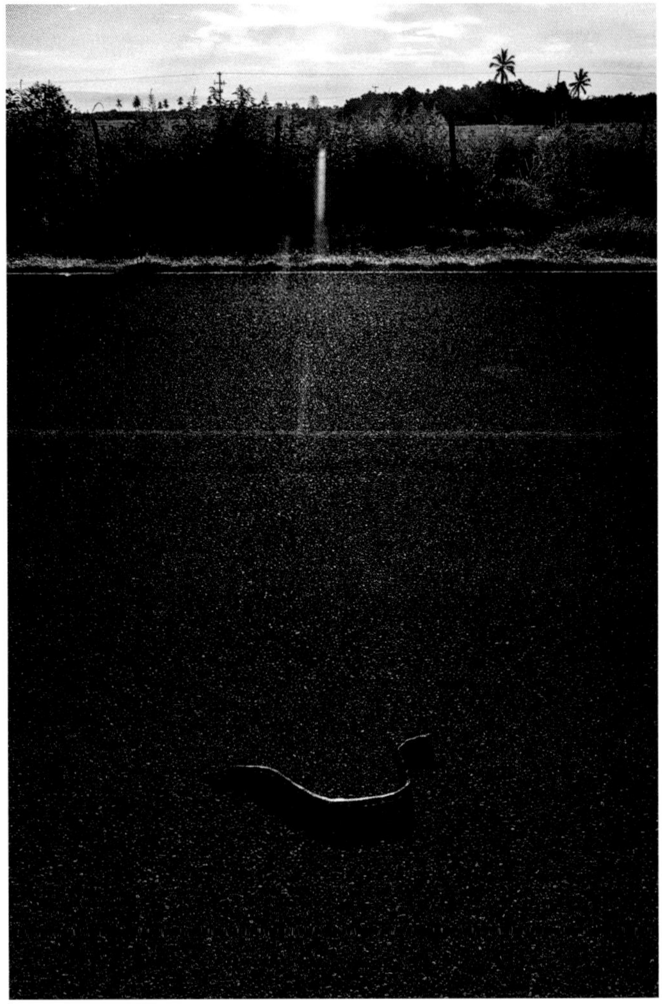

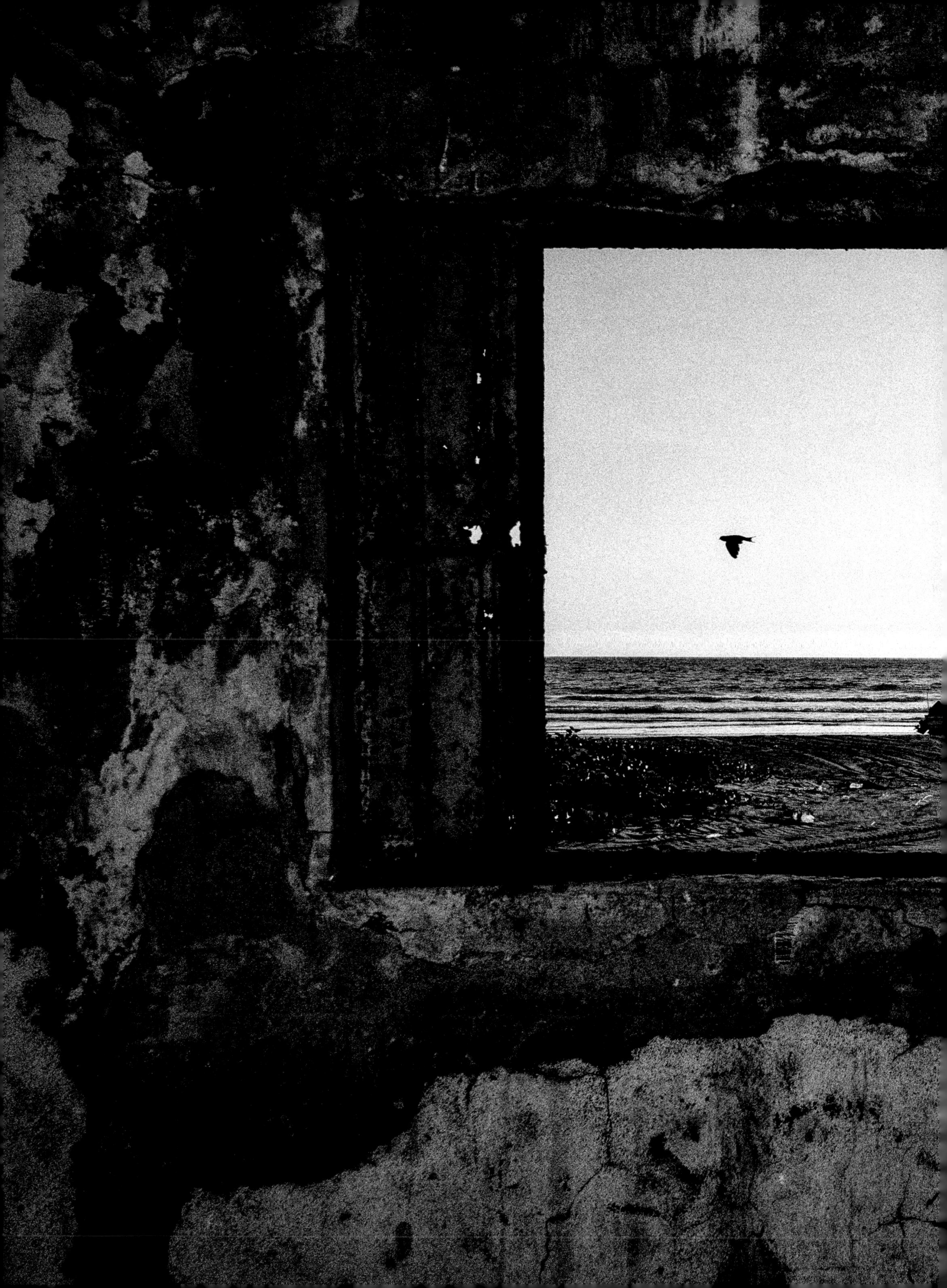

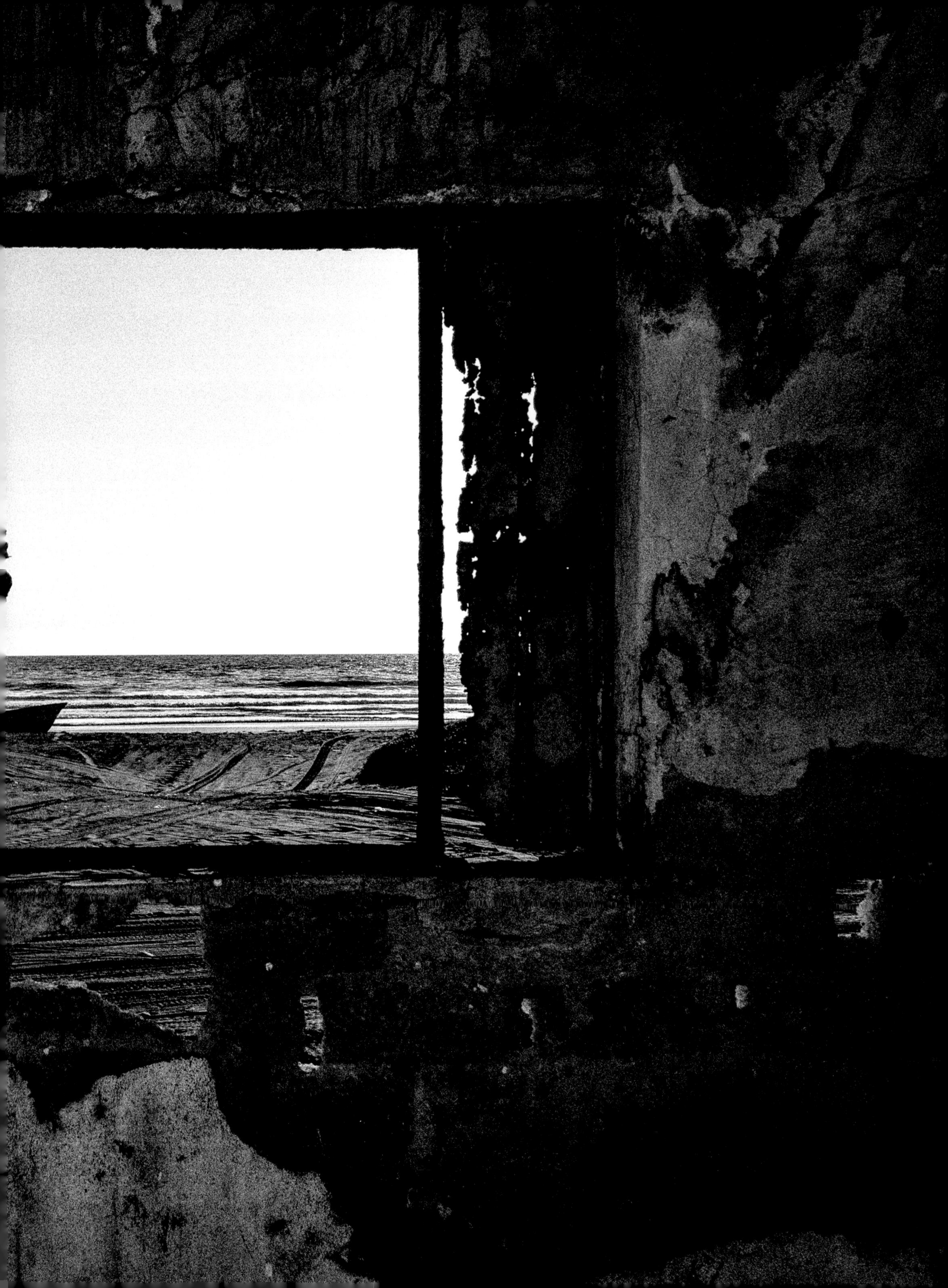

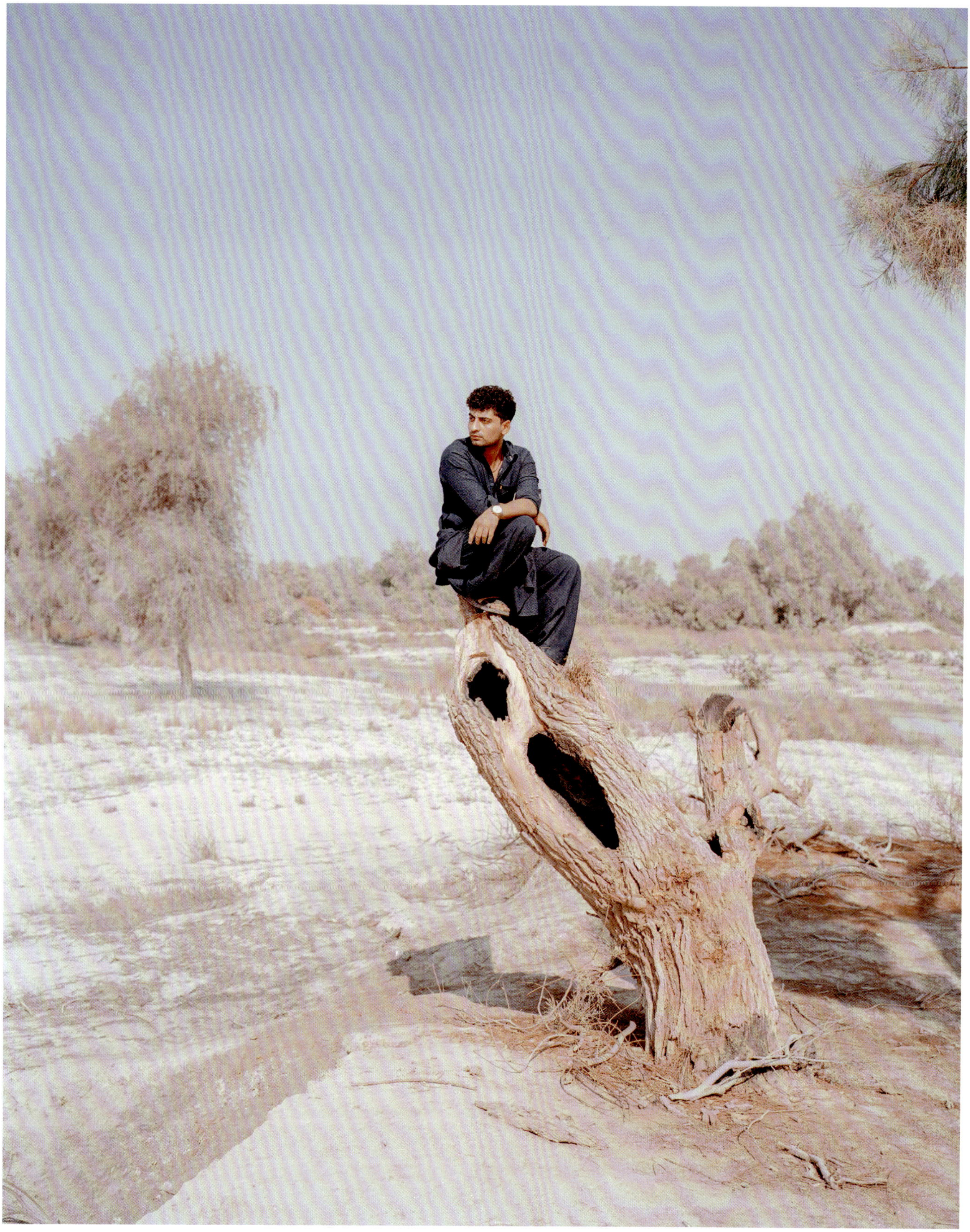

Kaelen Wilson-Goldie

Hashem Shakeri *Dry Spells*

If Hashem Shakeri's recent and ongoing series of photographs were a novel, its main characters would be a short-snouted crocodile and a resplendent *kahur* tree. Both are native to the wetlands of Balochistan, a region pounded by drought, covering the far southeast of Iran as well as southern and western portions of Afghanistan and Pakistan, respectively. Both carry heavy meaning for the people who live there.

The kahur, which grows in dry, salty soil and is able to thrive with minimal water, embodies the resilience and endurance necessary to withstand a climate of extreme heat, pervasive aridity, and brutal seasonal winds. The crocodile, known locally as *gando*, symbolizes life, blessings, and survival. The presence of healthy gandos is taken for a sign that water is plentiful. If gandos die or disappear, it is considered a bad omen, a warning "that the land has become thirsty," said Shakeri. Local residents consider gandos sacred. Some go to great lengths to care for the gandos and ensure their livelihood. Others are justifiably afraid. "A few years ago, I met Hawa, a ten-year-old girl who had gone to fetch water for her mother when a gando attacked her and tore off her right hand," Shakeri said.

The gando and the kahur face each other with sly majesty in a pair of images from Shakeri's series *The Kahur Does Not Fall Unless the Earth Wills It* (2018–ongoing). The crocodile, which lives in rivers and ponds and finds refuge in deep pits when water is scarce, is half submerged in an eerie green pool edged with tall grasses. The kahur, set against a sun-blasted landscape, is rendered in a vivid, electrifying red. A man in dramatic silhouette stands on its low branches. The red was initially a glitch that appeared on Shakeri's screen while he was at home in Tehran, scanning negatives.

This was during the 2022 Women, Life, Freedom uprising in Iran. "The people of Balochistan, especially in Zahedan, the provincial capital, joined the movement with remarkable persistence," Shakeri explained. "Every Friday, under the pretext of Friday prayers, they gathered to protest against injustice and oppression." During the first demonstration, Iranian security forces opened fire on the crowd, killing at least ninety-six people. The crackdown intensified, and protests across the country waned. But not in Balochistan. For Shakeri, the man in the kahur tree represents "the stubborn will to live

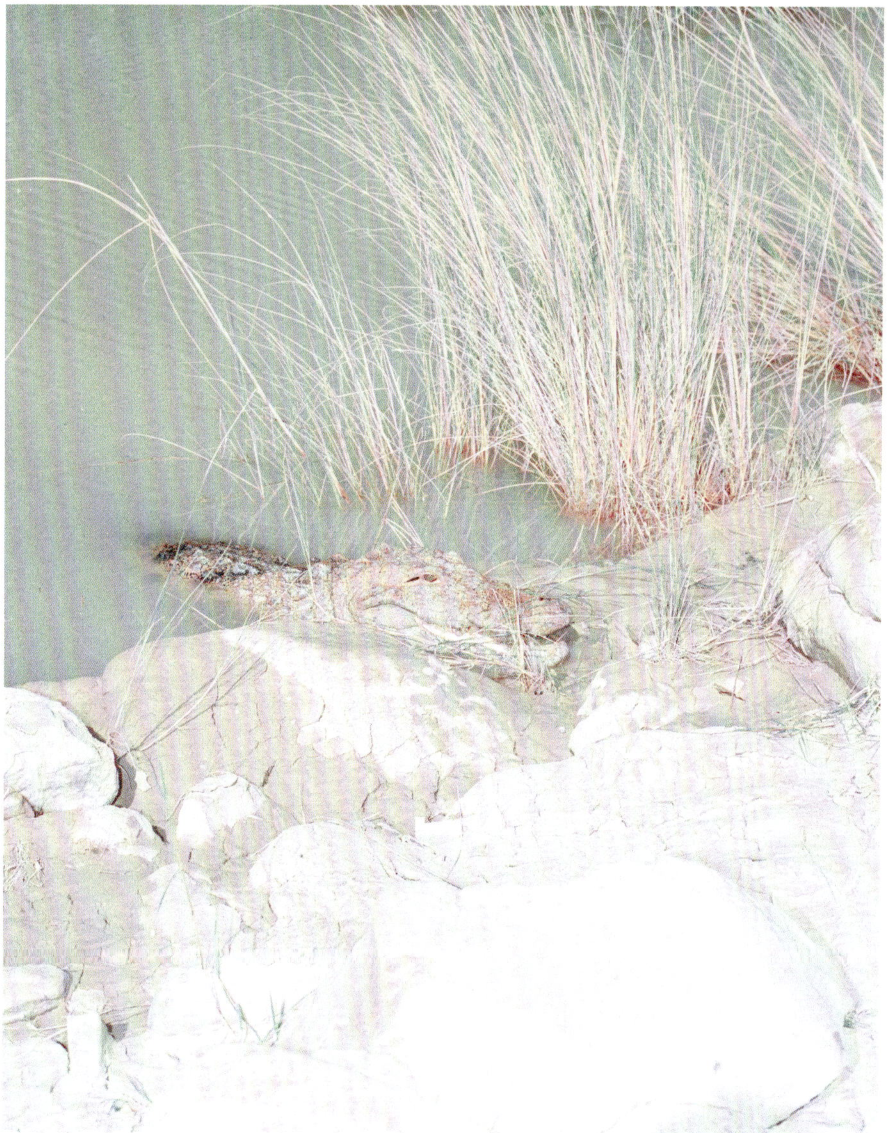

under the most unforgiving conditions," and Balochistan itself, "parched and wounded, yet unyielding."

Shakeri often describes himself as self-taught in photography. "My formal education is in architecture. I also have a background in theater." He explained that soon after entering university, "I saw an image from the Iran-Iraq War in a conference hall, and it affected me so deeply that from the very next day, I saw myself as a photographer and devoted myself to it with immense passion." That was nineteen years ago, and since then, Shakeri has proceeded largely through cycles of self-study and intuition. For nearly a decade, he has been pursuing a long-term project on the effects of drought, resource deprivation, and climate change among marginalized people living in the Iranian province of Sistan and Balochistan.

One component of that project is a trilogy: The first part is *An Elegy for the Death of Hamun* (2018–ongoing), about the seasonal lakes and reservoirs that dried up due to drought and the mismanagement (some would say corruption) of water resources in Sistan. The second, *Cast Out of Heaven* (2016–ongoing), looks at the housing crisis on the outskirts of Tehran, where people find themselves abandoned in so-called new cities that are ill-conceived and far away from the jobs the residents depend on to get by. The third, as yet untitled, considers the place of oil in the history, ecology, and culture of Iran. As proof of how capacious Shakeri's working method has become, *The Kahur Does Not Fall Unless the Earth Wills It* is also part of the same ongoing project.

Thousands of years ago, Sistan and Balochistan were covered by forests. For generations, these were agricultural lands. People lived by fishing, farming, and animal husbandry. Now, the drying lakes and wetlands have pushed the local population far below the poverty line. This situation appears in Shakeri's work in two ways. He forms deep bonds with inhabitants of this region, allowing him to capture the conditions of their lives, as seen here in the pictures of women doing laundry, men cutting each other's hair, and youngsters swimming in brown waters. Shakeri also tends to photograph in the middle of the day, so that the blinding intensity of the noontime sun sweeps across all his images, lending them a clear aesthetic. Shakeri describes his photographic world as melancholic, populated by "human beings who, after relentless exploitation of nature, now find themselves defeated by it." His narrative, his novel in visual form, pinpoints a crucial intersection between suffering and beauty: "To me, art is perhaps the only reason we can endure so much ugliness and monotony in life."

Kaelen Wilson-Goldie is a writer and critic based in Geneva.

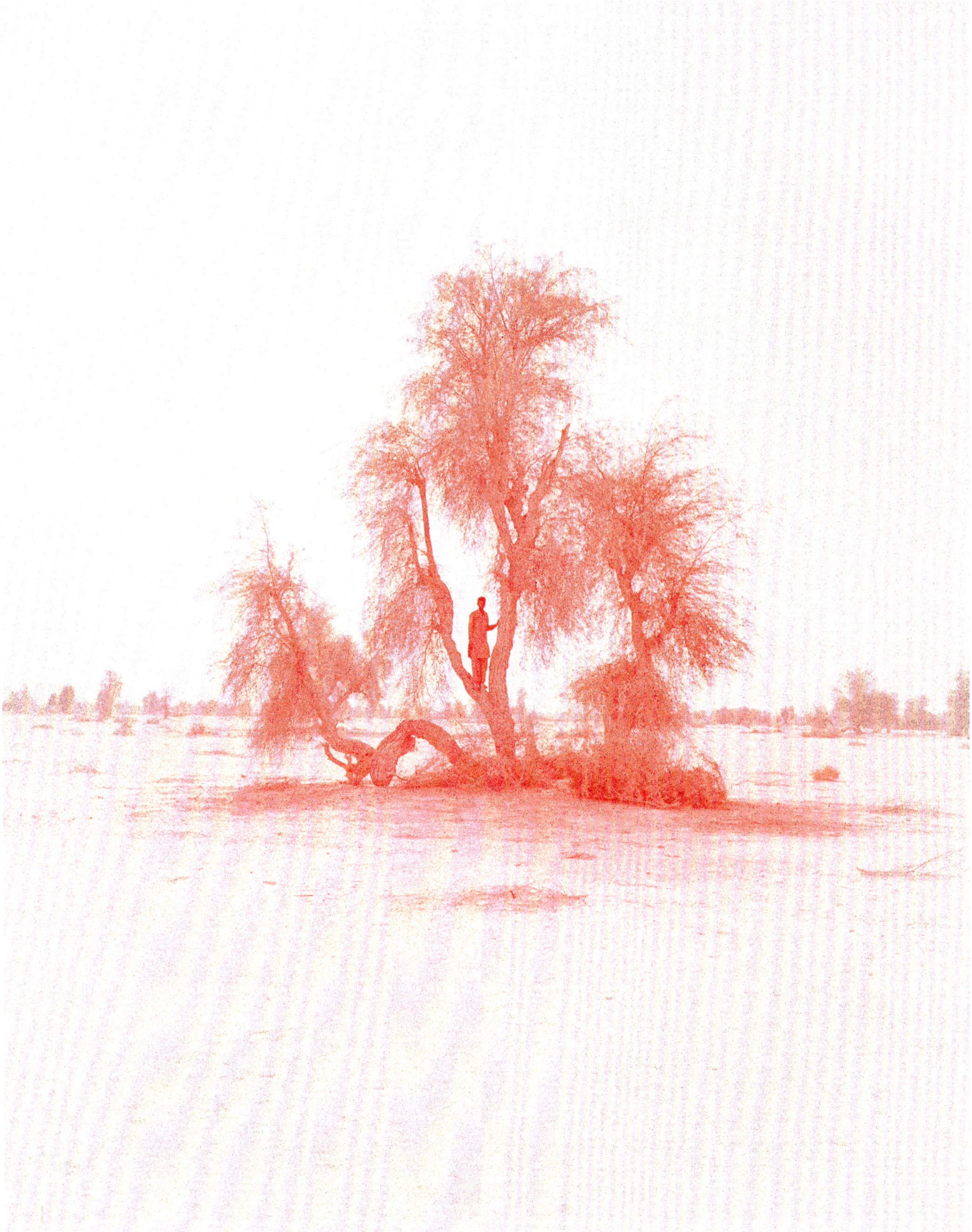

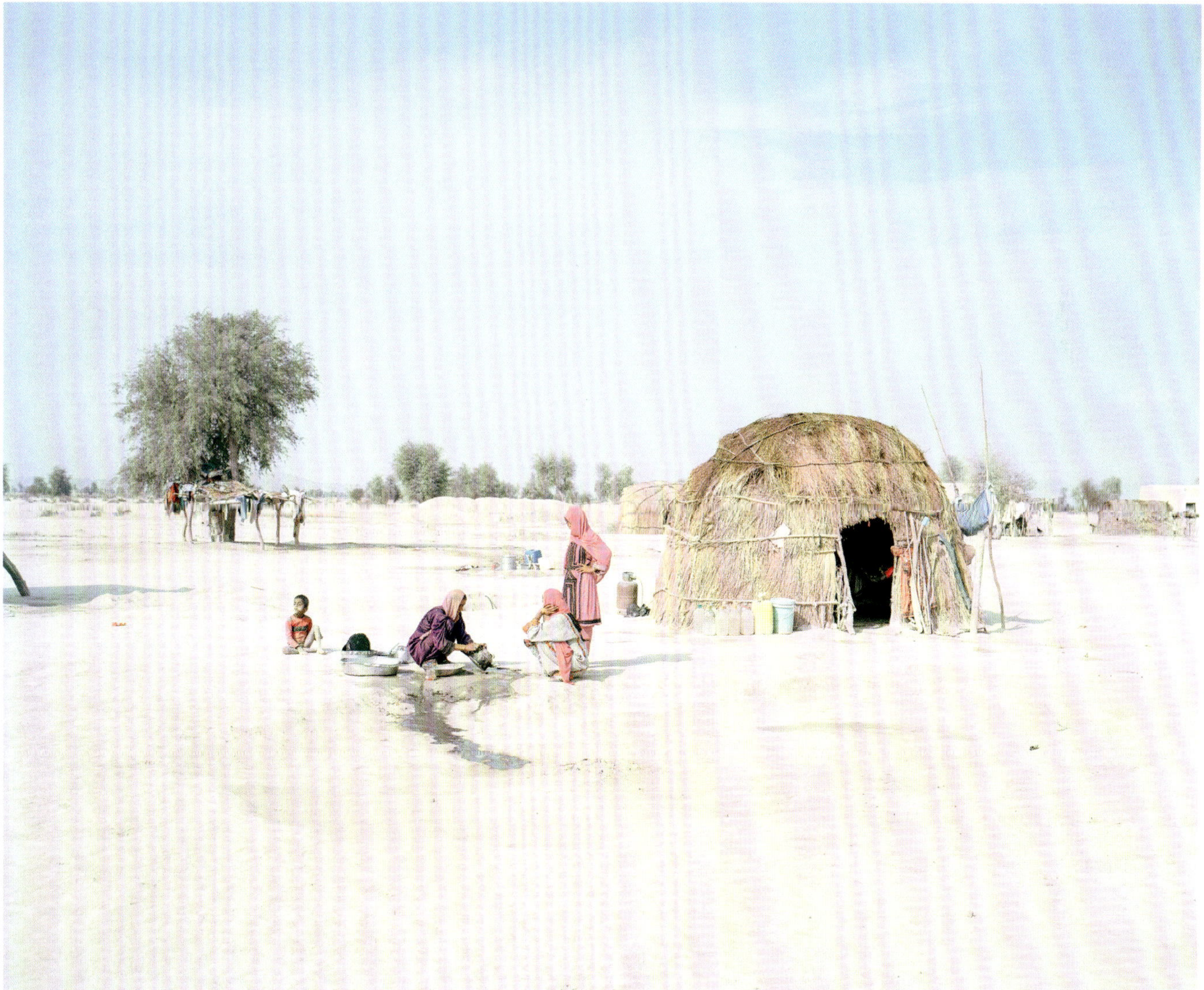

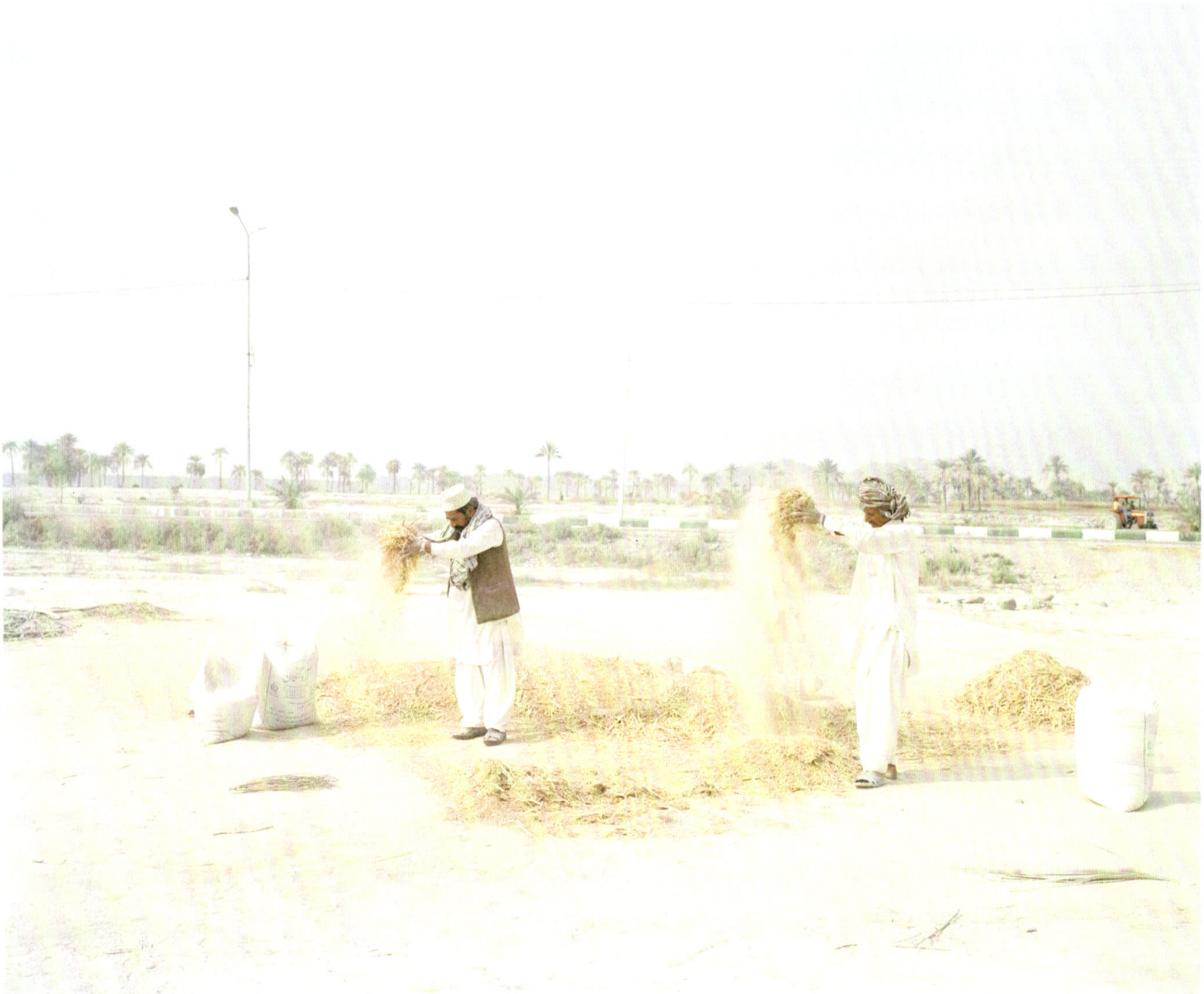

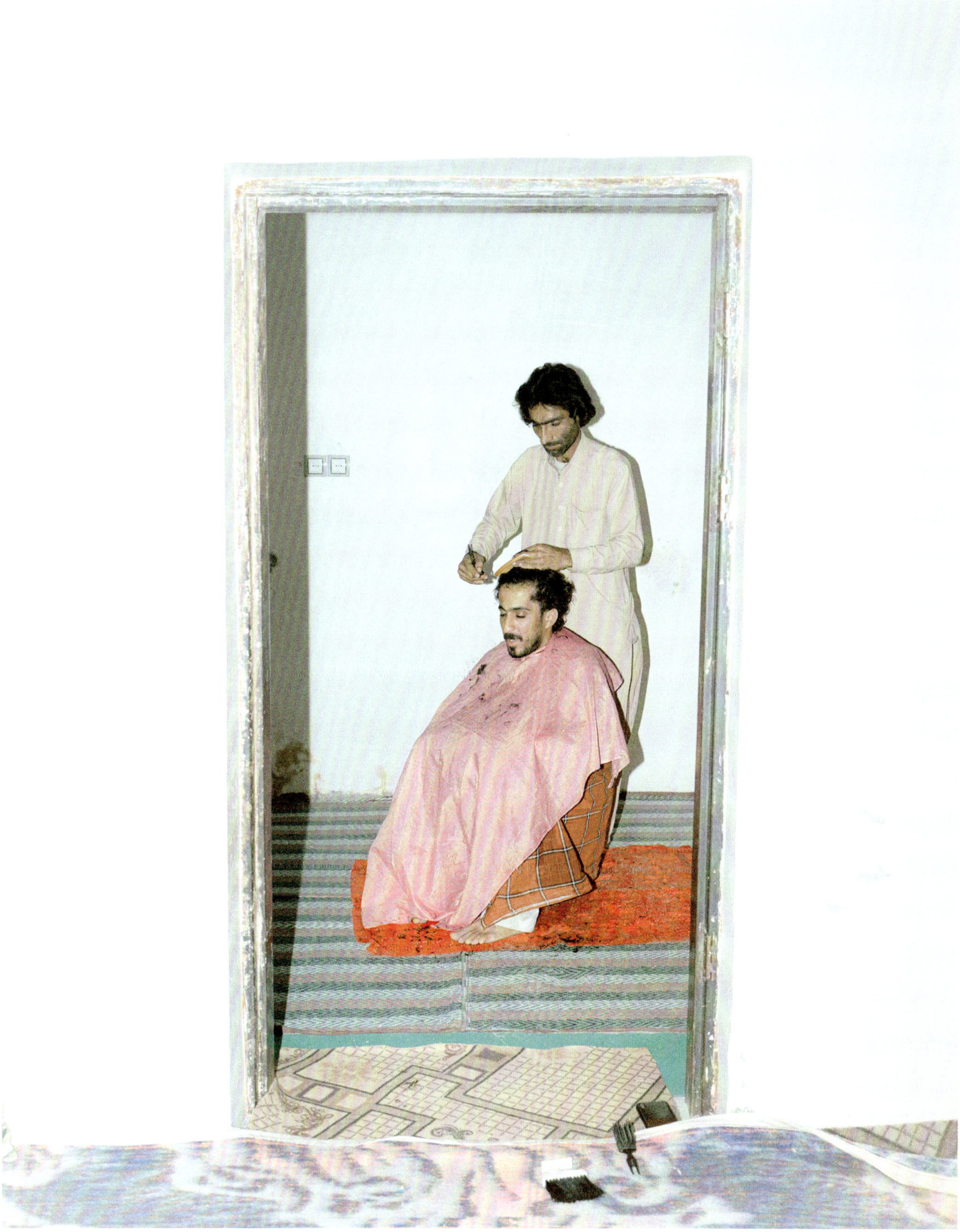

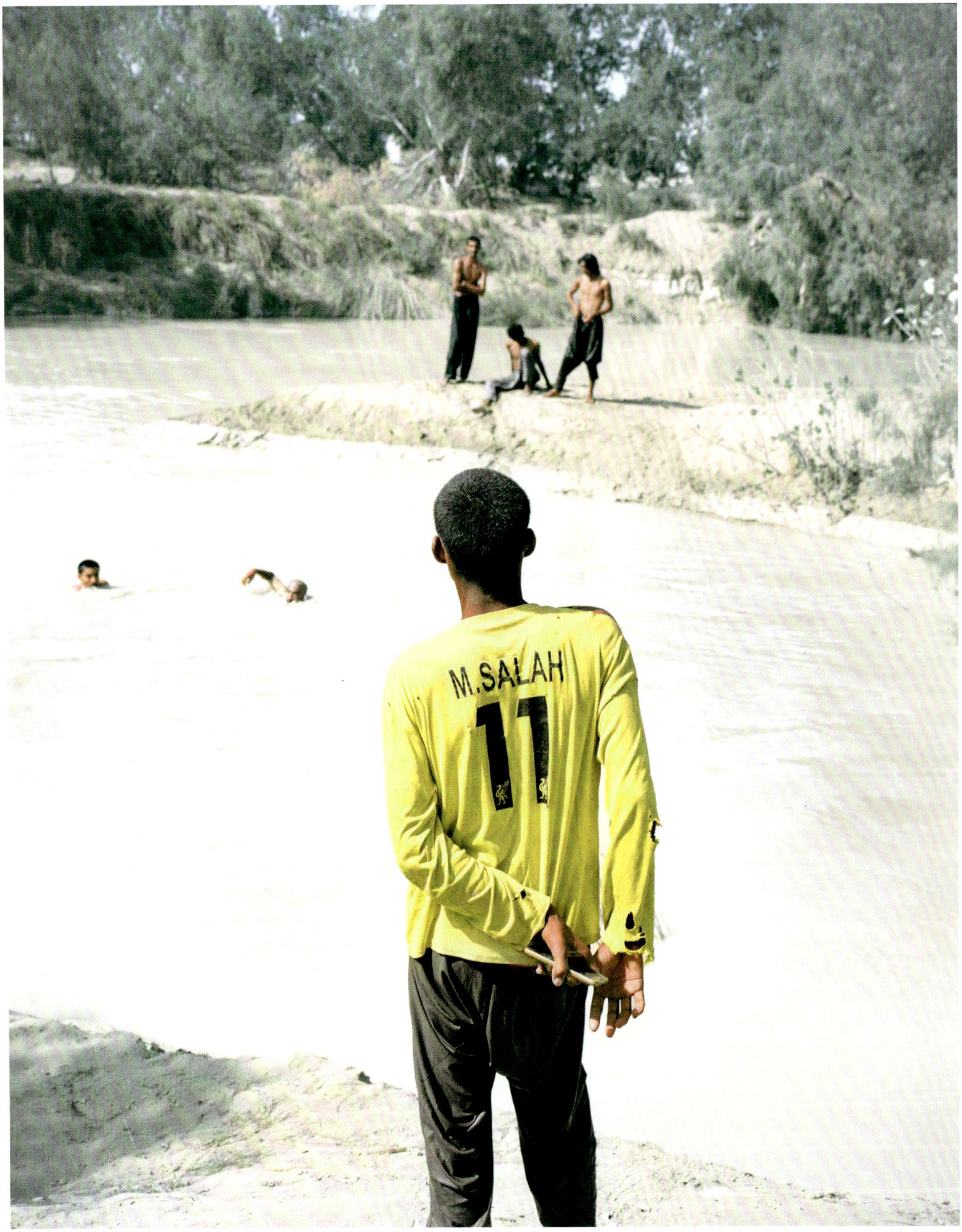
M.SALAH
11

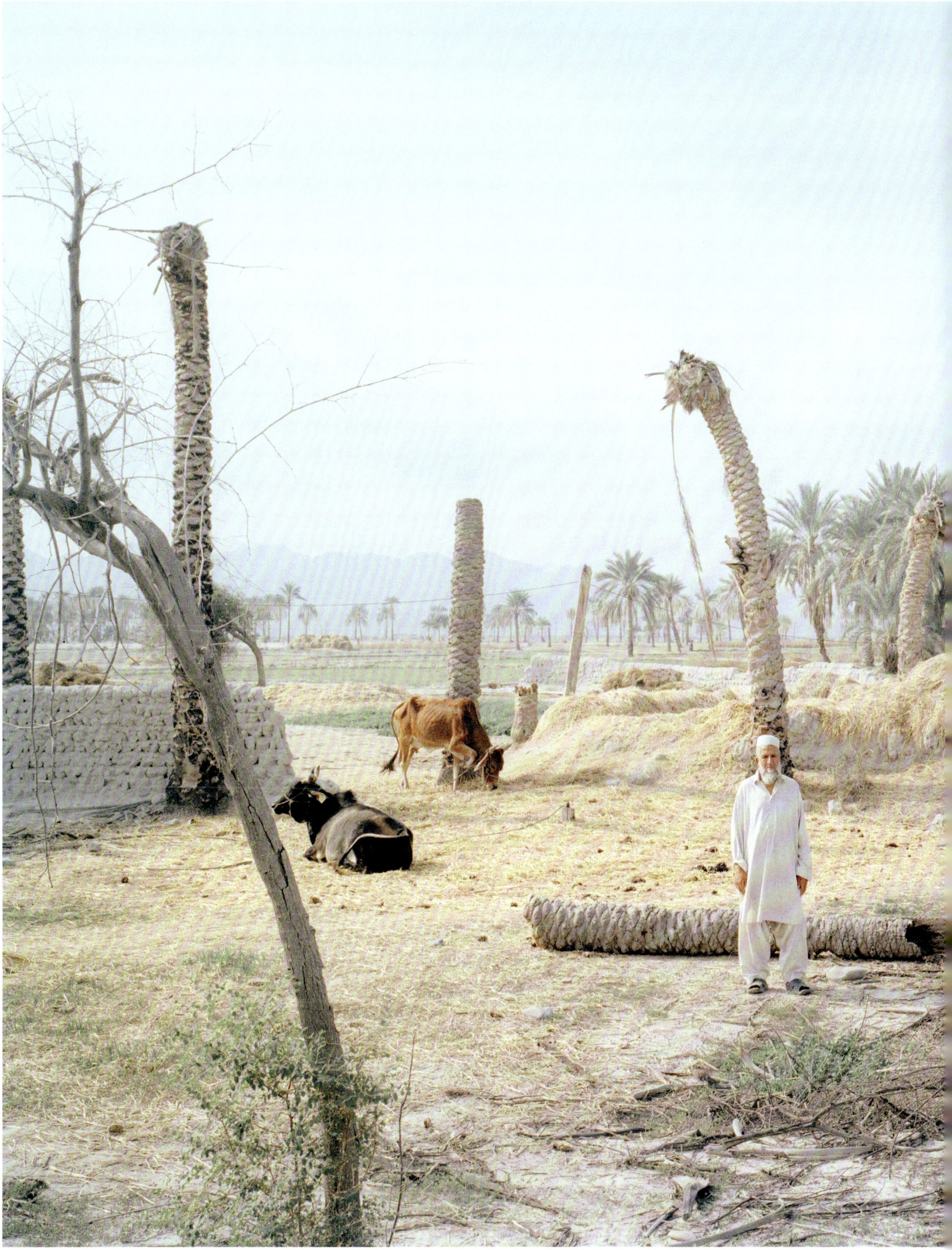

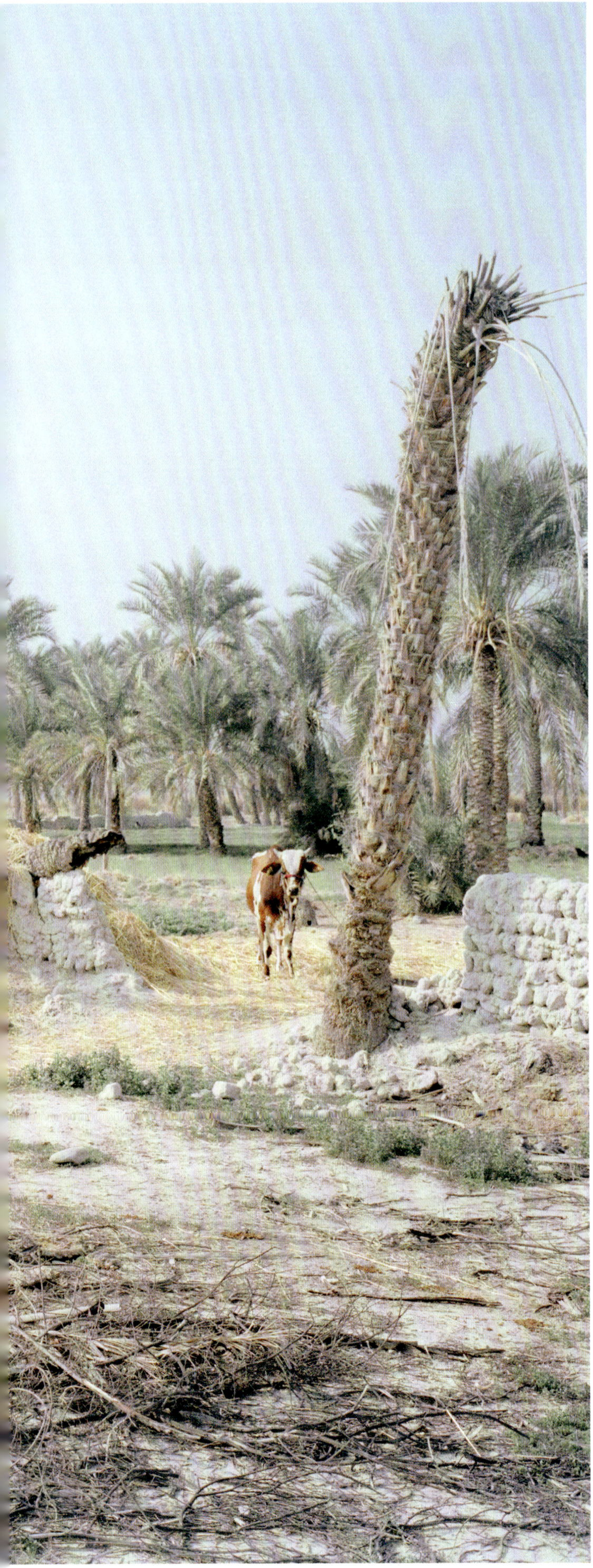

All photographs from the series *The Kahur Does Not Fall Unless the Earth Wills It*, Balochistan, Iran, 2018–ongoing
Supported by Magnum Foundation

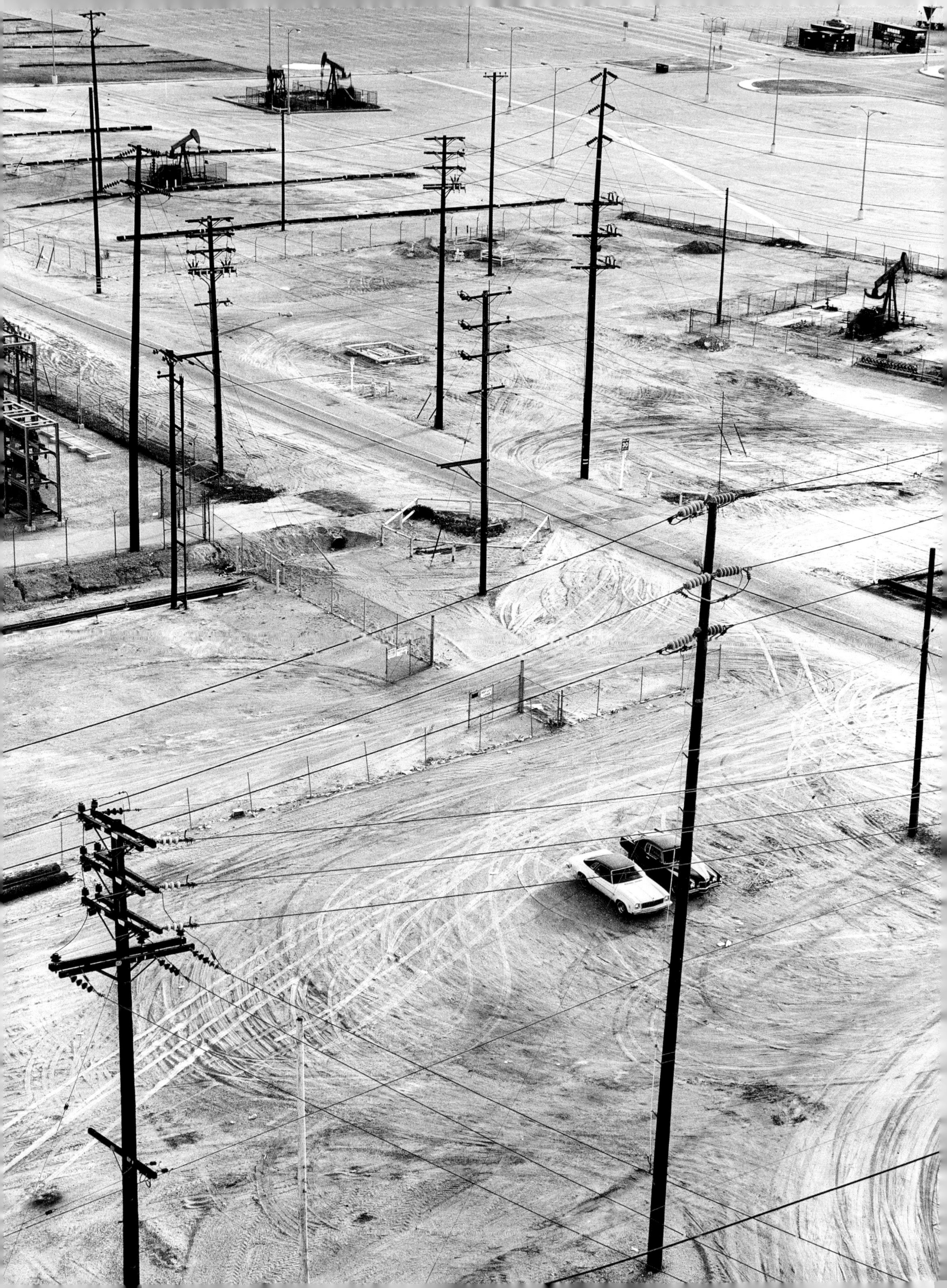

Contemporary life is underpinned by a system of extraction that often goes unseen. Yet the history of American photography was forged in the mines.

Ian Bourland

Beneath the Surface

IF YOU SPEND MUCH TIME IN THE AMERICAN WEST, the indelible traces of mining are impossible to miss. From abandoned shafts and ghost towns to gleaming refineries and places newly resplendent with fancy houses and fancier pickup trucks, the perennial boom-and-bust shapes the landscape. In Butte or the Bakken Formation, northern Utah or the Navajo Nation, it is clear that American history is a procession of resources being wrested from lodes far beneath the surface, its modernity a great speculative venture.

Photography's history, too, is a mineral one. As a spate of recent ecologically minded scholarship reminds us, the act of recording photonic energy is metallurgy in miniature: precious amalgams activated by other chemicals affixed to copper or tin. The rise of photography in the 1840s was made possible by new strikes of silver and gold. And many of those early camera operators set their lenses on those doing the sluicing, digging, and refining. Timothy H. O'Sullivan was famous for his battlefield images and harsh framing of the West's Rocky Mountains, but he was also among the first to document the rush towns of Nevada that cropped up after the Comstock Lode was found in the territory in 1859. From the beginning, American practitioners worked to forge new genres of portraiture and landscape photography centered around these pockets of extraction.

Today, *extraction* is a buzzword. Emerging from ecological humanities and theories of the Anthropocene over the past decade, it can now mean anything exploitative or inequitable,

Page 72:
Grant Mudford, *From Ocean Boulevard, Long Beach*, 1979

This page:
Timothy H. O'Sullivan, Savage Mine, Curtis Shaft, Virginia City, Nevada, 1868

From the beginning, American photographers created genres centered around pockets of extraction.

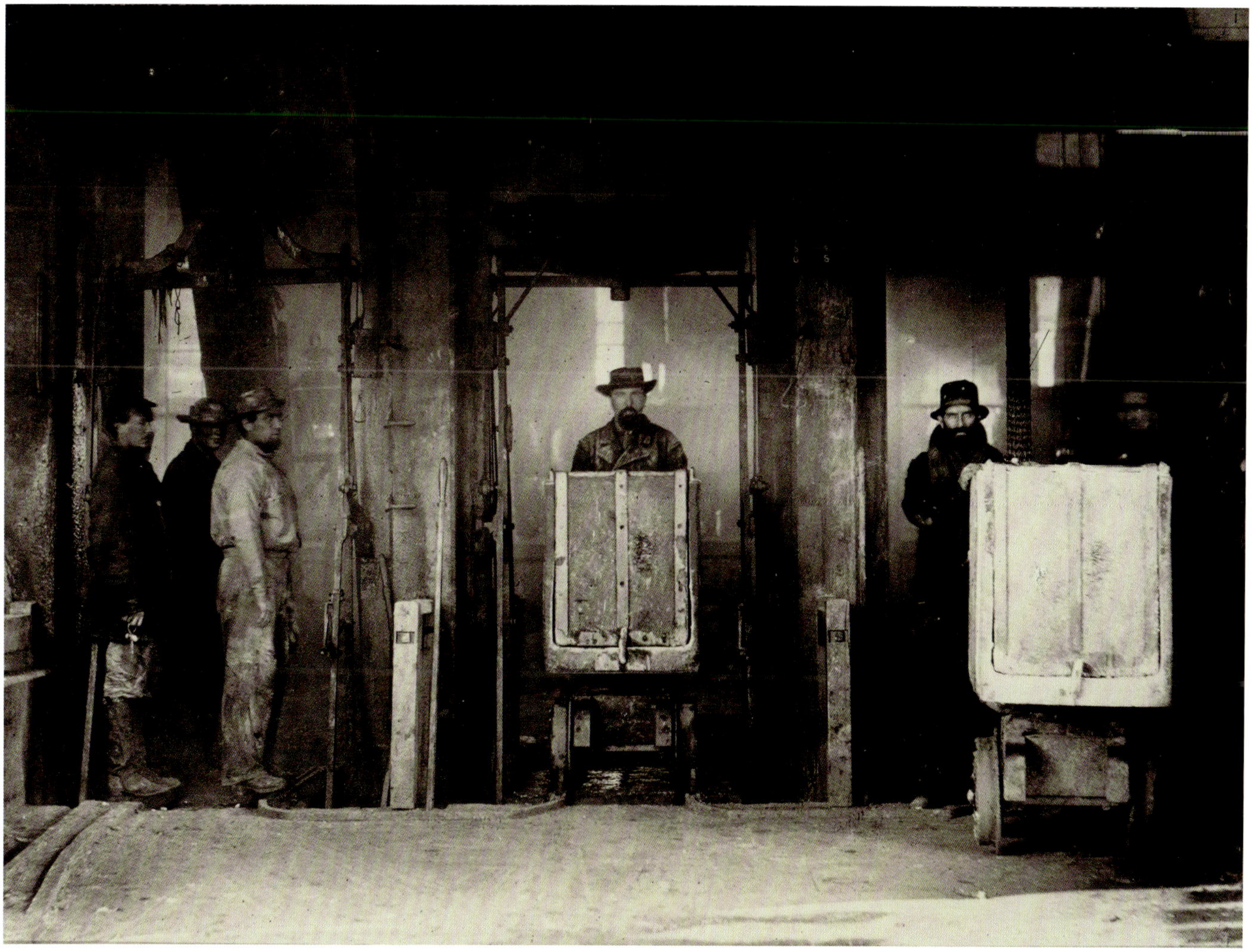

especially in economic relations. In mining history, the term simply describes the laborious—often brutal—process of moving matter from one place to another, converting it from its rawer forms into more refined yields. Extracting is something humans have done all over the world for millennia, and it was the key driver of many of the colonial endeavors that transformed the planet since the fifteenth century. Visualizing such a sprawling terrain is an elusive task, but one to which photography's relentless archival bent is well suited. Accordingly, the exhibition *Beneath the Surface: Mining and American Photography*, which opens a multicity tour this May at the National Gallery of Art in Washington, DC, draws together some 150 works and makes explicit an undercurrent running through the medium's nearly two-hundred-year trajectory.

Marshaling such a vast range of objects could have been a task without end, spanning the gamut of countless corporate, popular, and fine-art photographs. Based on my conversations with the curators, Diane Waggoner and Kristen Gaylord, *Beneath the Surface* is a trenchant exhibition—one that shows American mining as not just a Western story but one that crisscrosses the United States, not merely a curiosity of a subset of photographers but a leitmotif visible in unexpected places. According to Waggoner and Gaylord, this focus allows viewers to newly "understand photography as a central tool in both depicting and critiquing the industries that enable our contemporary world, and to help us all better understand how photographers have deployed it throughout the medium's history."

Much recent writing on photography and mining focuses on the connections between extractive industries and colonialism, stretching back to the Iberian quests across the Atlantic in search of precious metals and up to our current moment. Even now, a scramble is on for rare earth metals to power our cars, microchips, and military technology. Versions of this story wend through *Beneath the Surface*, as in several works by the Diné artist Will Wilson that adapt the surveillant mode of the aerial image to reveal the insidious cycle of a colonial paradigm that persists out West: the speculation of new minerals on Indigenous land, the abandonment of those who live there, and the depredations of the waste left behind. His *Shiprock Disposal Site, Shiprock, Navajo Nation, 36* (2020) foregrounds a sprawling pentagonal complex in New Mexico that one might mistake for a Michael Heizer earthwork. Off in the distance, storm clouds dapple a high desert sunset near the titular Tsé Bit'a'í (the Navajo name for Shiprock), a rock monolith of cosmological significance to the Diné. In this way, Wilson juxtaposes two kinds of mapping—the ruthless abstraction of the surveyors' grid and the emplaced topographies of the people on the ground.

Tens of millions of tons of uranium were cleaved from Indigenous land during the twentieth century, used to make warheads, reactors (J. Robert Oppenheimer built his bomb just a few hours away), and X-ray photography. The disposal site contains the radioactive residues of that process. New Mexico is honeycombed in this way, with deep caverns from which ore was taken, and others in which its dangerous by-products are entombed. Just hidden from view in Wilson's landscape is the San Juan River, a fragile lifeline in this arid region.

Still, photographers have long known that a perverse beauty persists in such instrumental images; even the chemistry of toxicity has its chromatic appeal. This is especially true in the hands of David Maisel, whose interplay of the photographic and painterly has long sought to chart the tailings and holding ponds

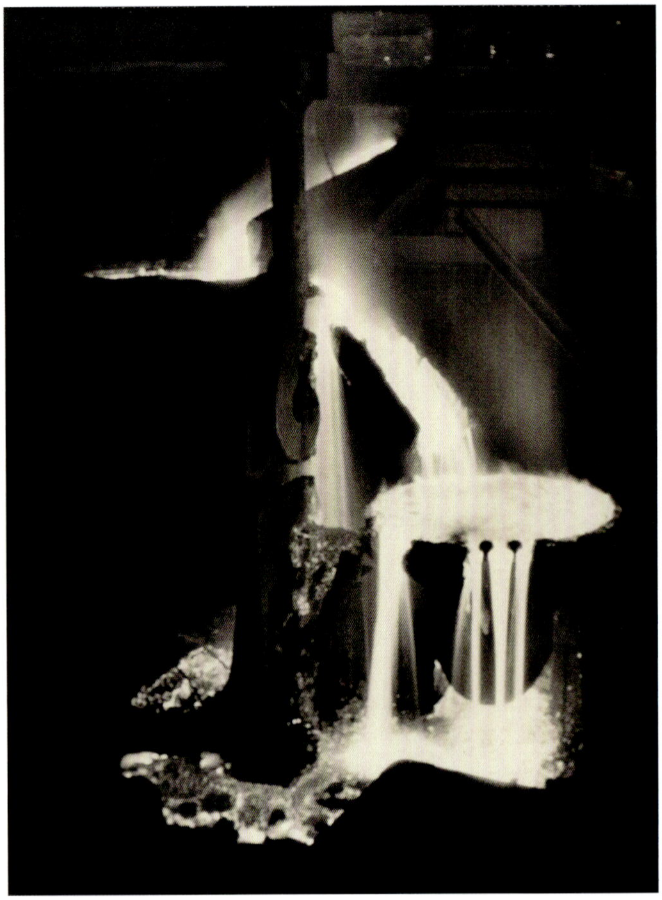

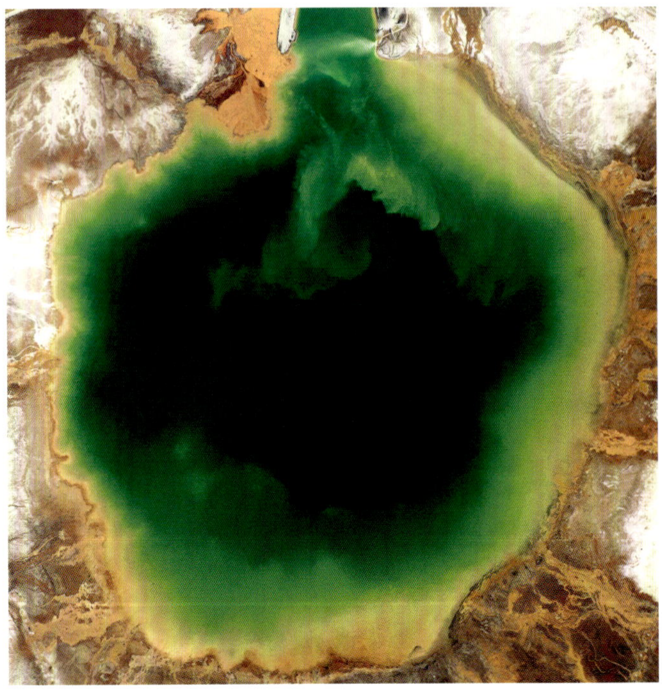

Top:
Margaret Bourke-White, *Four Thousand Fahrenheit, Otis Steel Company*, ca. 1927–28

Bottom:
David Maisel, *American Mine (Carlin, Nevada 1)*, 2007
Courtesy the artist and Haines Gallery, San Francisco

Will Wilson, *Shiprock Disposal Site, Shiprock, Navajo Nation, 36*, 2020

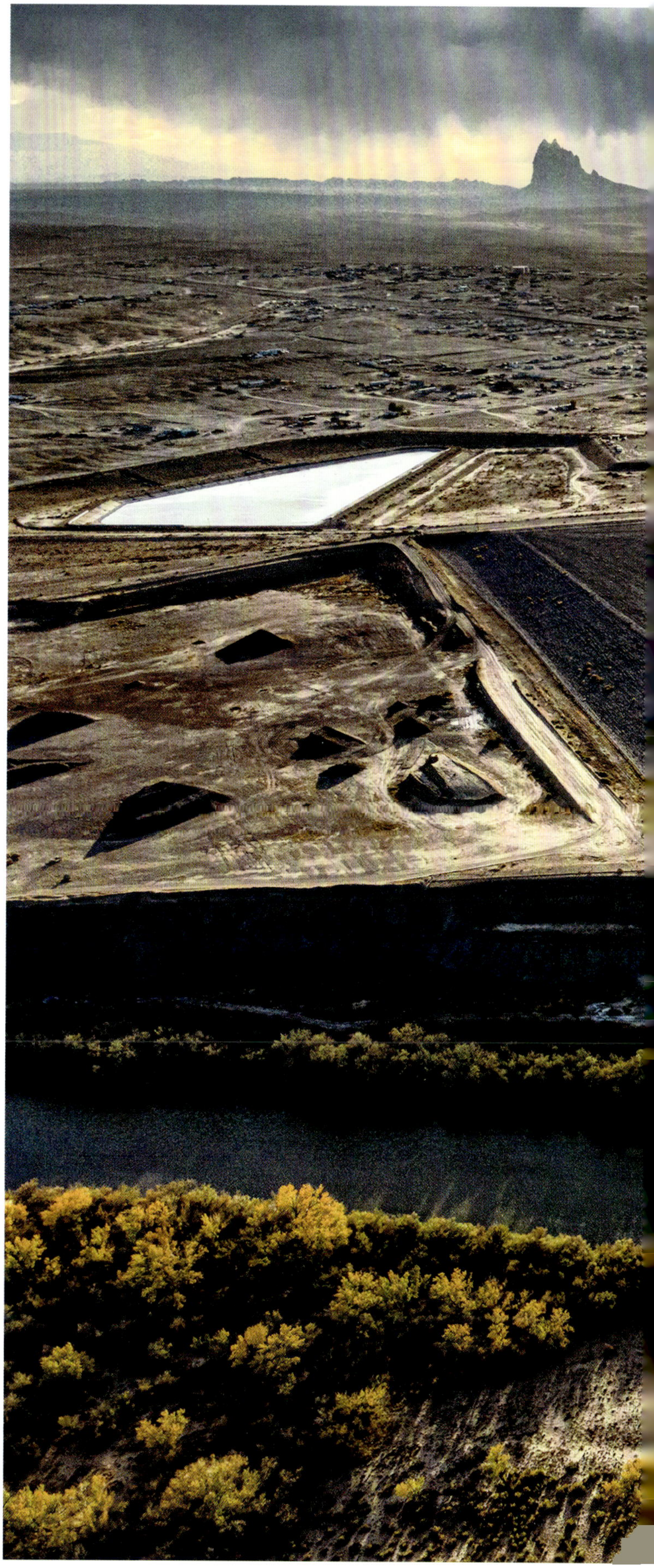

left in the wake of mining industries. Gold processing, for instance, relies on cyanide and sulfuric acid treatments, and yields contaminated wastewater, laden with heavy metals that pollute the surrounding ecosystem. Maisel notes the asymmetry, that "the word *pond* connotes something idyllic, perhaps a site where Thoreau might reflect on the natural world. . . . But no human-made tailings pond is wholly impervious to failure; they are essentially earthen dams." His *American Mine (Carlin, Nevada 1)* (2007) depicts such a pond, which seeps across the frame in what Maisel calls a cyanide-infused "lurid green."

For both Wilson and Maisel, this tension between the aesthetic allure and political-economic critique captured in their work needn't be resolved. Describing his depictions of Nevada's Carlin gold district, Maisel told me, "We may be seduced by its beauty and then feel a sense of betrayal when we comprehend the darkness of its subject. I like that contradiction, that ricochet between beauty and horror, seduction and betrayal." And given their siting in desert basins removed from most Americans' daily lives, this sort of mapping is all the more urgent. At the same time, the products and wealth generated by those sites suffuse every facet of our financial system and built environment. This is one reason LaToya Ruby Frazier's many series foregrounding the rust belt back East continue to resonate—because they show us the dense social worlds emanating from the more familiar landscapes of the mill, foundry, or factory.

Frazier was raised in Braddock, Pennsylvania, where Appalachian coal country converges with the industrial imperium of the early twentieth century. This Pittsburgh region was built on steel, a beacon for a new middle class and Black families on the Great Migration. But by the time of Frazier's childhood, in the 1980s, much of the US Steel plant and its jobs were gone, while the toxicity remained. She and her family were left to contend

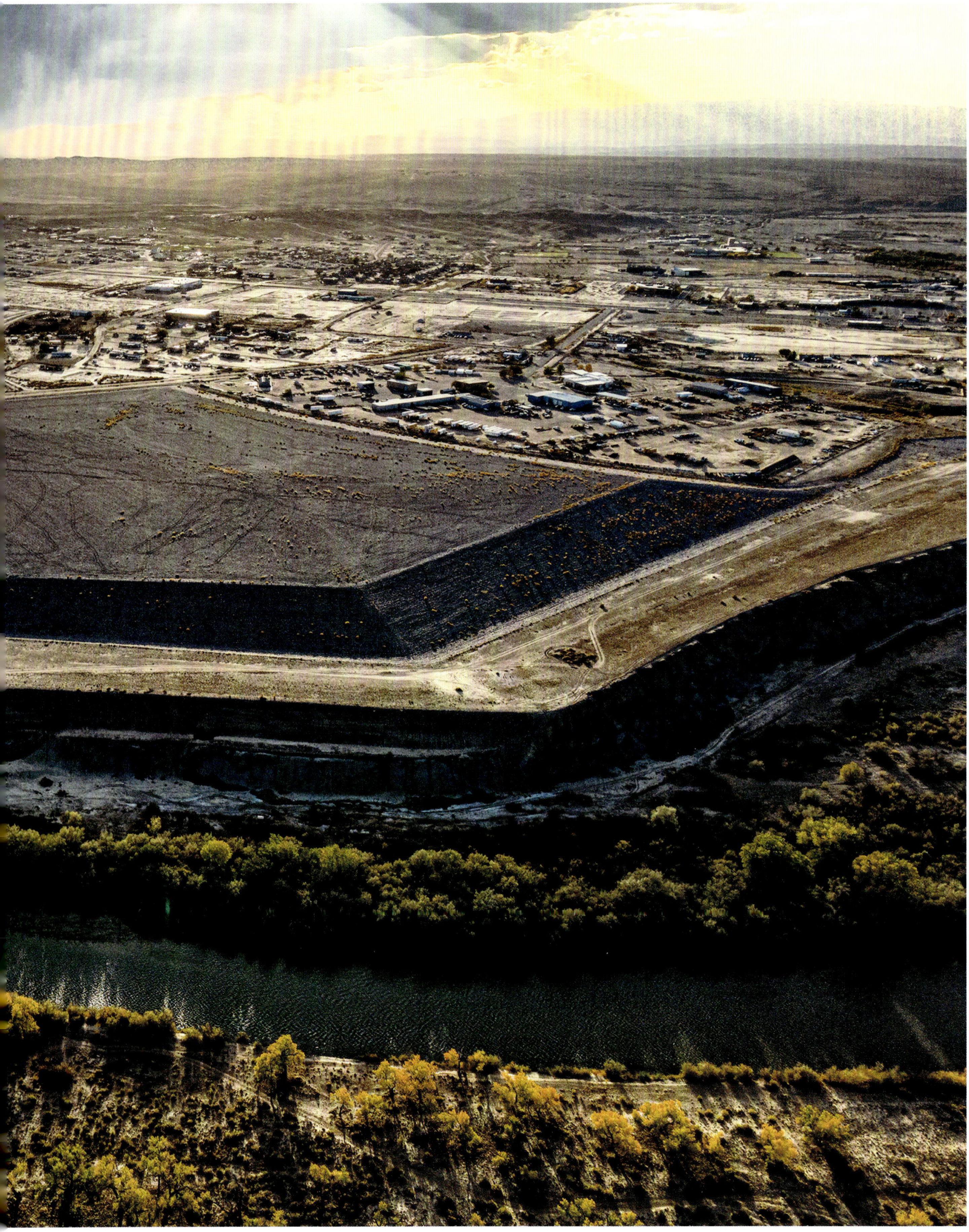

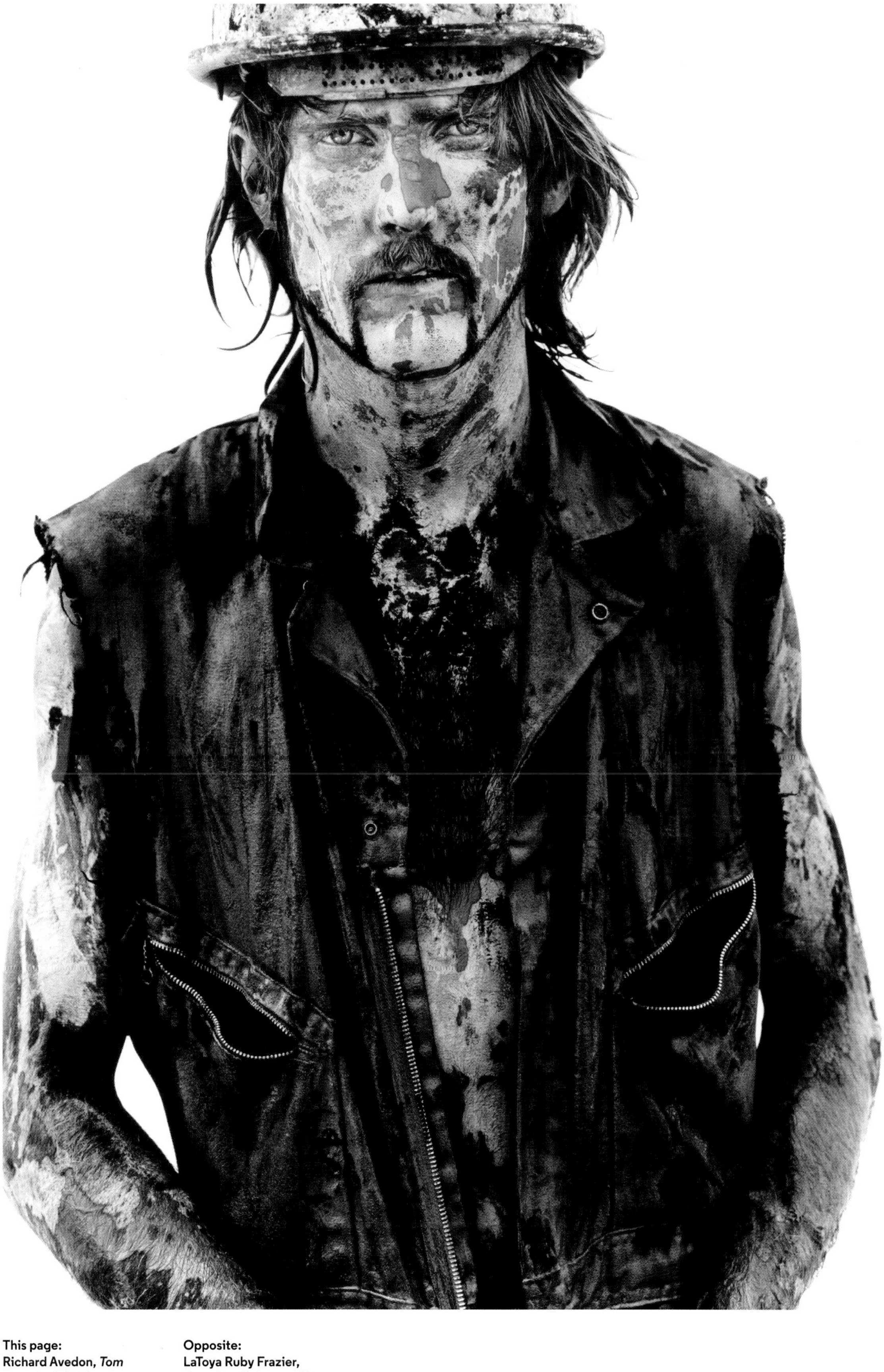

This page:
Richard Avedon, *Tom Stroud, oil field worker*, Velma, Oklahoma, June 12, 1980
© The Richard Avedon Foundation

Opposite:
LaToya Ruby Frazier, *Grandma Ruby and Me in Her Livingroom*, 2007
© LaToya Ruby Frazier and courtesy the artist and Gladstone Gallery, New York

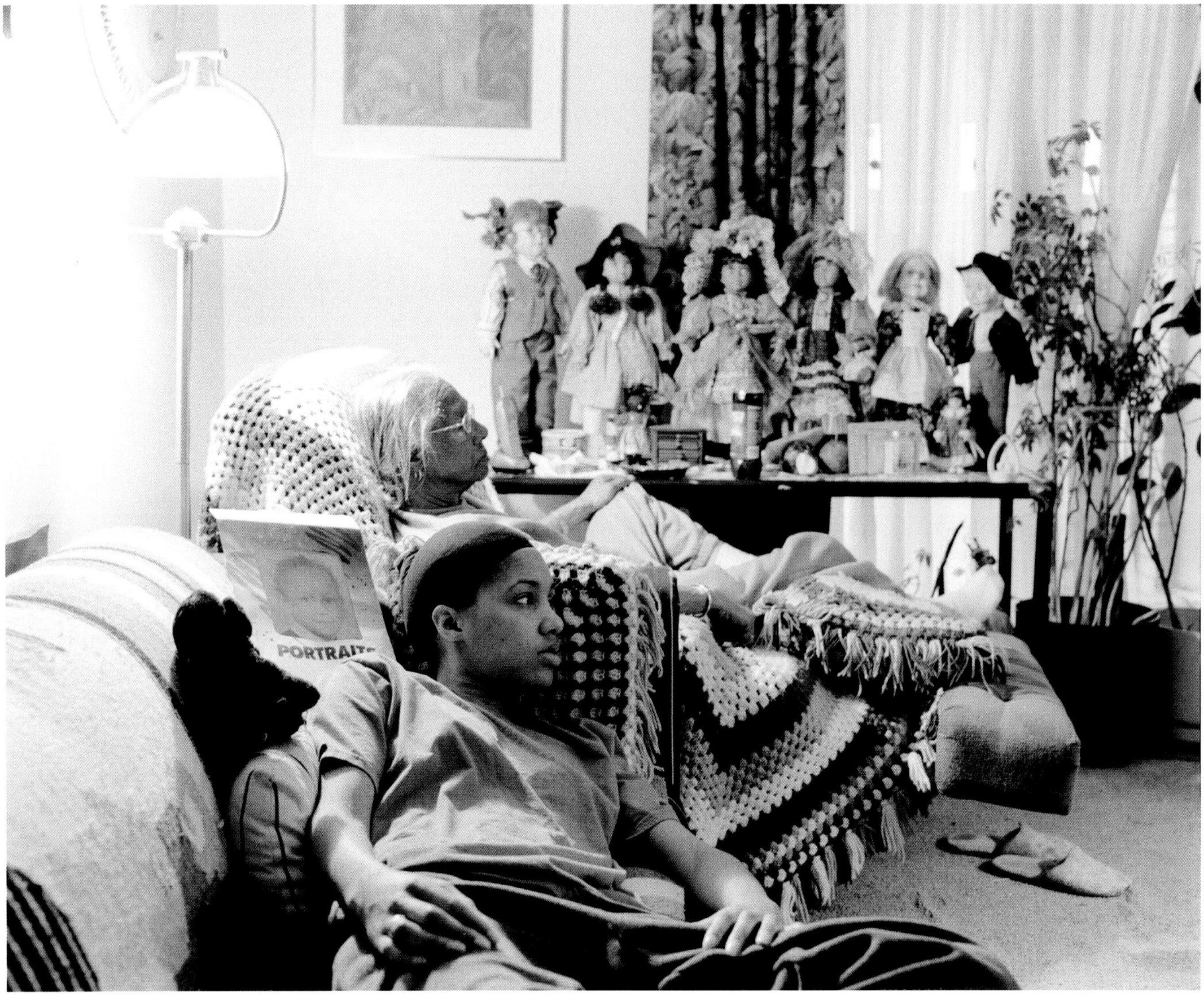

with a contemporary ghost town, where even the local medical center closed its doors, leaving the borough to the vagaries of foreclosure or gentrification. One of several Frazier photographs in *Beneath the Surface* is drawn from her celebrated photo-essay of domestic interiors. Another shows the Monongahela River arcing picturesquely around two remaining operational furnaces, interlaced by highway and railcars: The black-and-white scene was taken in 2013 but could be a postcard from another era, in which such vernacular architecture manifested the mined world in human terms.

For all the power of these industrial topographies, Frazier is best known as a portraitist of the American working class. In this way, her immersive projects are of a piece with journalistic forebears such as Gordon Parks and Margaret Bourke-White (both featured in the show, with their entrancing geometries of oil pipelines and poured molten ore, respectively). Yet Frazier's contemporary icons breathe in new ways in *Beneath the Surface* when seen alongside a host of anonymous mine workers captured in the antique tonalities of the nineteenth century. While extractive capitalism is the structure in which modern mining unfolds, that same mining is done by the countless humans toiling at the ore face. This has always been rough labor conducted at excruciating temperatures in the stygian depths. There is a reason that mine head frames (which hoist people, animals, and ore up and down their cableways) are called "gallows": Drowning, explosion, asphyxiation, and tunnel collapse have always been present dangers; deafness, silicosis, black lung, and other maladies stalk those workers years later.

Beneath the Surface's task, then, is to strike a difficult balance, telling a story of extraction from its widest conceptual angles while grounding it in the human tableaux in which involute systems are animated. It is an important time to revisit this American story, not only because versions of it are playing out around the world right now but also because we are still navigating the contradictions and residues of a modernity hewn from the mines. Photography, it is clear, has long drawn our focus to the stakes of that modernity: It's there in what and how we consume, where we prospect anew, and in the forms of solidarity we seek. Just because what happens beneath the surface so easily eludes our vision does not mean it does not reverberate up here in the light.

Ian Bourland is a critic and historian at Georgetown University.

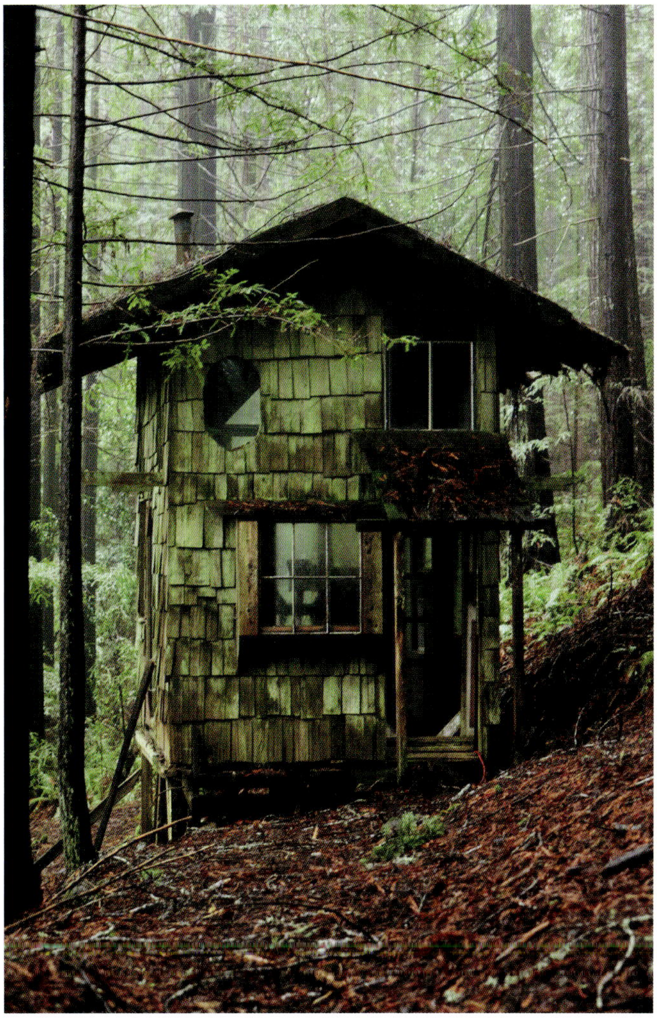

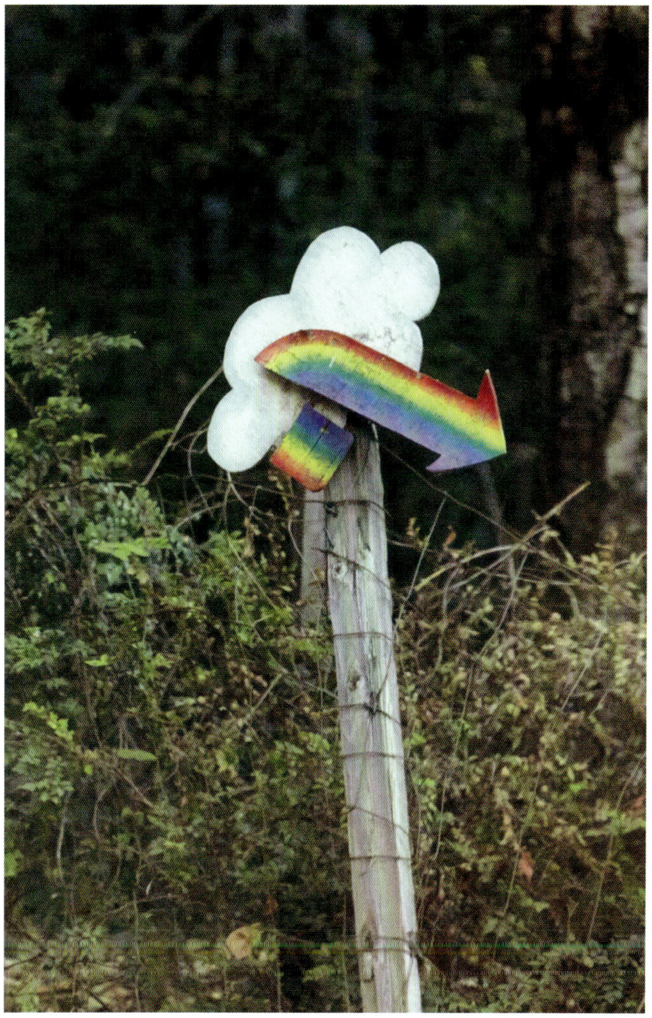

Michael Schmelling

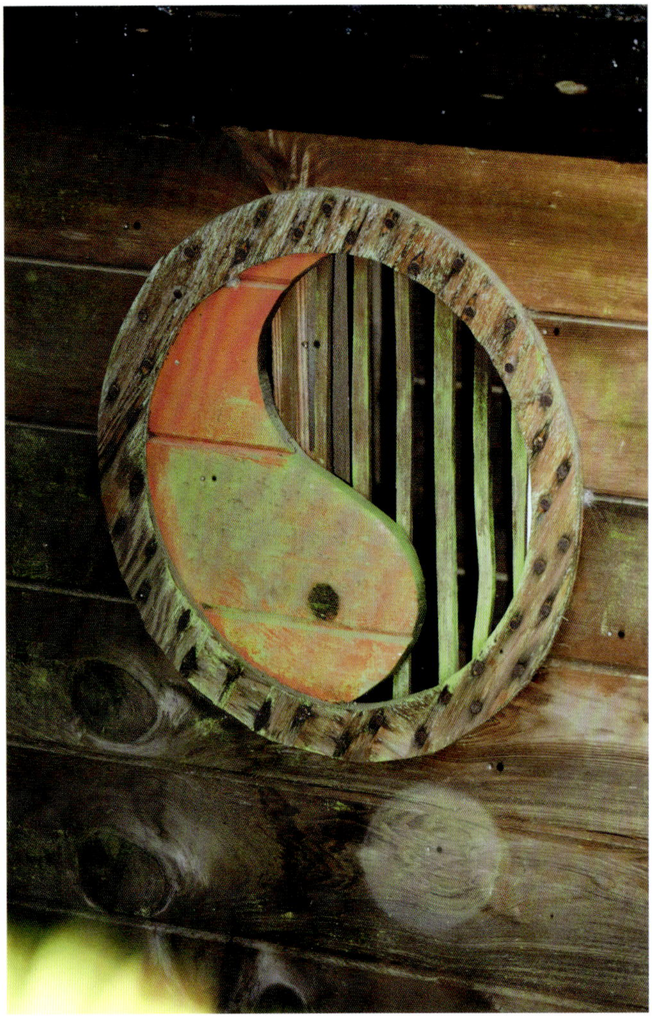

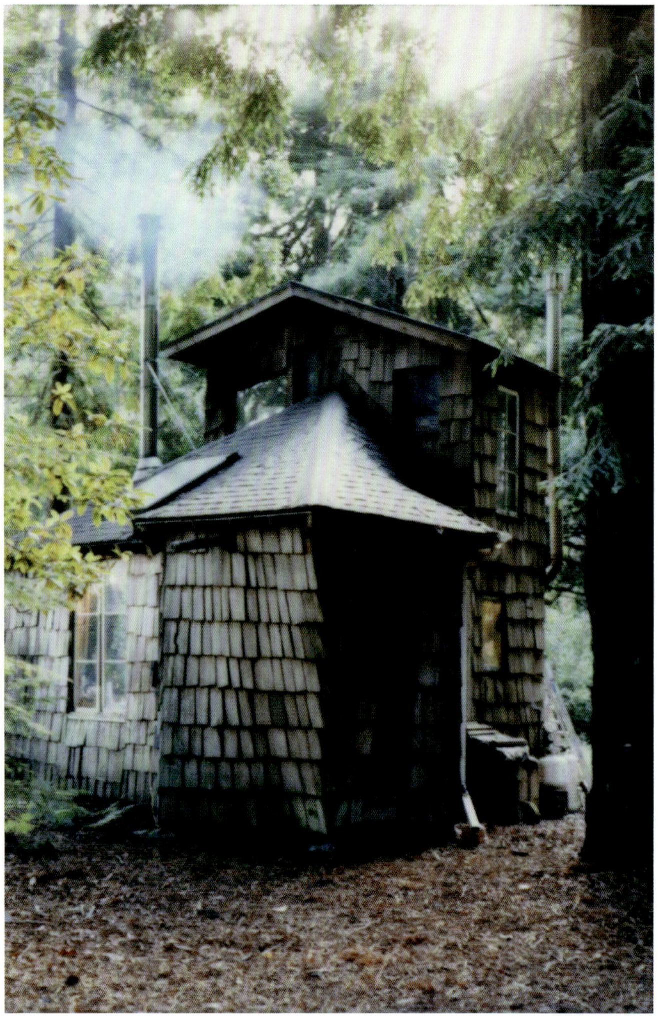

Back to the Land

Jeremy Miller

When we think of pioneers, the image that probably springs to mind is that of a migrant on a covered wagon crossing an endless prairie—a vision rooted in the myth of manifest destiny. But there was a second wave of pioneers, less mythic yet no less ambitious. From the mid-1960s through the 1970s, thousands of young idealists, disillusioned by the Vietnam War and industrial capitalism, left the cities for the fringes of the American wilderness.

The back-to-the-land movement was a global phenomenon, but according to the Los Angeles–based photographer Michael Schmelling, its spiritual home was Northern California, in the wooded enclaves of Mendocino and Humboldt Counties. "This was the epicenter of the movement for the entire world," he told me.

For the last five years, he and his collaborator, David Jacob Kramer, have traveled thousands of miles of back roads in Mendocino and Humboldt, collecting images and oral histories of those pioneers for their book *Handmade Utopia: Back-to-the-Land Architecture in Northern California*, which will be published this summer. "You had people going north into this huge stretch of territory," Schmelling said. Driven by the idealism of the era and the do-it-yourself ethos articulated in Stewart Brand's *Whole Earth Catalog*, these transplants purchased parcels and set to carving out simple lives far from the urban throngs. "A lot of the land had been completely clear-cut. So big parcels could be bought for cheap. And on top of that, there was a lot less regulation," he explained.

Schmelling's photographs are saturated with the deep greens and dark earthen tones of the Pacific Northwest. Rectangular cabins, geodesic domes, yurts, kite-shaped barns, and myriad other unconventional structures—many tacked together from planks of rough-hewn pine—seem to have sprouted from the rugged hillsides of the Coast Ranges.

Traces of the counterculture run through the architecture: a stained-glass

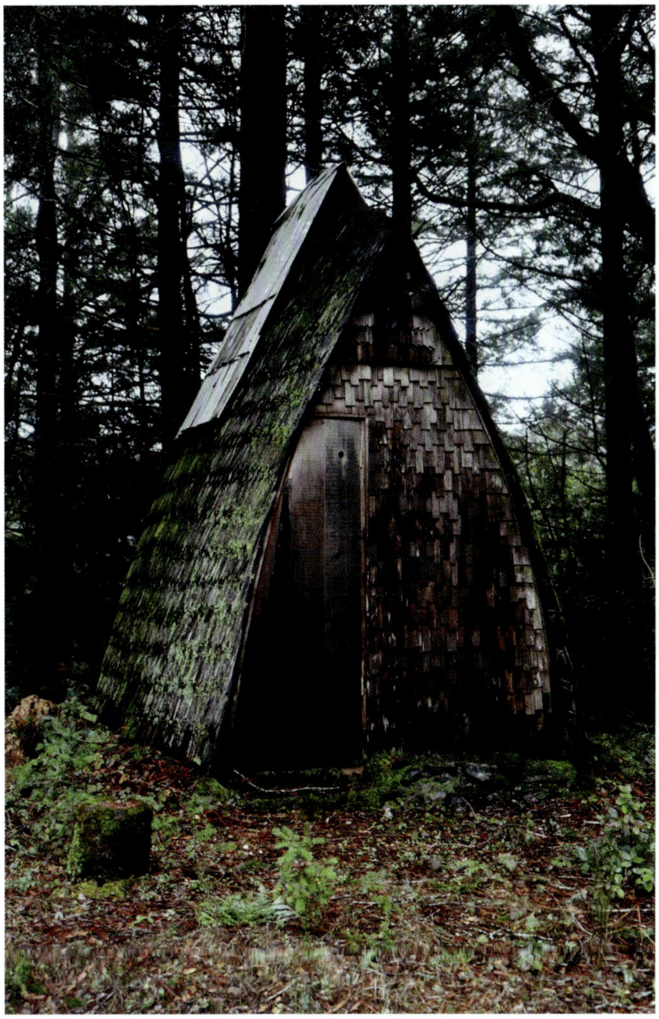

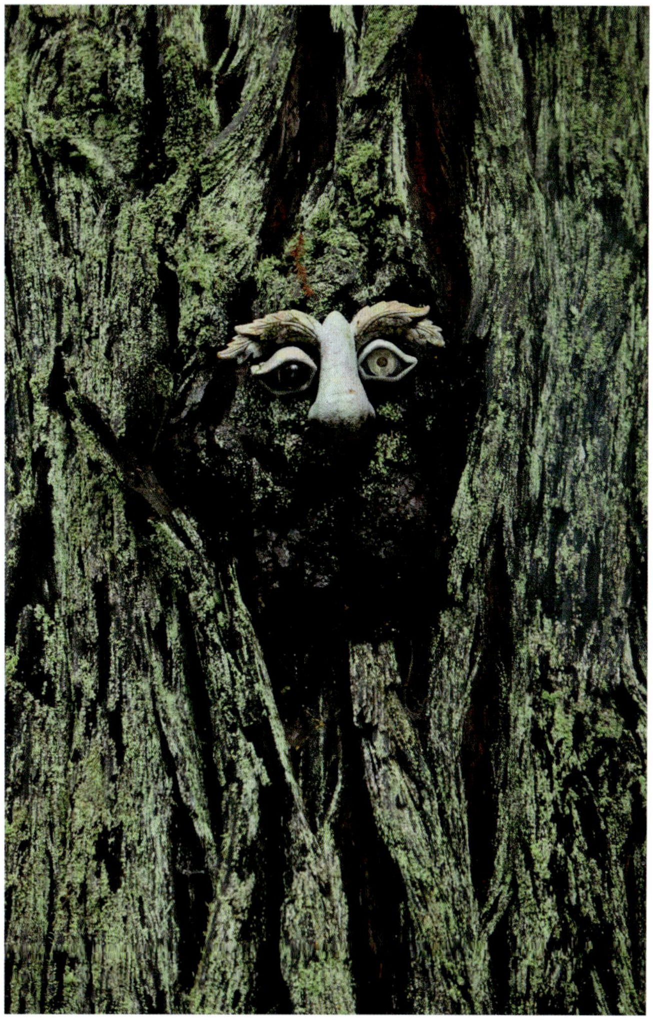

window in the shape of a psychedelic four-leaf clover; a yellowed newspaper urging the government to "lace the air with LSD." Yet Schmelling insists the movement was not mere escapism. "Back-to-the-landers were early adopters of solar power, organic farming, and sustainable living," he said. "They helped lay the groundwork for modern environmentalism."

Though no two houses are the same, the dreamlike edifices, inspired by "hippie modernism," form a cohesive style of architecture. Trees were cut and milled on-site; windows and doors were salvaged from demolition sites. The aesthetic is defined in equal parts by necessity, imagination, and willpower. Despite the rough edges, the homes in Schmelling's photographs exude an undeniable sophistication. Some hover on stilts over lakeshores. Others teeter precariously on steep hillsides. All are of a piece with the local environments in which they were built—a rarity in an age dominated by carbon-copy tract homes.

But Schmelling and Kramer's interests run deeper than architectural oddities. It is the personal stories of the men and women who built these homes that most interest them. There is Frannie Leopold, a Berkeley anti-war protester who came to the forests of Humboldt County for a party and found a vibrant community. There is Laird Sutton, a minister from San Francisco who, before moving to the woods, distributed instructional videos in hopes of educating his congregations about the many variations of human sexuality. And there is Tom Hessler, a former weed grower who lays out, in simple terms, his rationale for his many years in the woods: "I wanted to get away from everyone. I wanted to get the hell out of there. All the bullshit."

Schmelling's project is driven by a sense of urgency. "These people are aging out," he said. "We felt the need to get up there and document them before they are gone. Most of the people we photographed, like their sons and daughters, have moved back to cities. Most of these homes are empty already. You can see how they're kind of getting taken back by nature—they are going back to the land themselves."

Jeremy Miller is a writer in Richmond, California.

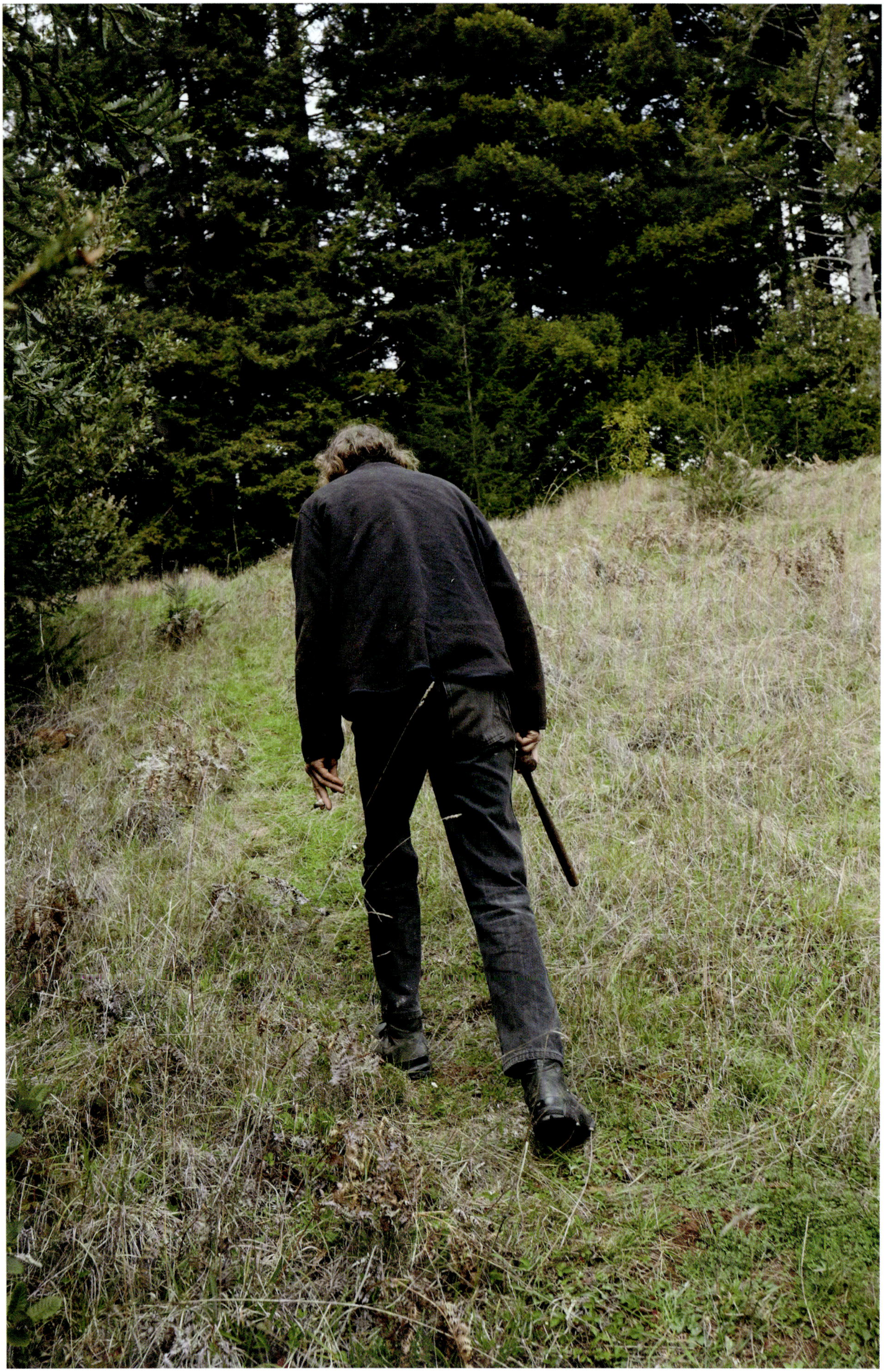

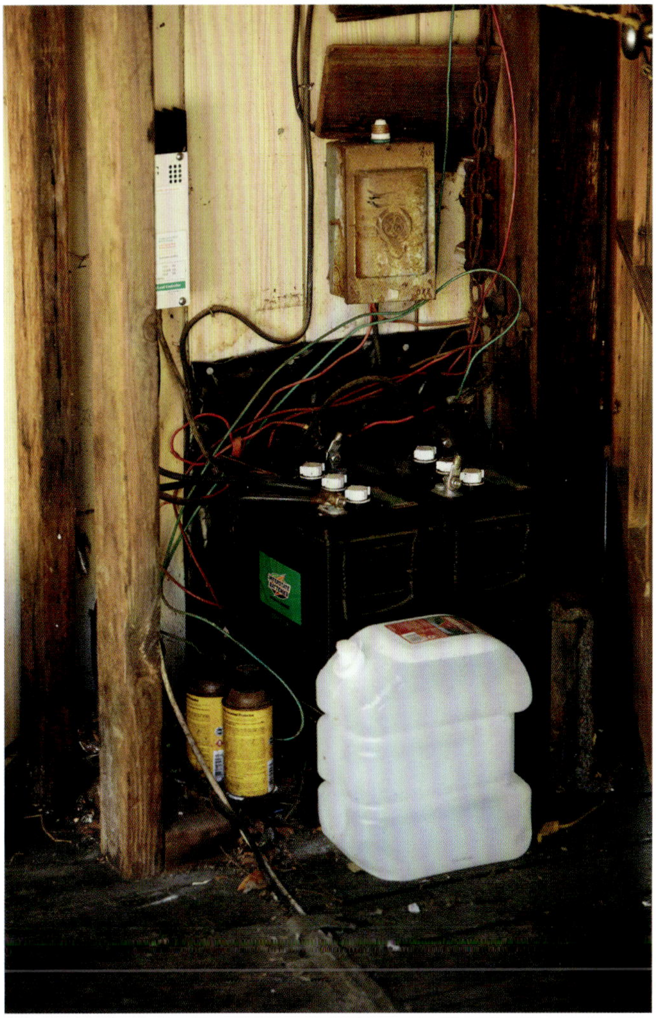

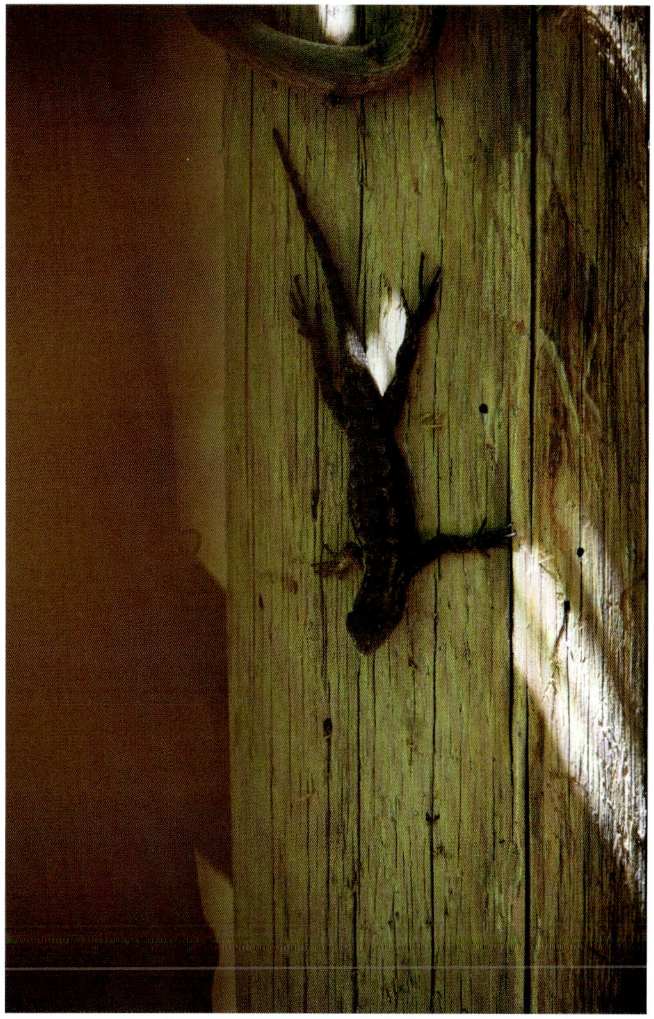

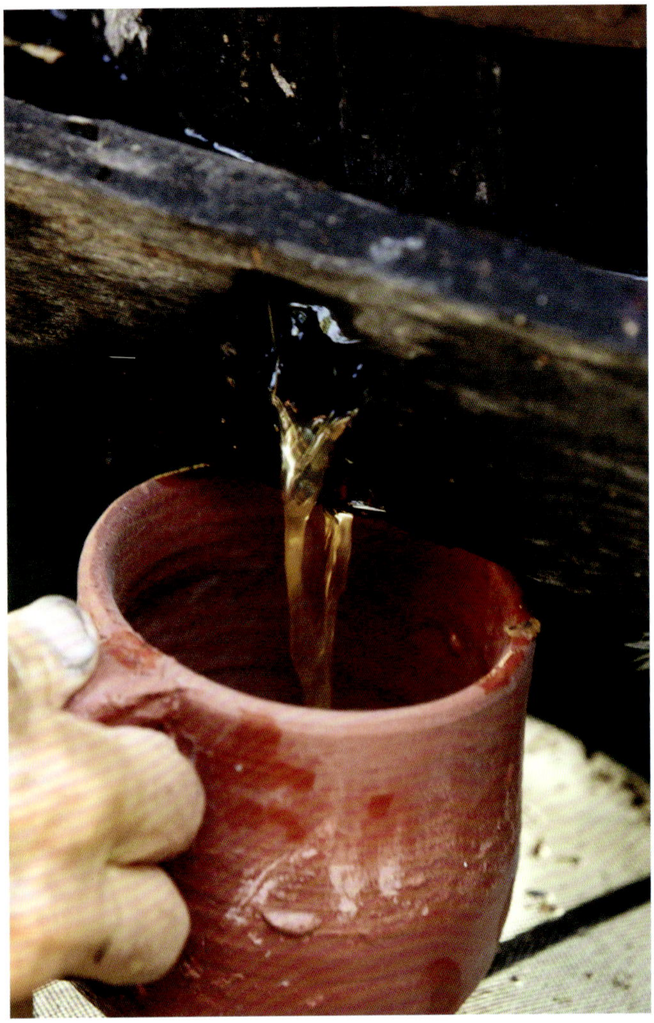

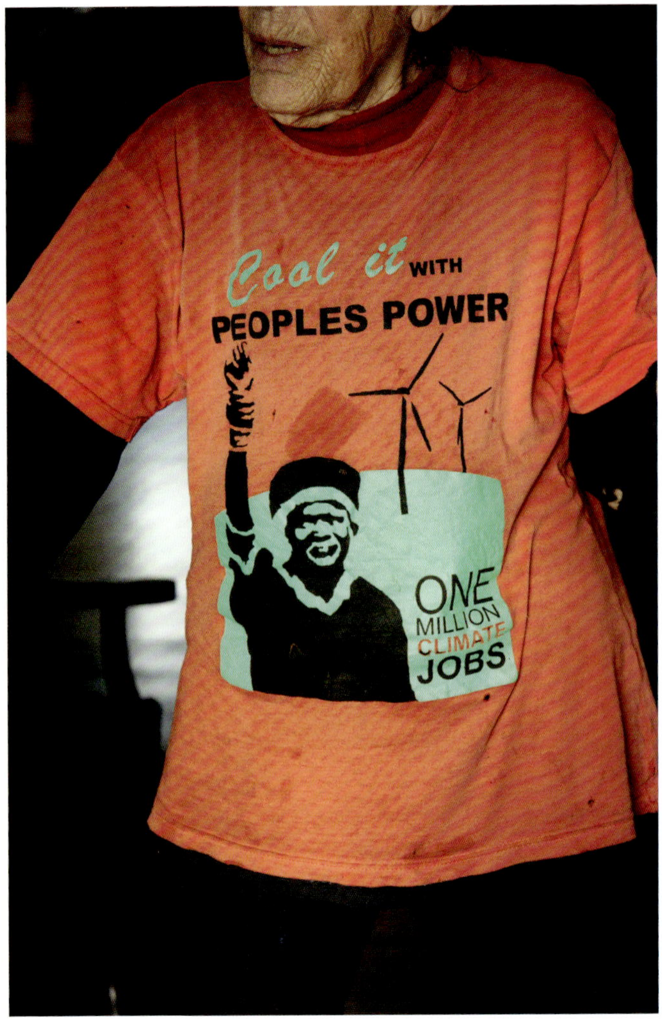
Cool it WITH
PEOPLES POWER
ONE
MILLION
CLIMATE
JOBS

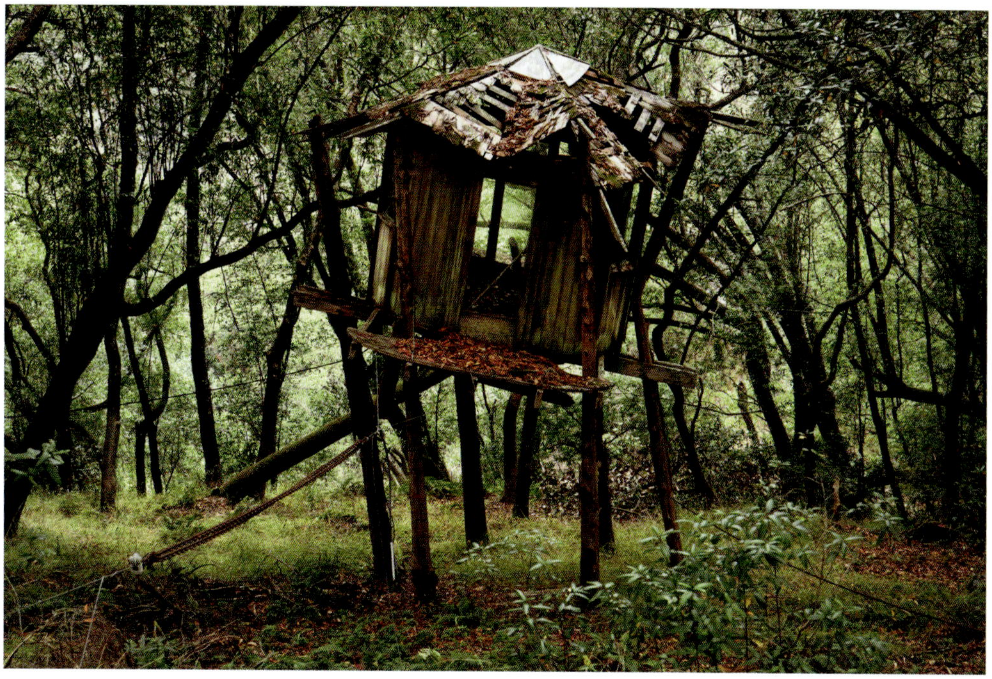
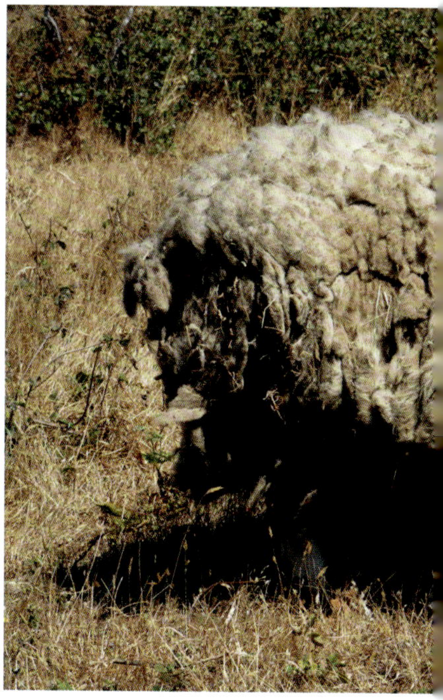
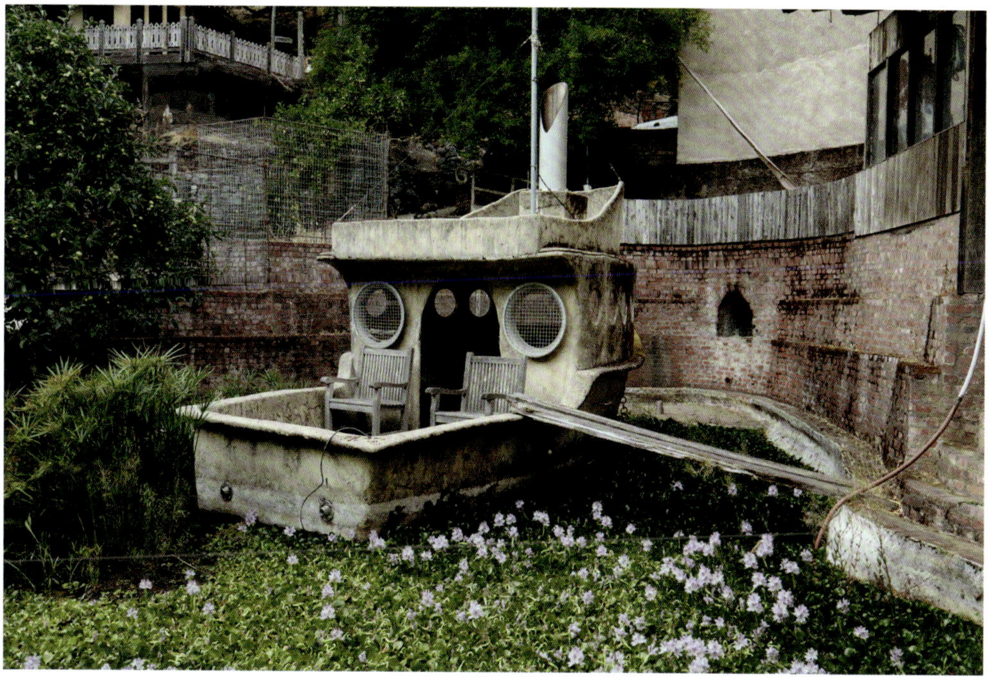
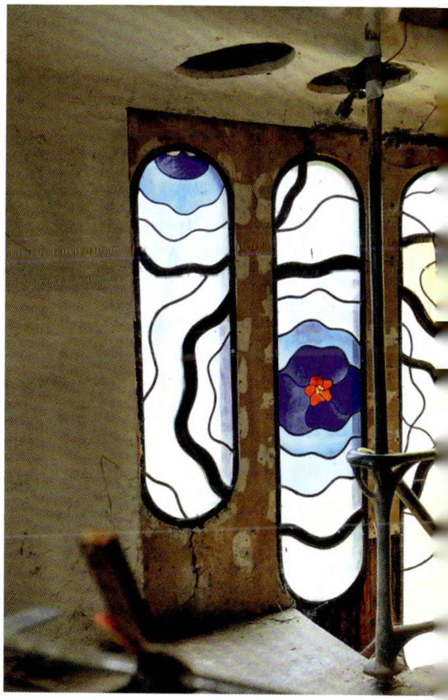
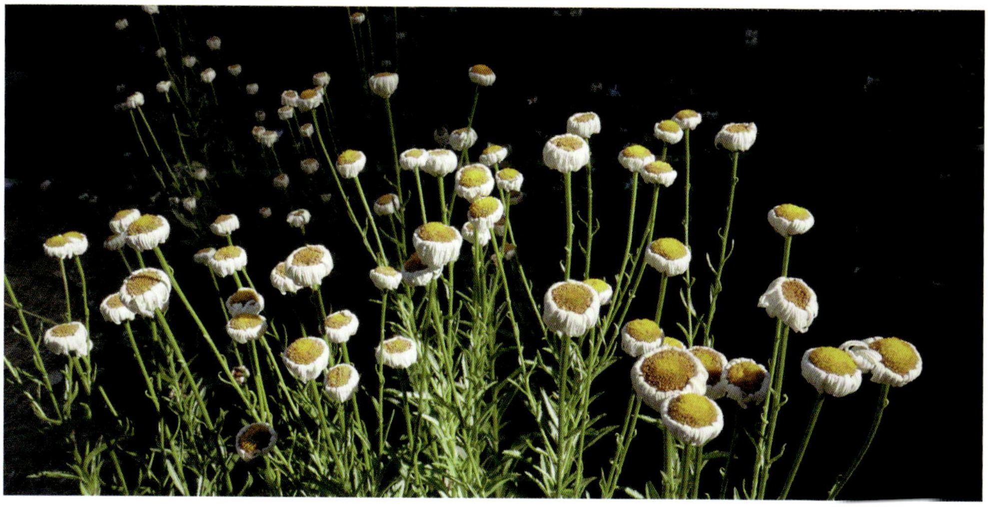
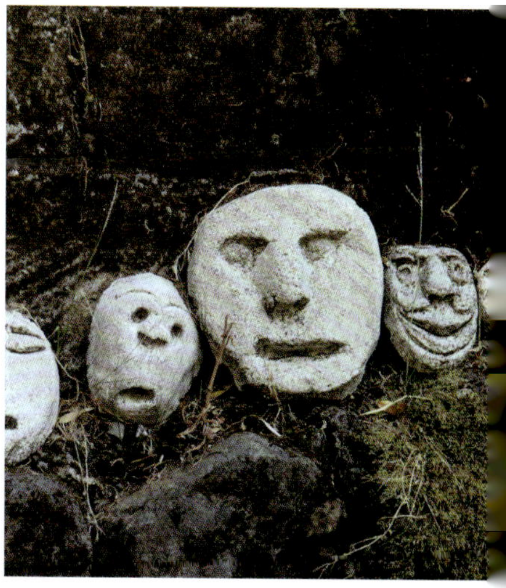

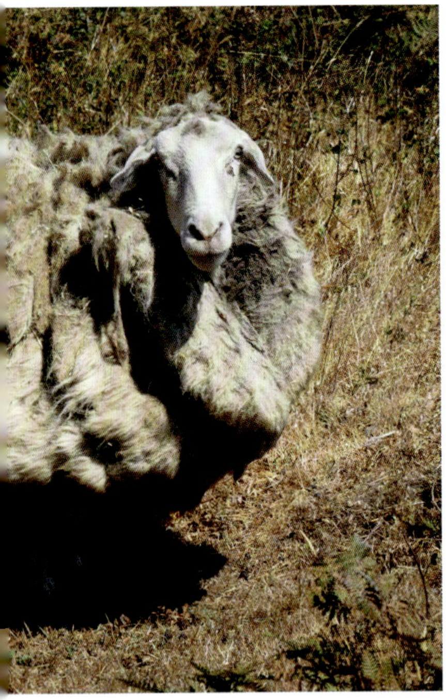

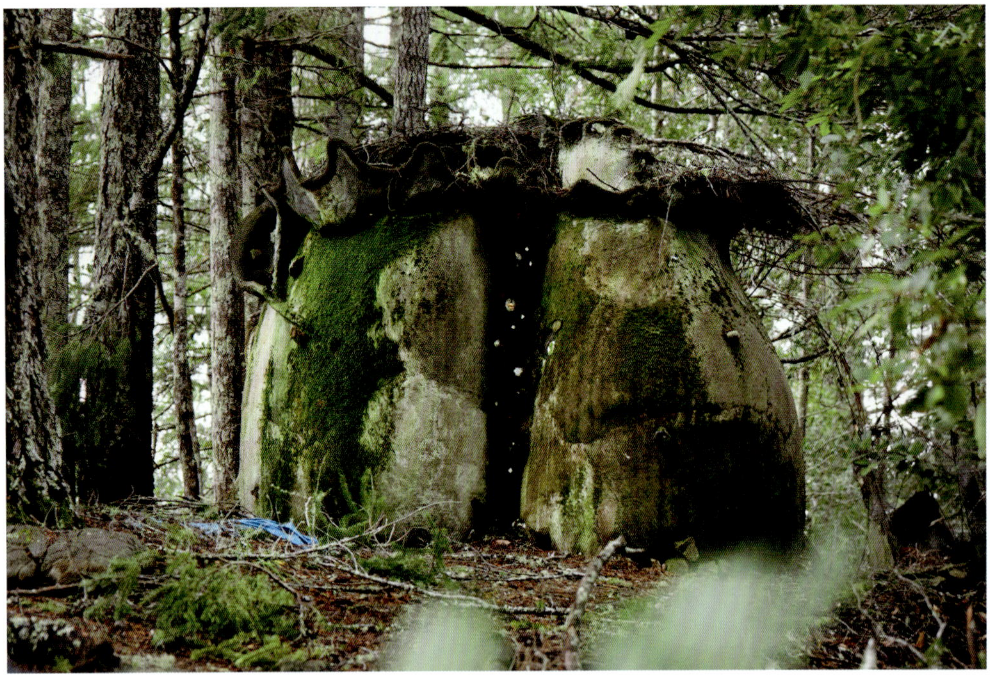

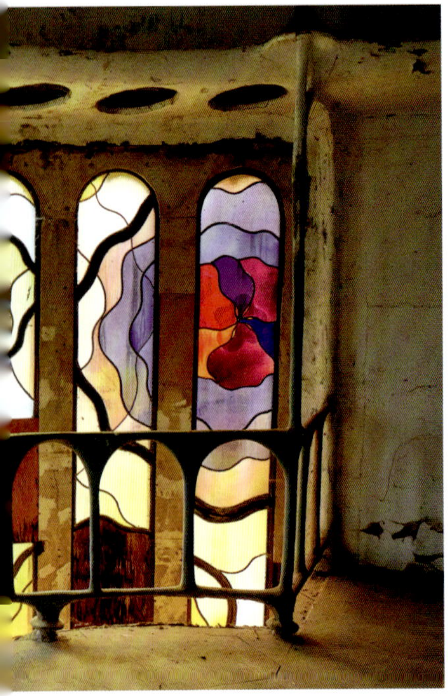

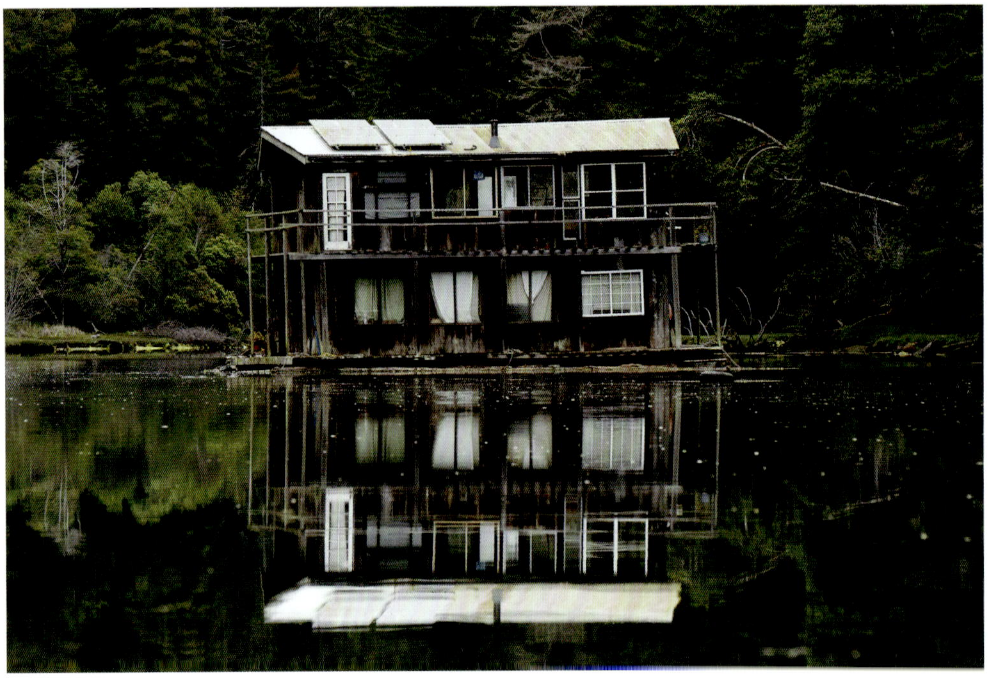

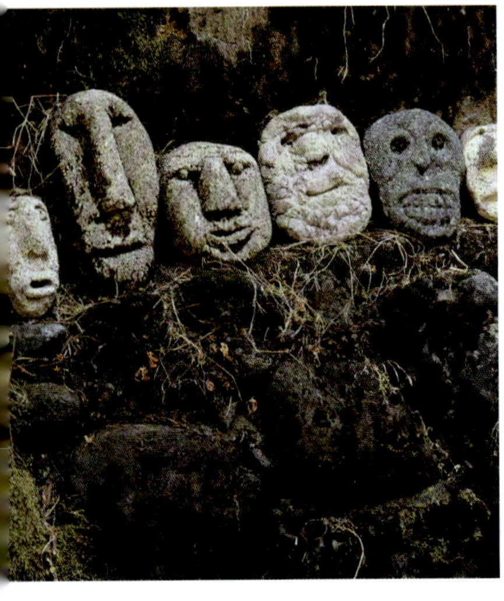

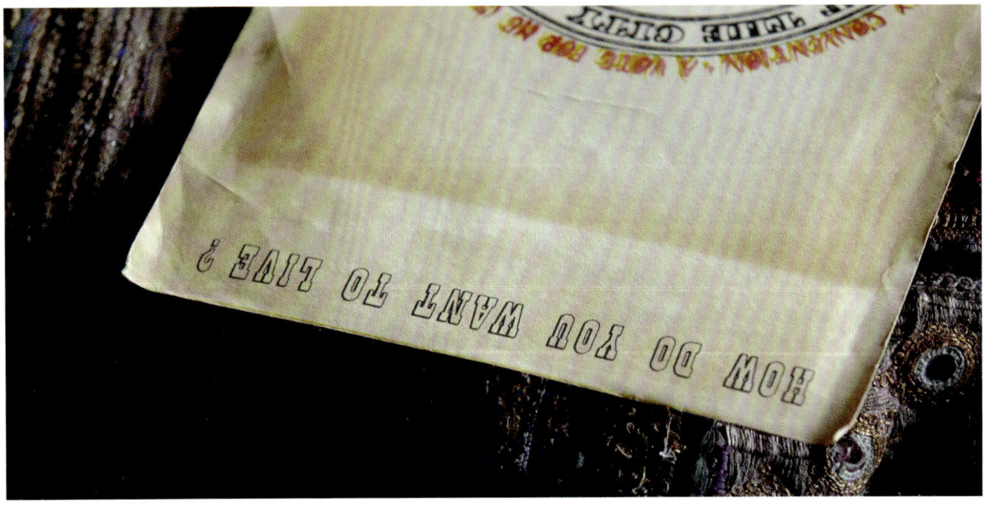
HOW DO YOU WANT TO LIVE ?

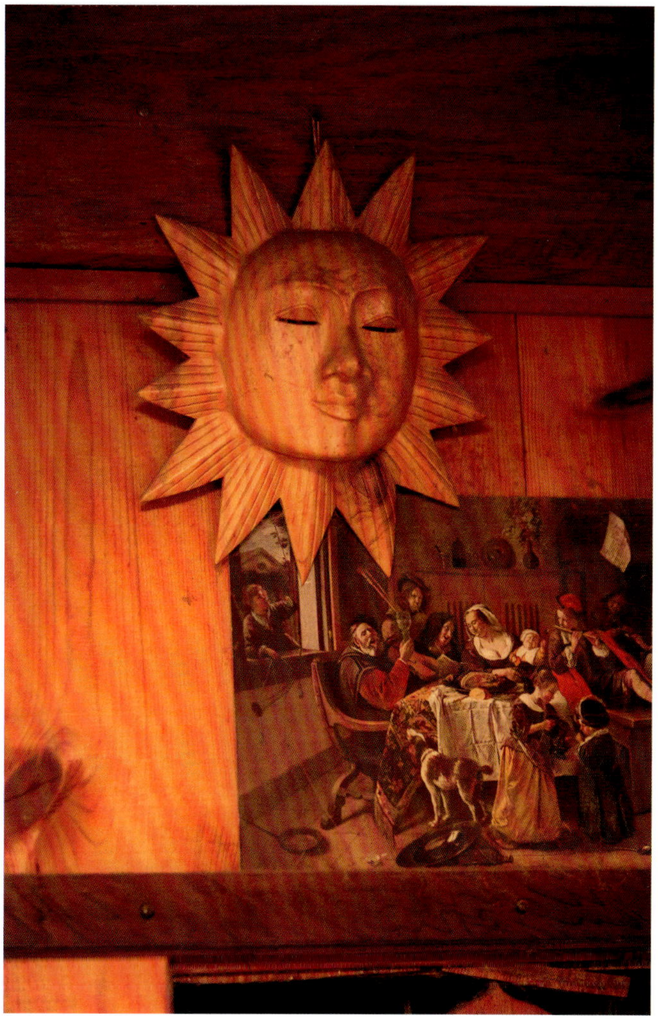

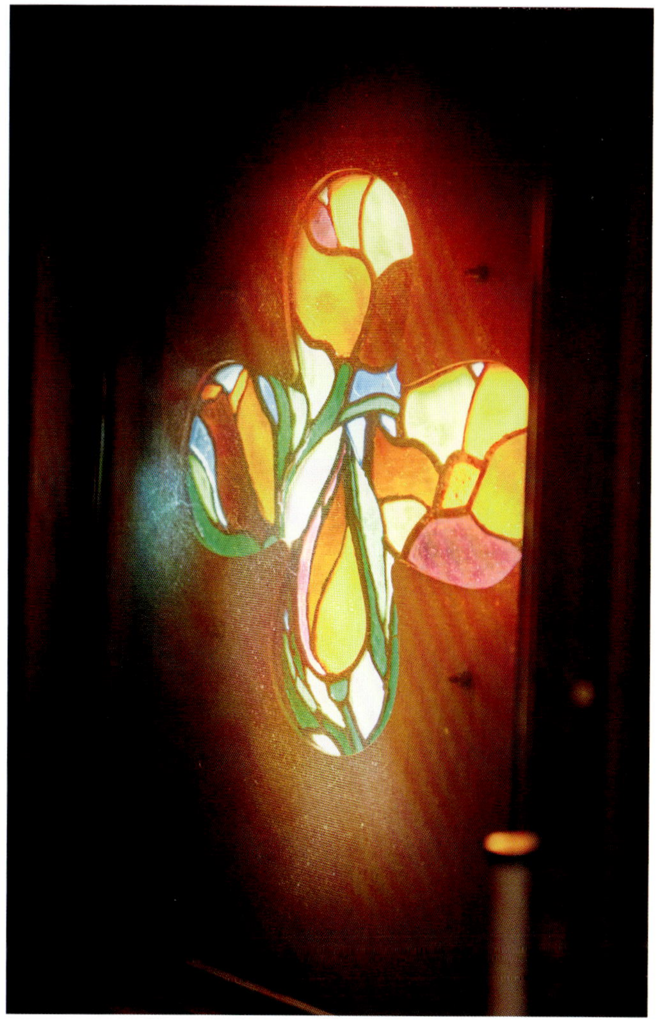

All photographs from the series *Handmade Utopia*, 2021–25
Courtesy the artist

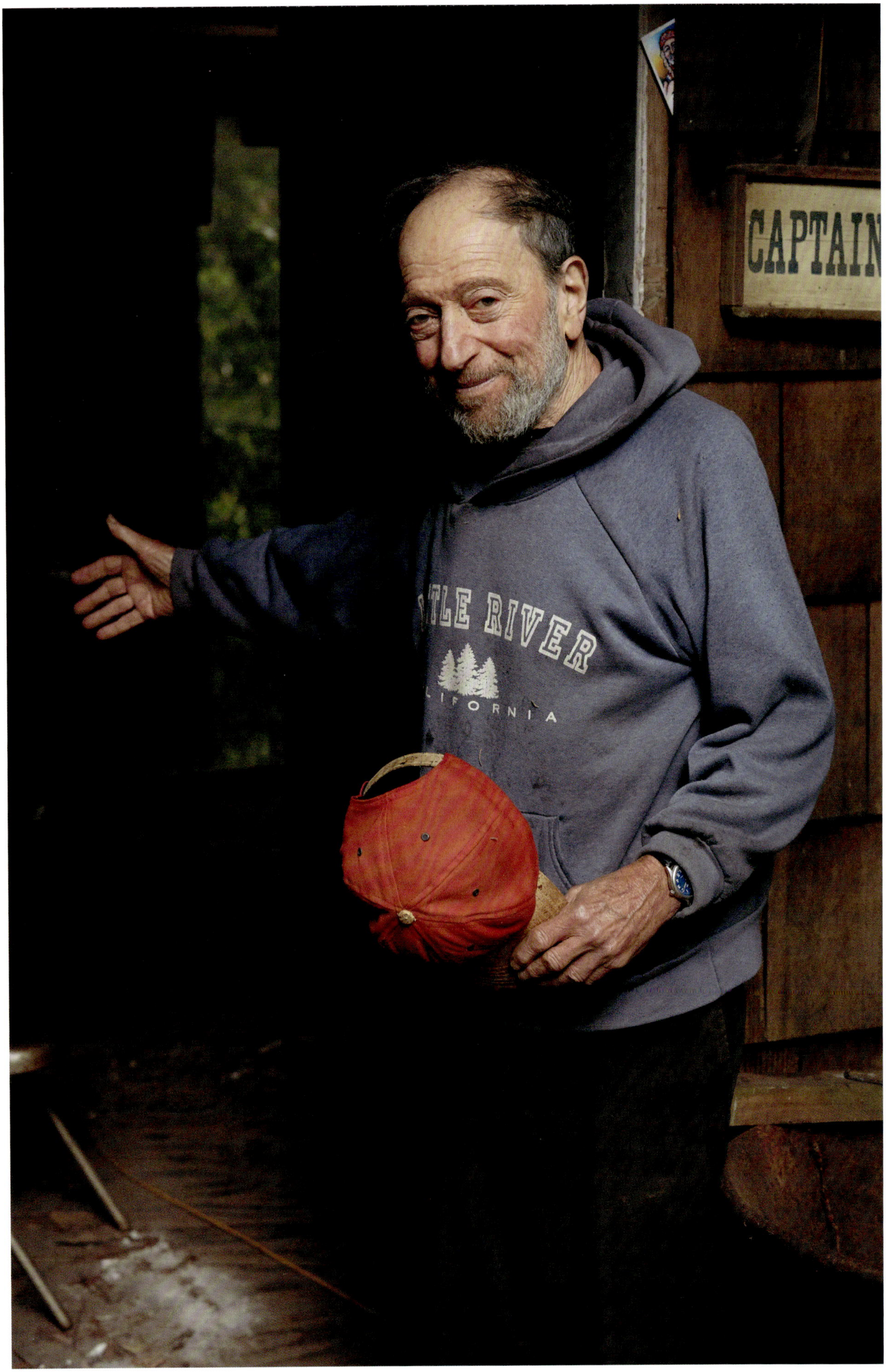
CAPTAIN
RIVER

Gayatri Ganju
The Pregnant Tree

Amitava Kumar

For the past several years, Gayatri Ganju, who was born in 1989 and lives in Bengaluru, India, has traveled south into the dense Nilgiri forest in Tamil Nadu to take pictures among the Kurumba people, one of the several Indigenous groups inhabiting the land. Her companions are two Kurumba men: Murthy, who is in his thirties, and Subbu, in his sixties; both serve as her guides and translators. Ganju needs a translator because she makes images only after close listening. During her treks, she asks the Kurumba to share their stories about the forest, this forest that is sacred to them and the site of their ancestral habitation. These meetings enact a ritual, with everyone sitting in a circle, sharing what they remember, and often what they are forgetting.

It is not always easy; there has been some suspicion of Ganju as an outsider. Early in her project, Ganju participated in a discussion with Kurumba representatives, and it was decided that the stories she collected would remain behind, among the people. Ganju was given permission to take only one story out into the world. This is the story that she received—a story about how the forests came to be born:

God made the world and then told the birds that there were no trees yet, and he was going to give them seeds to take back and put into the soil. The birds began their journey, but a wicked giant had overheard the conversation, and, as he didn't want any trees, he took the seeds from the birds. The giant put the seeds in a big, hot pan and began to roast them so that they would die. There was one very clever little bird called the *pirikki* who understood what the giant was doing. She dived into the pan to save the seeds. In the process, some of her feathers were burned and turned black, and that is how the black-and-white pirikki got the marks on its feathers. The pirikki carried the seeds in her beak and planted them in the earth. These seeds turned into huge thriving forests.

When I first encountered the pictures in Ganju's series *The Pregnant Tree* (2016–ongoing), they appeared mysterious. The story that Ganju had heard among the Kurumba offered an explanation. Even now, these images seem to belong to a play; they are staged, a dramatic moment caught in a long performance. However, as I looked at them more, it began to seem that the real silence that the photographs hold within them is the silence of the forest itself. Ganju told me that official records indicate that over the last two hundred years, there has been an 80 percent loss of the Nilgiri grasslands mosaic. This is an ancient, prolific ecosystem with 3,500 flowering plants and 1,500 endemic species; it is recognized by UNESCO as one of the world's most biodiverse areas. We do not witness in Ganju's work the depredations carried out in the name of development, or the lives of the people forced out of the forest and now living in urban slums—displaced people, like seeds being roasted in a pan over a fire. This, too, is a part of the silence and mystery of these photographs. They possess the quiet calm of trees in a forest. There is much for the viewer to learn and find moving in that world that is still there.

Amitava Kumar is the author, most recently, of the novel *My Beloved Life* (2024).

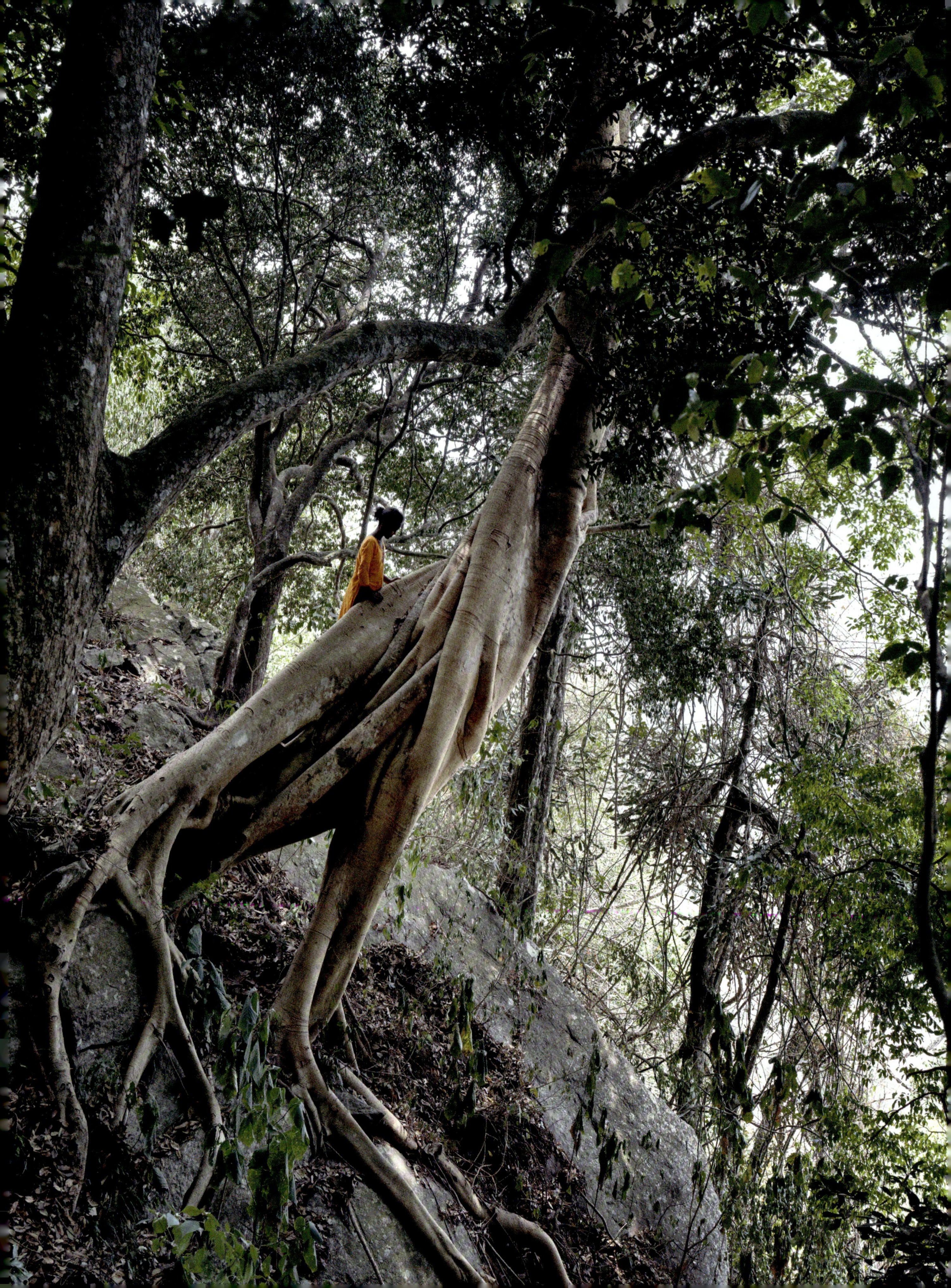

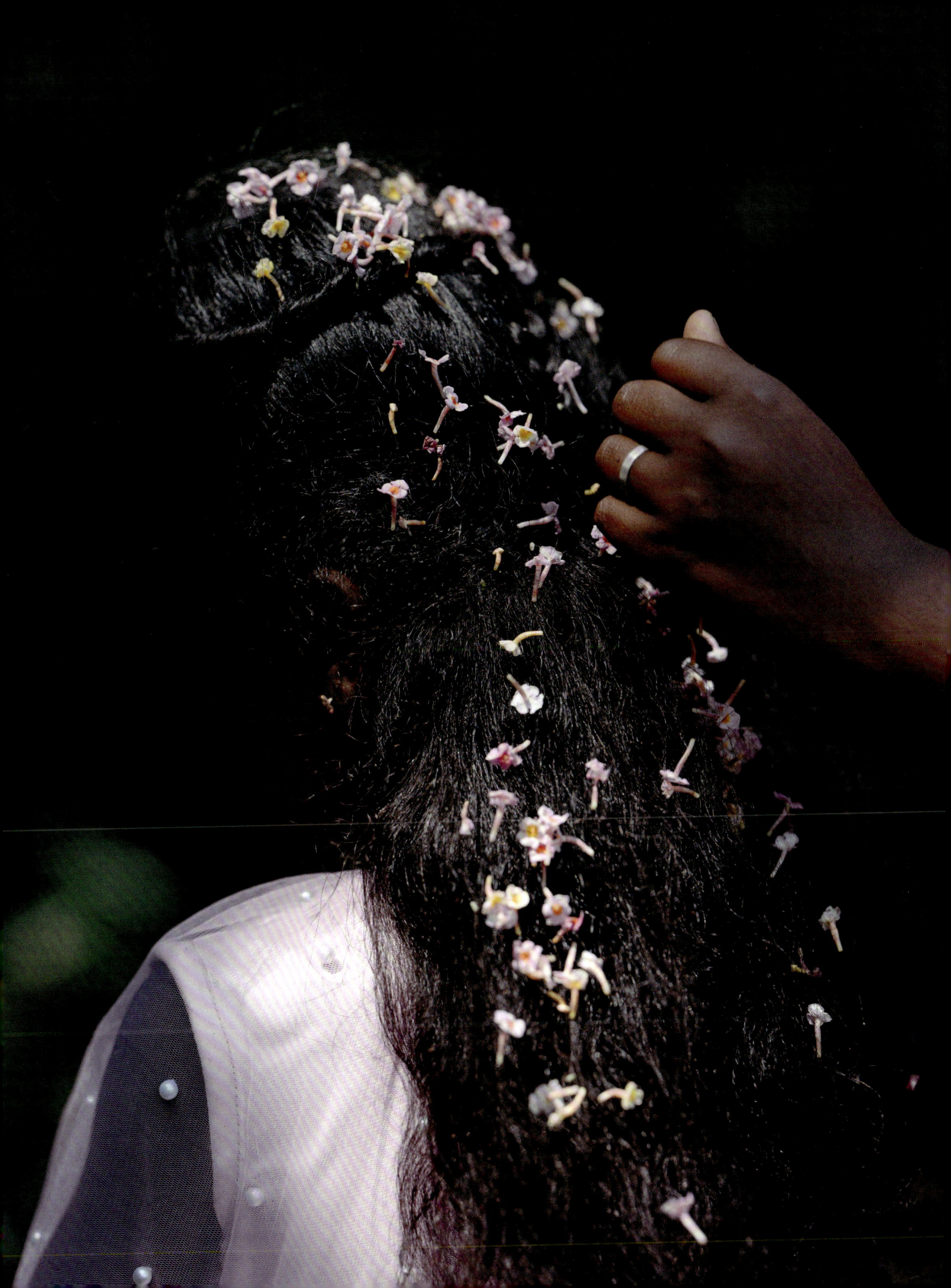

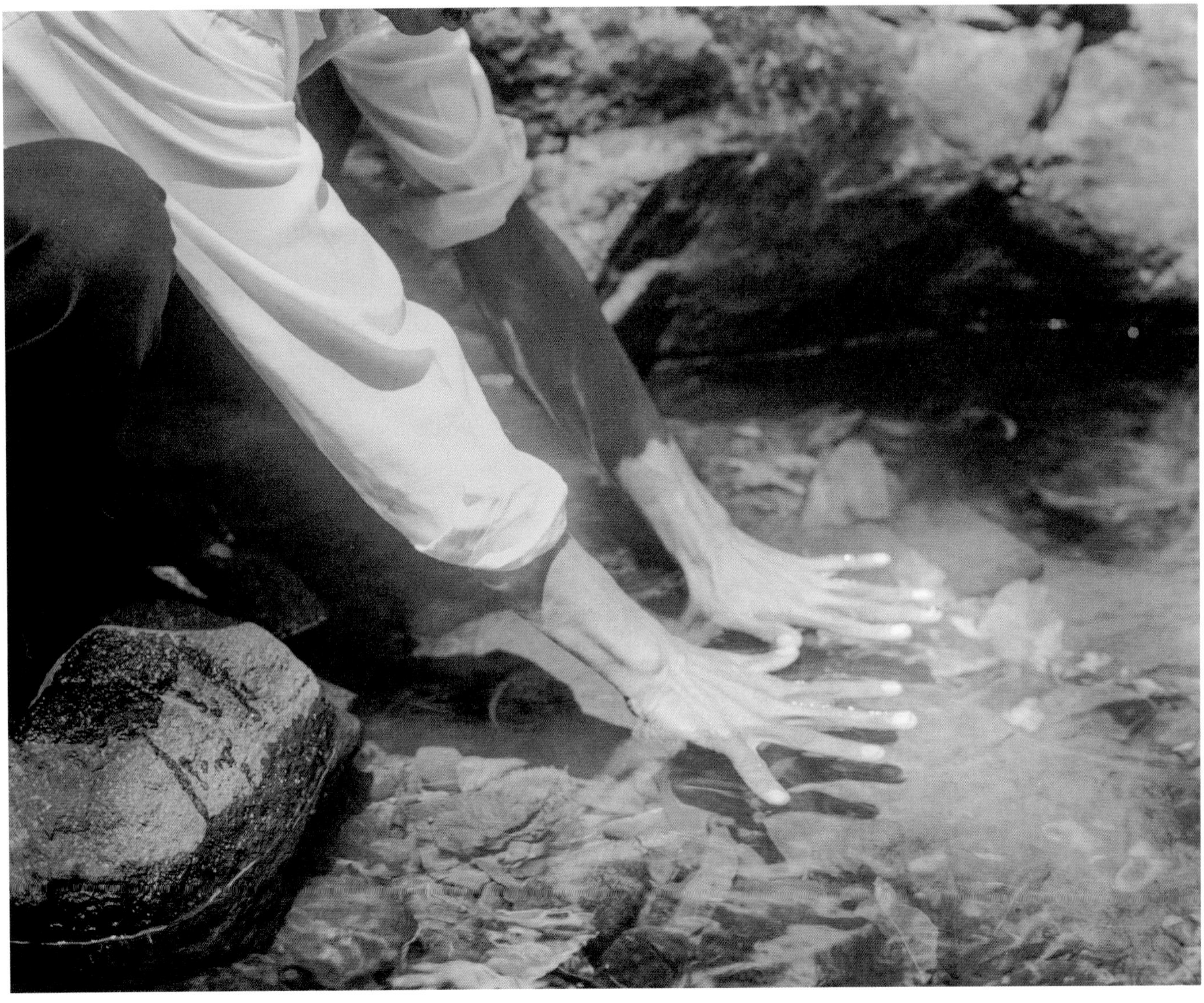

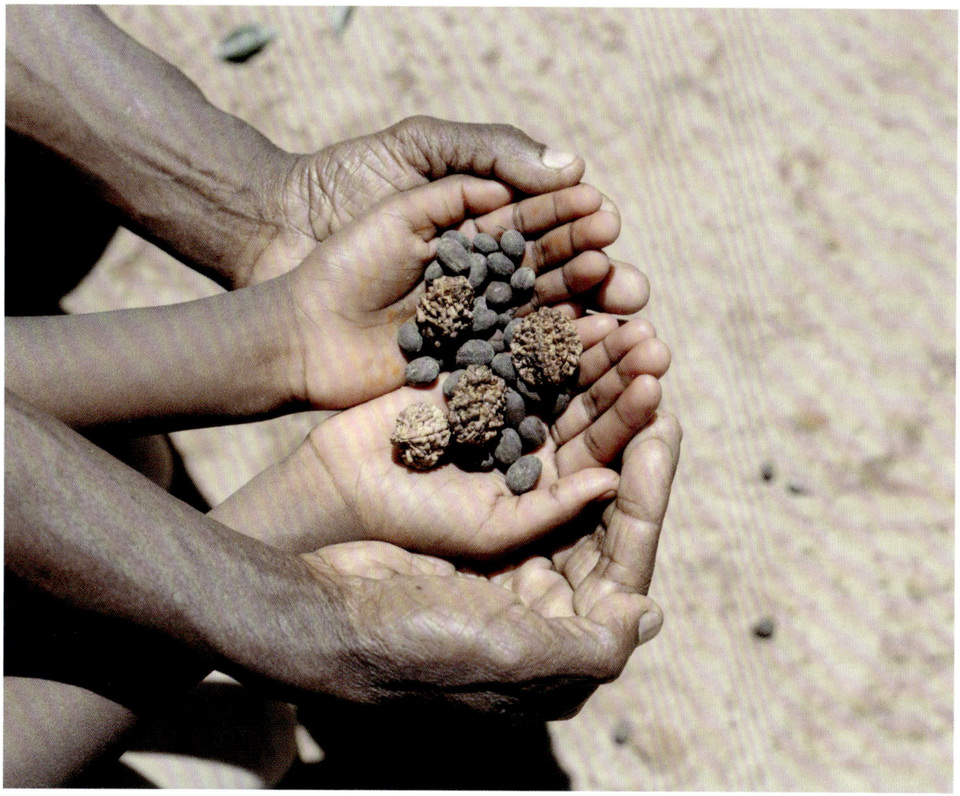

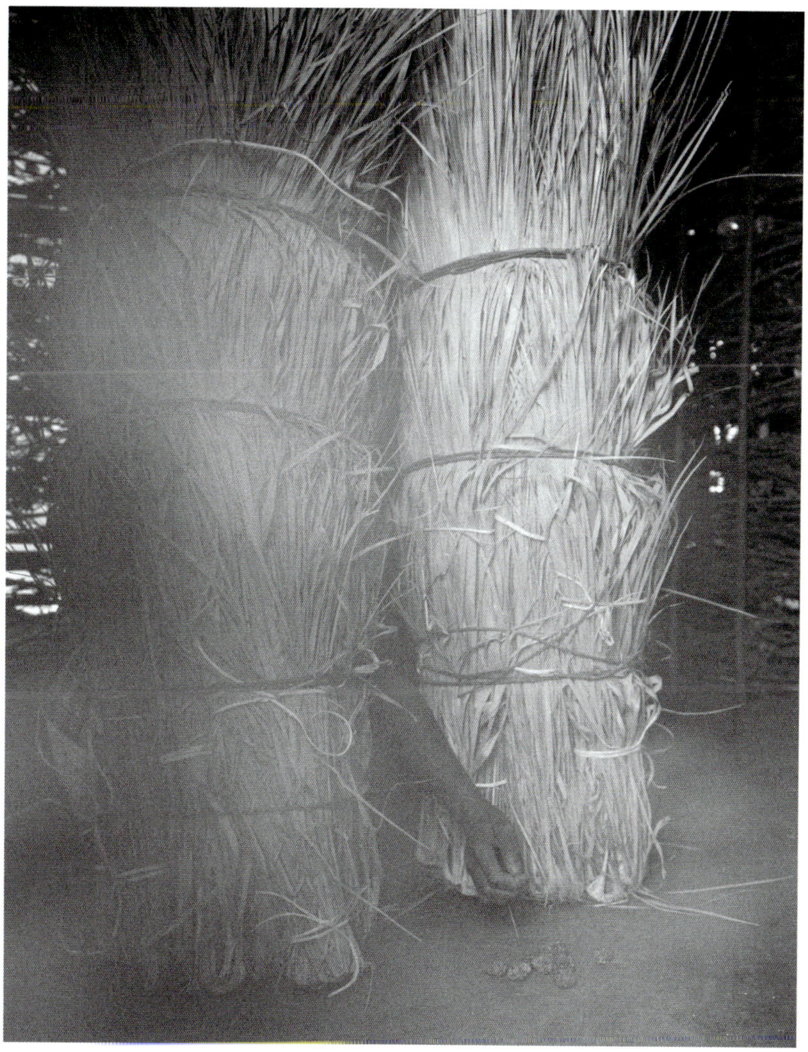

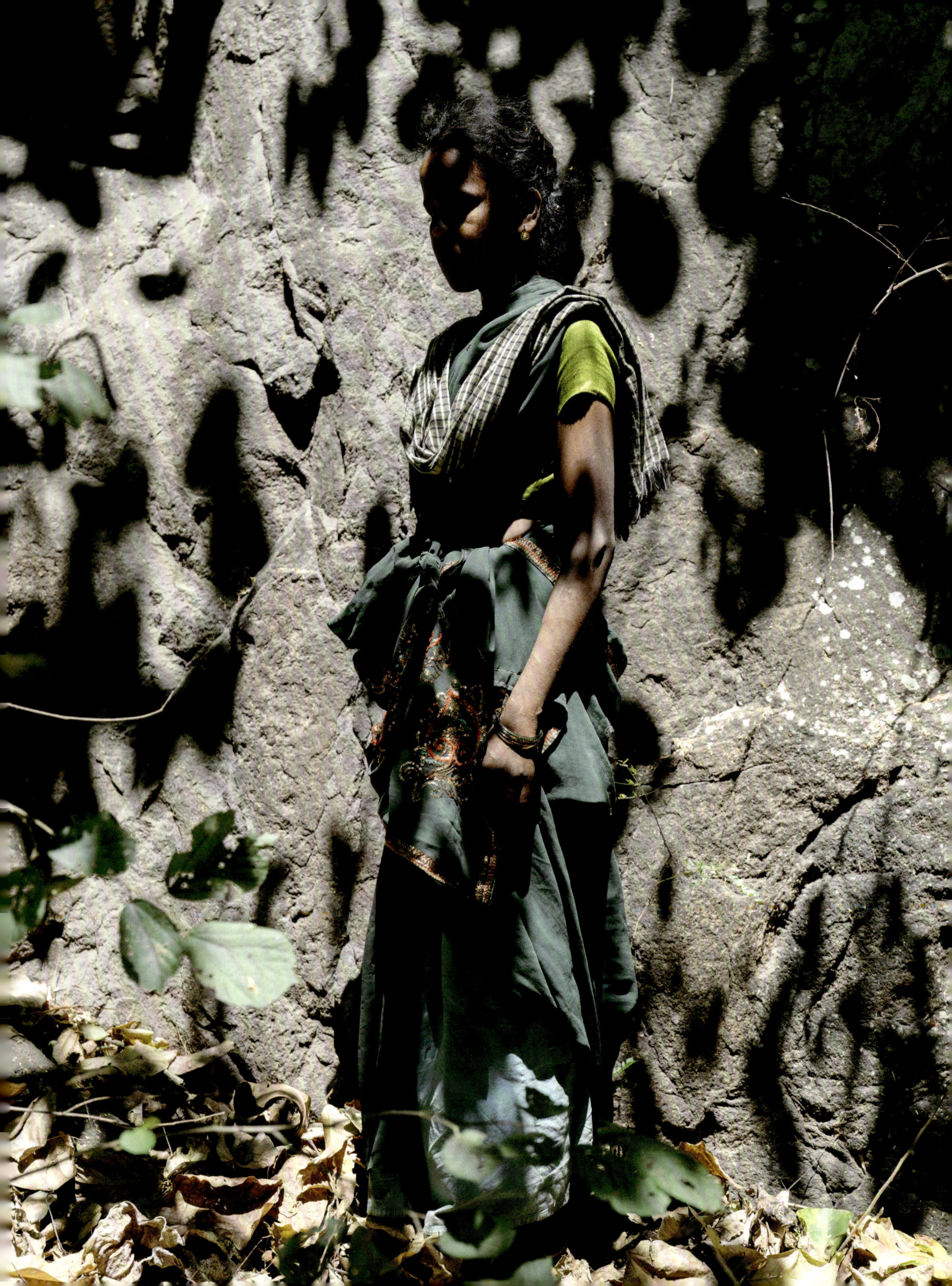

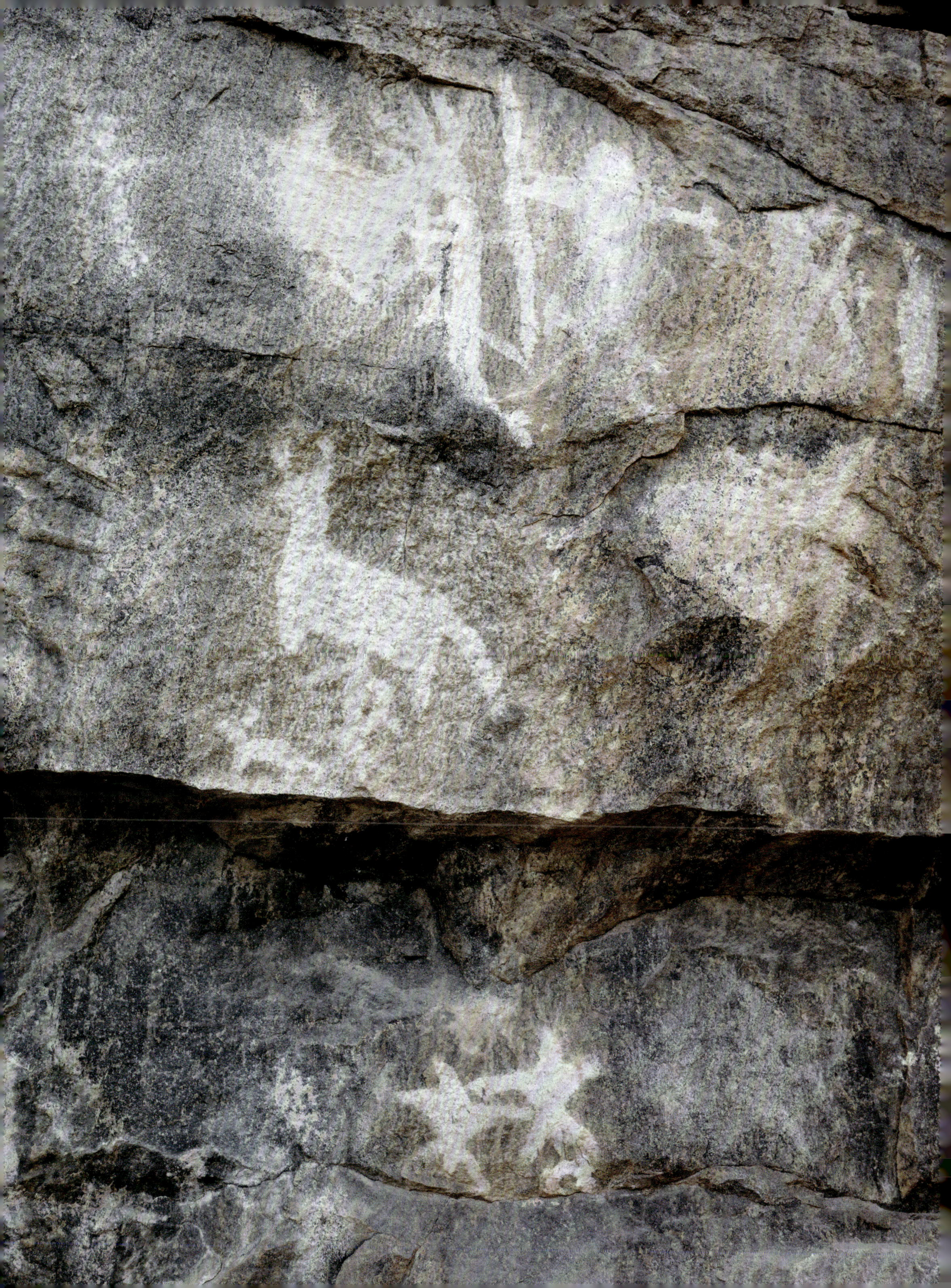

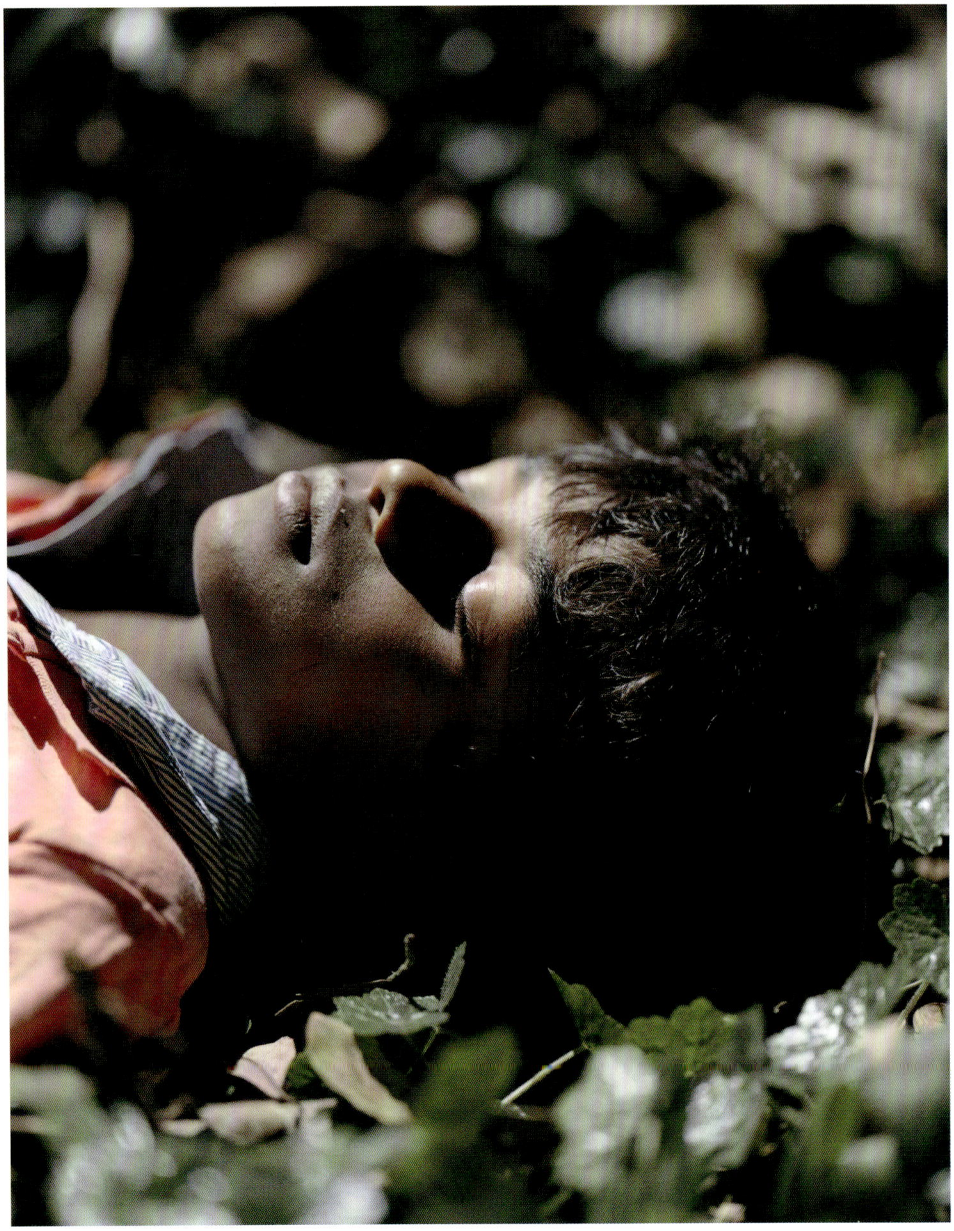

All photographs from the series *The Pregnant Tree*, Tamil Nadu, India, 2016–ongoing
Supported by Magnum Foundation and Museé du Quai Branly

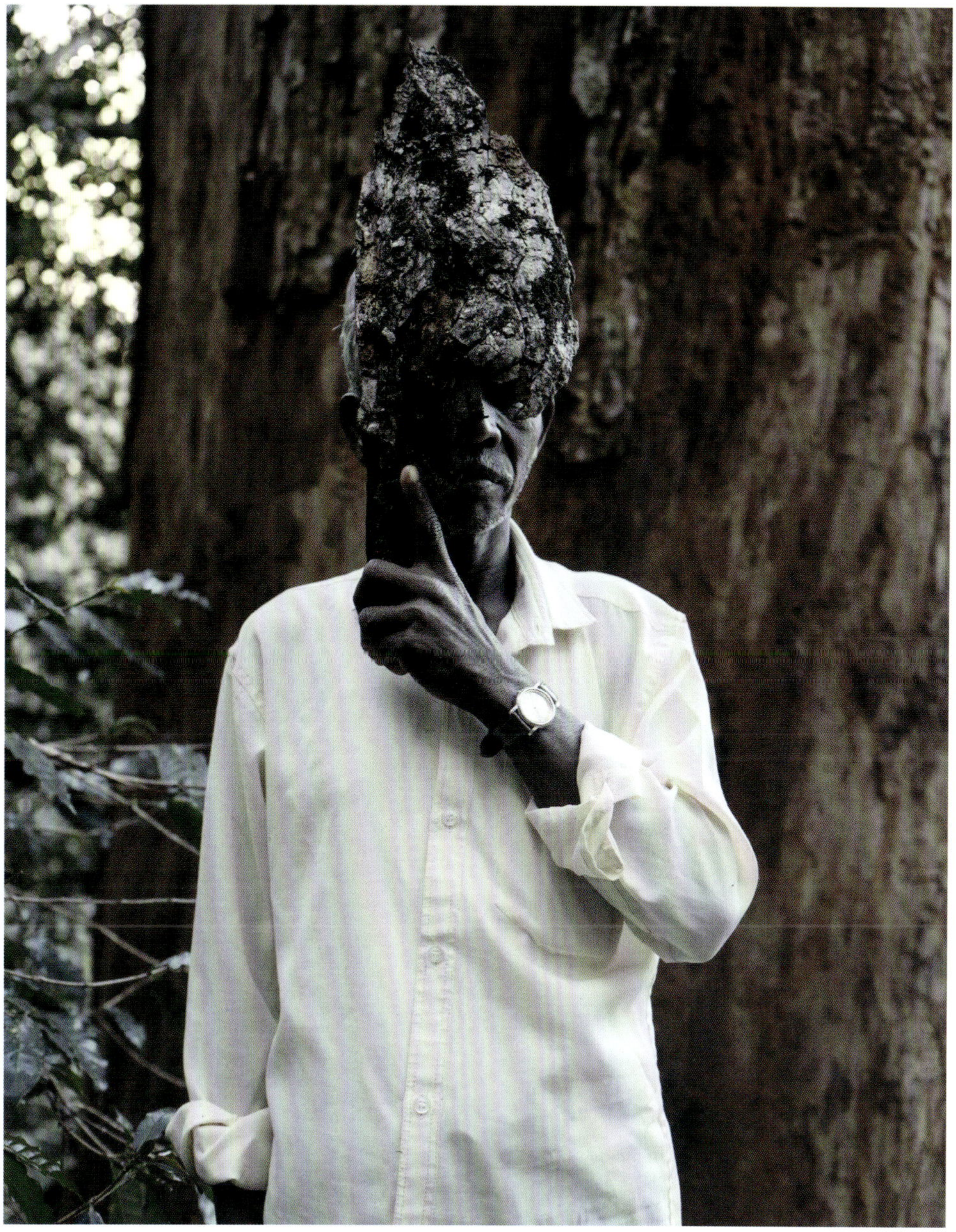

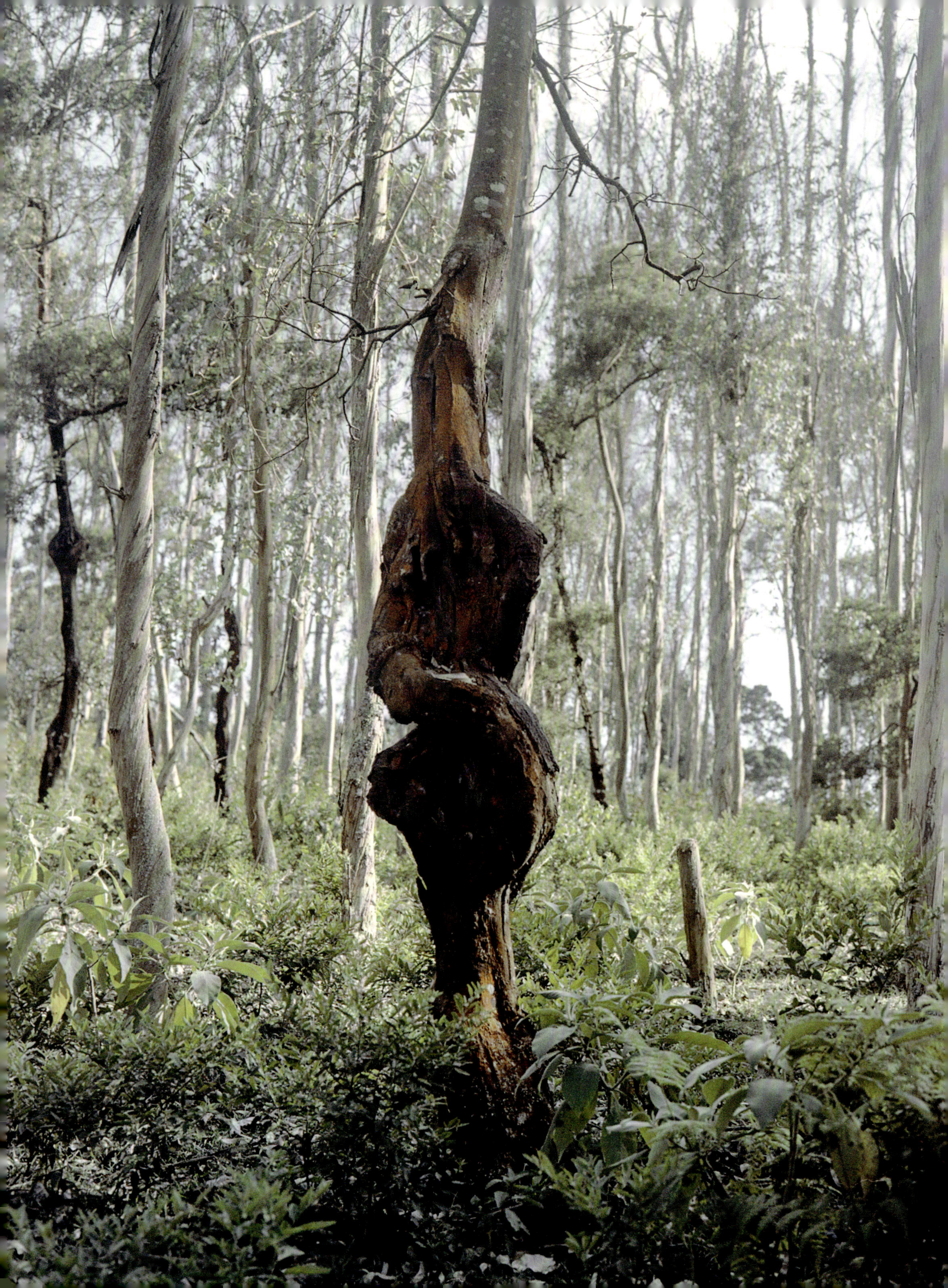

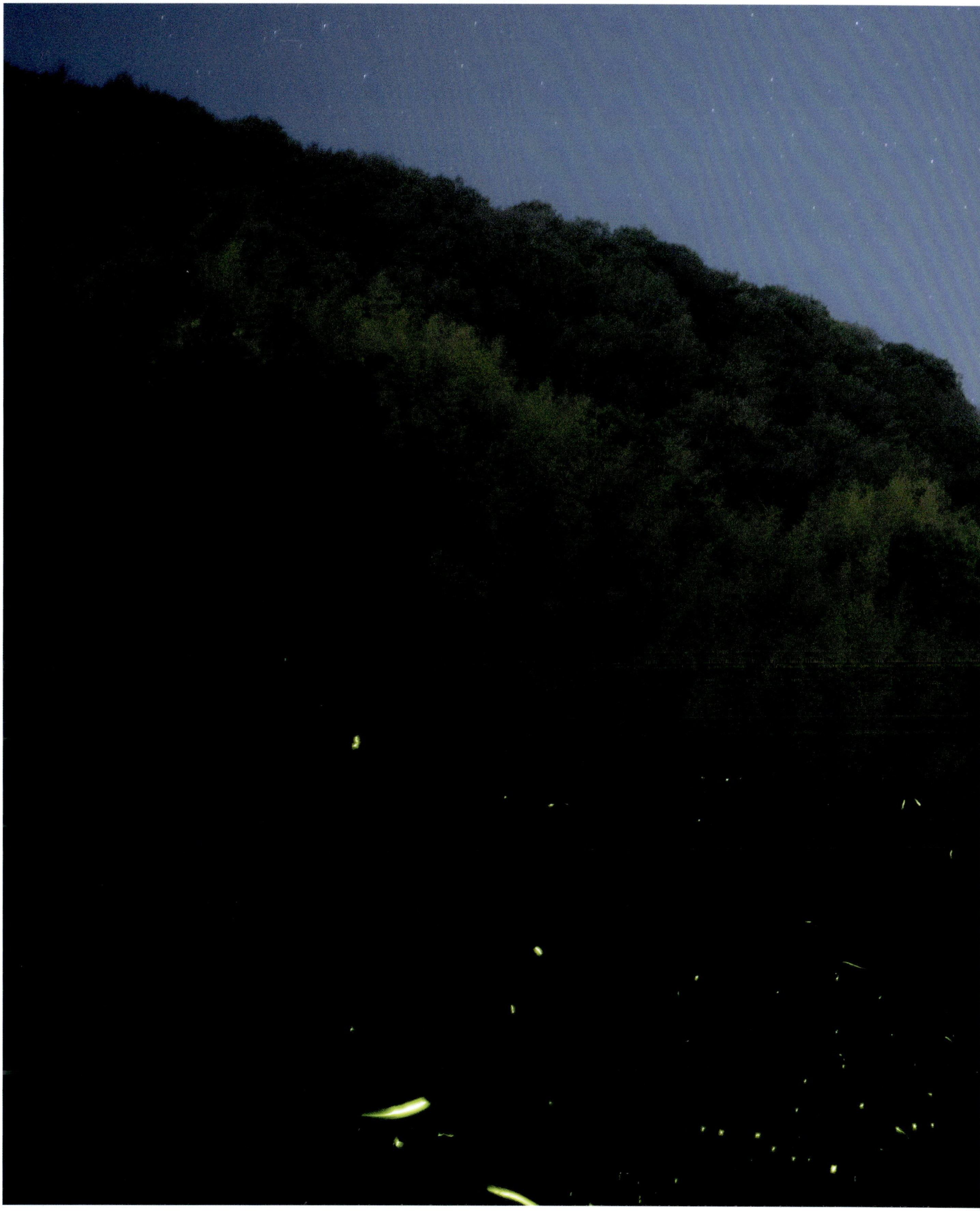

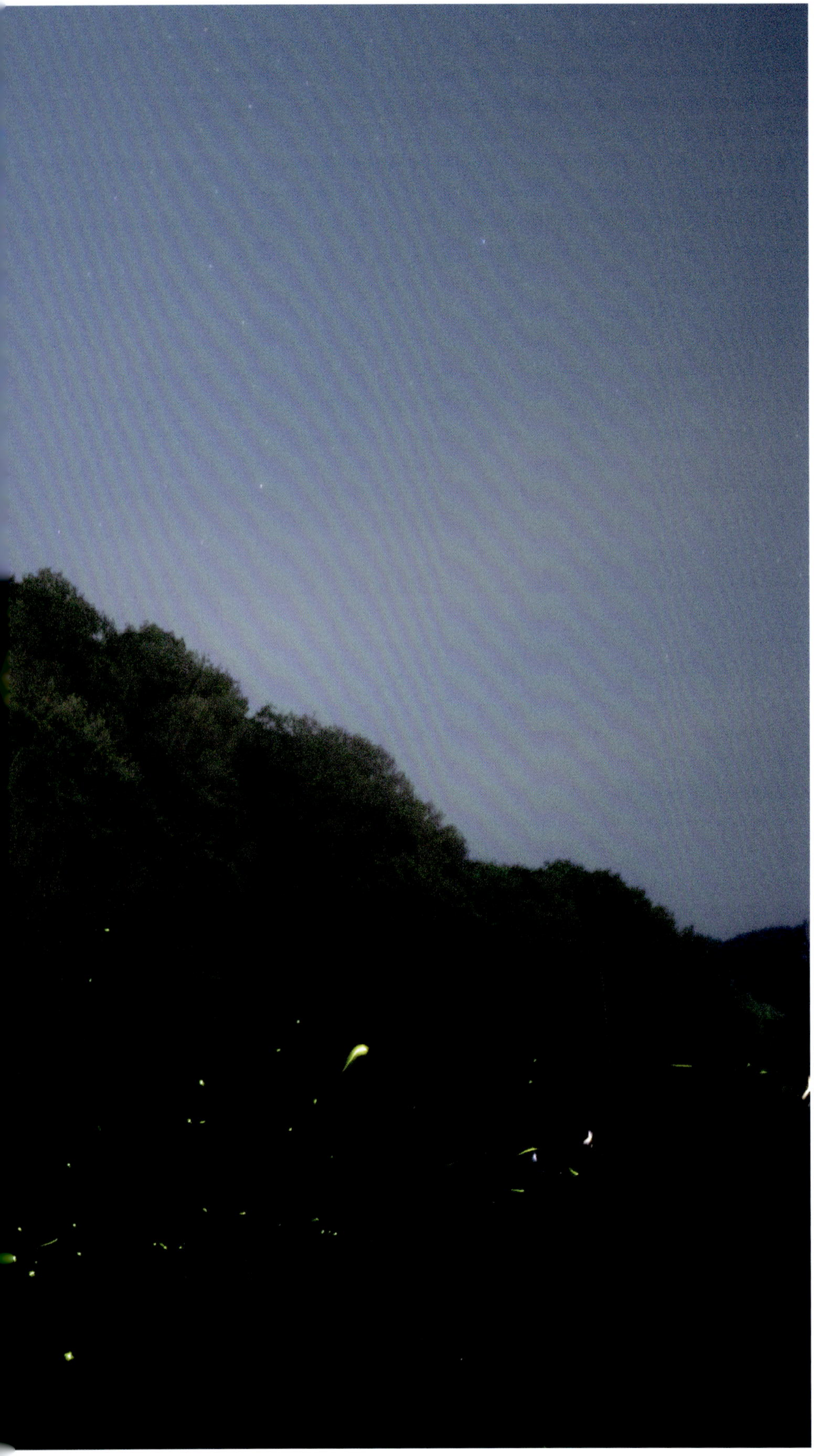

Rinko Kawauchi *Alight*

Pico Iyer

If you take a slow train and then an occasional ferry to Teshima, in Japan's Seto Inland Sea, you'll find yourself on a long-forgotten fisherman's island that moves at a human pace. Board the island's only small bus, and fifteen minutes later you come to a grassy hill overlooking the still blue waters in the distance. Walk around the slope—birdsong, rusting maples, flashes of bright sea—and you will arrive at a huge cave of sorts, the Teshima Art Museum, shaped like a drop of water.

Across roughly two hundred feet there is nothing—you gradually discern—but drops of water coaxed out of the ground in a work the museum houses, *Matrix* by the artist Rei Naito. On each side of the large space is an opening in the ceiling, through which you can follow crows, scudding clouds, perhaps light drizzle. There's nothing there, and everything. You could spend a day in the emptiness and the view through both openings would never be the same. The droplets running across the ground and forming small puddles become a world in themselves.

I can never help thinking of the Teshima Art Museum when I meet Rinko Kawauchi's exquisite spots of time. Not just because she sometimes gives us drops of water, but more because her gaze is always turned to all that is larger

than we are, and smaller. Much like Utagawa Hiroshige, she regularly places humans in a natural setting, so that you can see how much they are a part of something vaster. And as in a classic haiku, she takes the smallest of moments or objects and finds in them a universe. The artist passes her unwavering attention on to us.

Attention, sometimes likened to prayer, arises out of stillness, and I sense a tremendous stillness in Kawauchi's work, the stillness of one who has no need to race around to find or generate her transports. I also sense the transformative innocence I associate with my neighbors in Japan, among whom I've lived for thirty-eight years. They have no longing to be fancy or striking or theoretical; simple, clear observation is enough.

Nor is there any need to distinguish between high or low, significant or trivial: Every object—from snail to leaf—is created or sanctified by the eye one brings to it. It's no surprise to learn that Kawauchi made some of her work in an Okayama forest where, as she writes, "stillness and movement, light and darkness" coexist. Other uncanny images came to her in Iceland, and in the bitter cold of Hokkaido. Our lives, she might be telling us, are made by how we look at them.

Kawauchi's eye I imagine to be wide open as well as rigorous and precise; I suspect she looks past nothing in any room through a wish to alight on what's important or essential. She is showing us what's important, which is to say almost everything. In Japan more than in most places, the artist knows that her task is less to find what she loves than to love whatever she finds.

The first time I visited Teshima, I wondered why I had to walk around the hillside, taking a long, roundabout course before entering the empty cave. Now I realize that the walk is a form of preparation, a way of slowing down and emptying yourself out so as to receive most fully all that awaits you. Perhaps the same kind of cleansing should precede an encounter with Kawauchi's work. In every one of her images, she seems to be giving solidity to what looks flimsy and permanence to what seems to be just passing.

Pico Iyer is the author of *Aflame: Learning from Silence* (2025), about monasticism, wildfires, and sitting still.

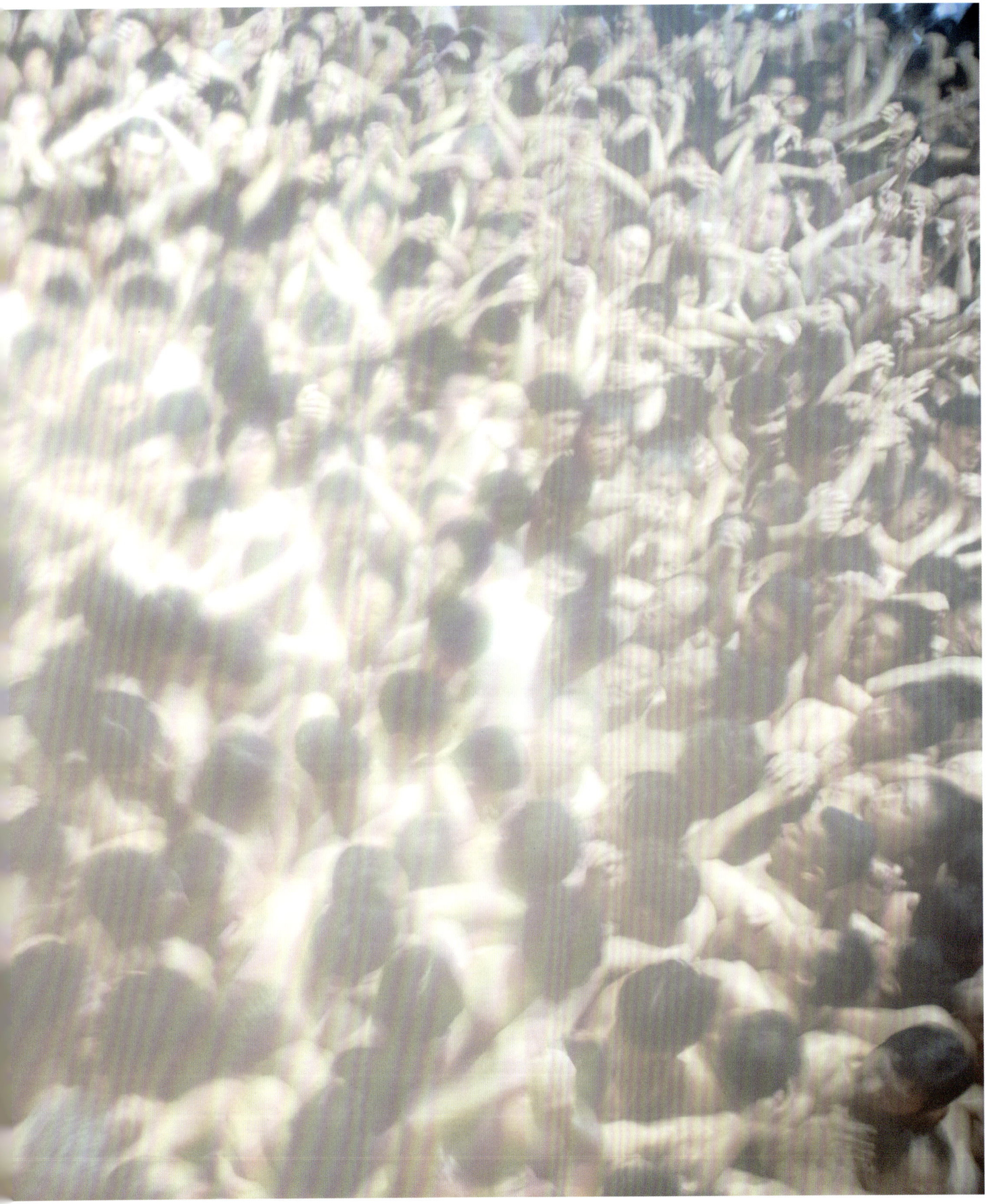

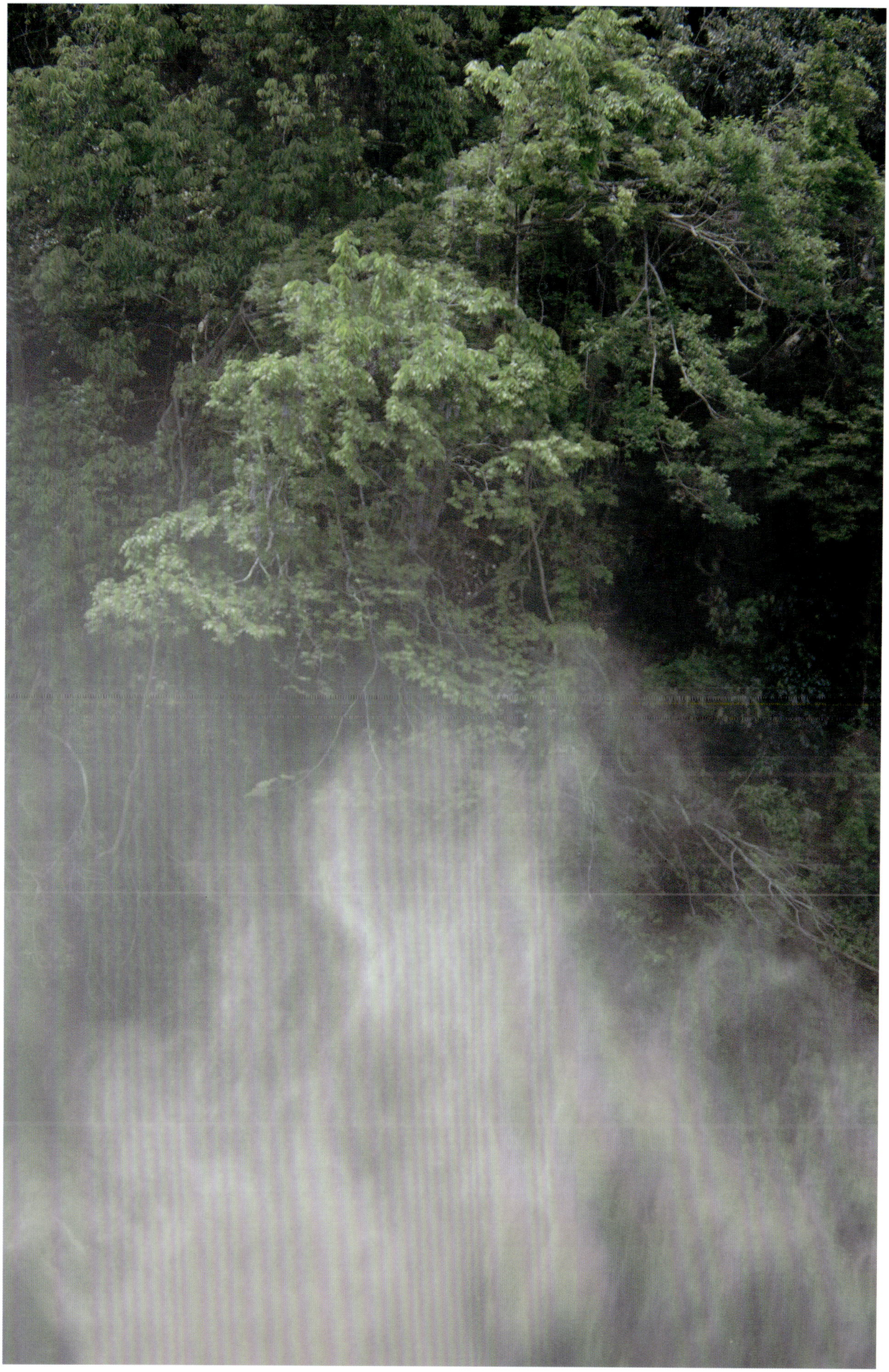

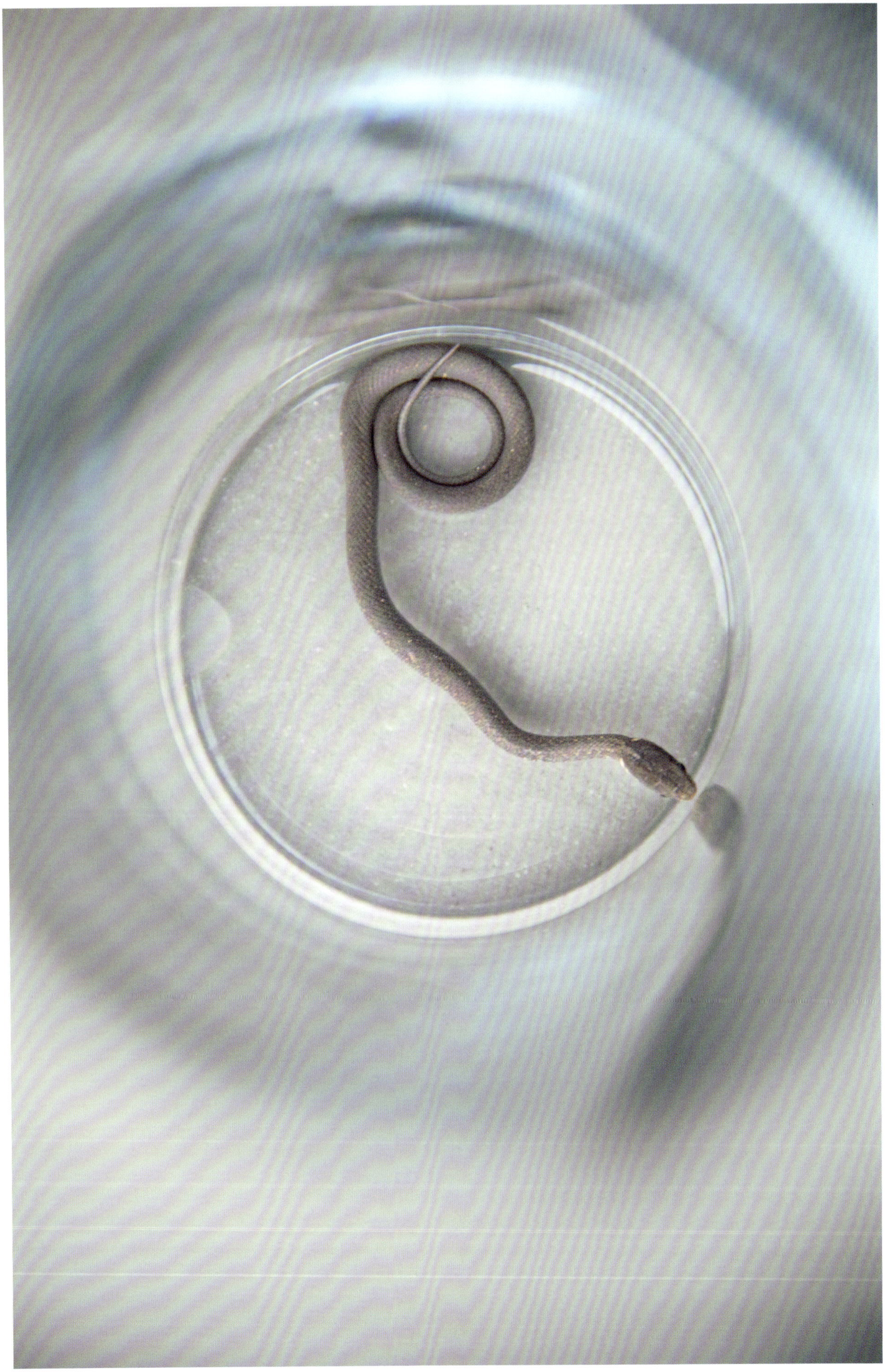

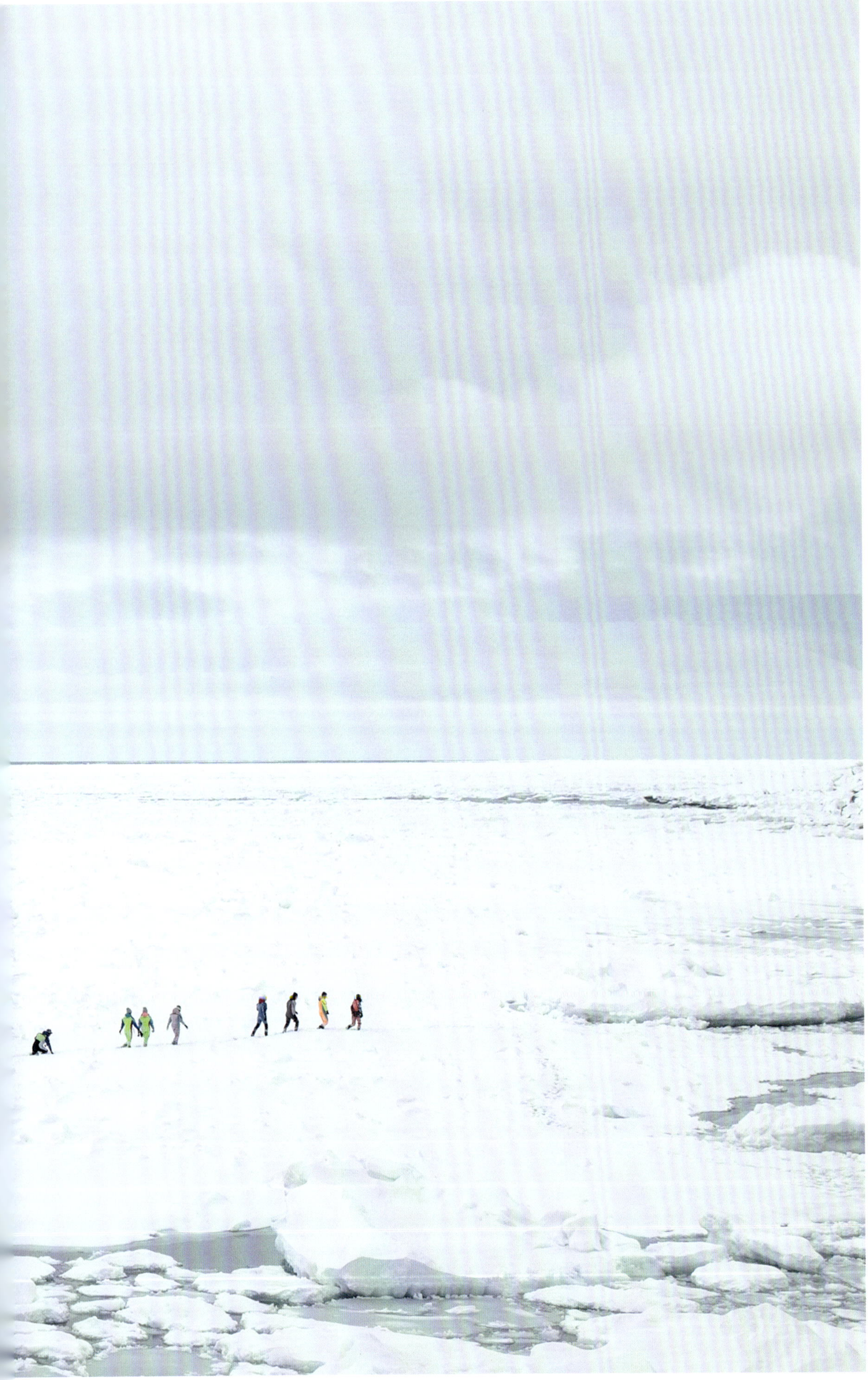

Pages 100–3 and 106–7: *Untitled*, 2024, produced by Forest Festival of the Arts, Okayama; pages 104–5 and 108–9: *Untitled*, 2020, from the series *M/E*; this spread: *Untitled*, 2022, from the series *M/E*
Courtesy the artist

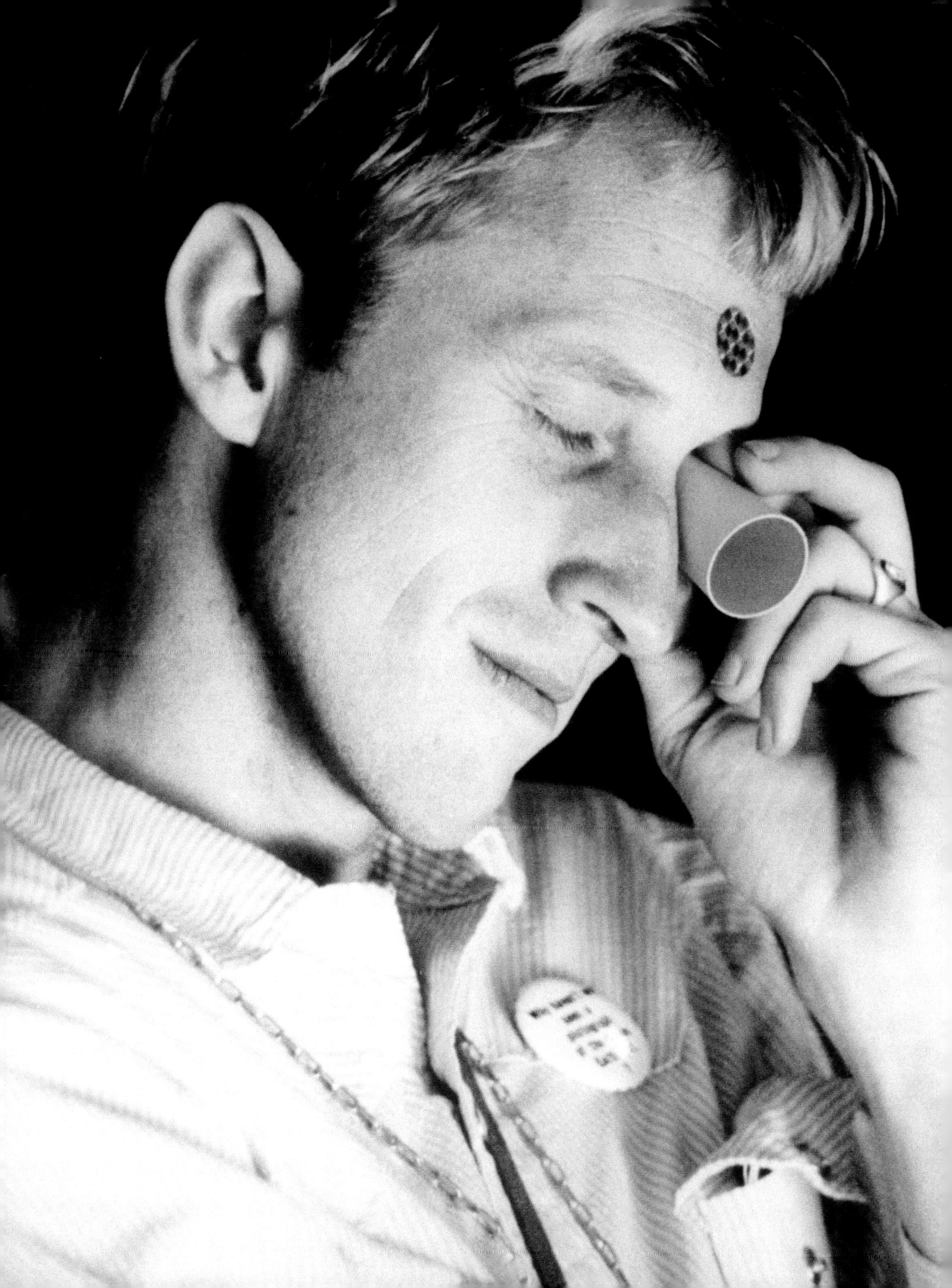

The Far Side of the Earth

Since sparking environmental consciousness six decades ago, Earthrise remains shrouded in misconceptions.

Eva Díaz

Stewart Brand wearing his "Whole Earth" pin, October 1966
Photograph by Gene Anthony. Courtesy Wolfgang's Vault

WHILE TRIPPING ON LSD IN SAN FRANCISCO IN 1966, Stewart Brand "came to the notion that seeing an image of the Earth from space would change a lot of things." He proceeded to produce buttons asking, "Why haven't we seen a photograph of the whole Earth yet?," which he sold on street corners near the University of California, Berkeley, and sent to members of the US and Soviet space programs, US senators, and countercultural gurus such as Marshall McLuhan and R. Buckminster Fuller. Apparently only Fuller replied, responding with a brief note: "Dear boy, it's a charming notion but you must realize you can never see more than half the Earth from any particular point in space."

Two years later, Brand published the first issue of the influential *Whole Earth Catalog*, its cover graced by a November 10,

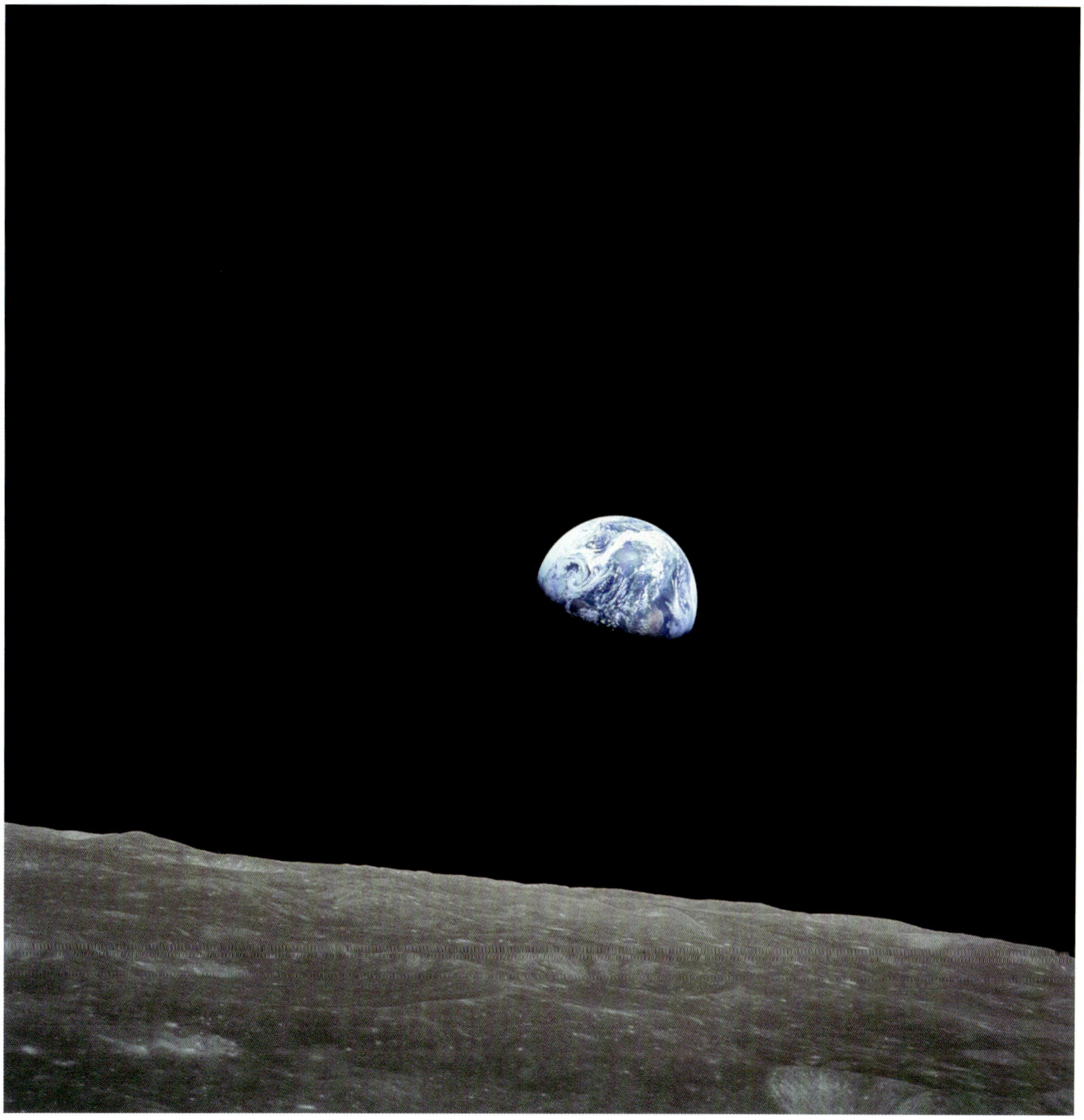

William Anders, *Earthrise*, 1968
Courtesy NASA

Earthrise helped to galvanize growing ecological consciousness about the vulnerability of terrestrial life.

1967, color image taken by NASA using the ATS-3 satellite. The back cover repeated the image with the caption, "We can't put it together. It is together." Its next volume featured the astronaut William Anders's so-called *Earthrise* photograph, taken from lunar orbit on December 24, 1968. The famous image was actually rotated 90 degrees when it first appeared in *Life* magazine, and also appeared this way on the *Whole Earth Catalog* cover, making it seem that Earth was "rising" over the horizontal surface of the moon. In fact, Anders snapped the image as the *Apollo 8* spacecraft orbited the lunar equator, when Earth was appearing to the side of the moon, seen vertically.

This manner of picturing Earth from outer space did indeed "change a lot of things." *Earthrise* helped to galvanize growing ecological consciousness about the vulnerability of terrestrial life and the need for holistic planning about the planetary future. *Life* later called it one of the most influential photographs ever taken. A few months after Fuller's note, the two men met in person at the Esalen Institute, in Big Sur, and Fuller continued to inspire Brand. The "blue marble" image was "motivating for a lot of people," Brand said, "because it gave the sense that Earth's an island, surrounded by a lot of inhospitable space. And it's so graphic, this little blue, white, green, and

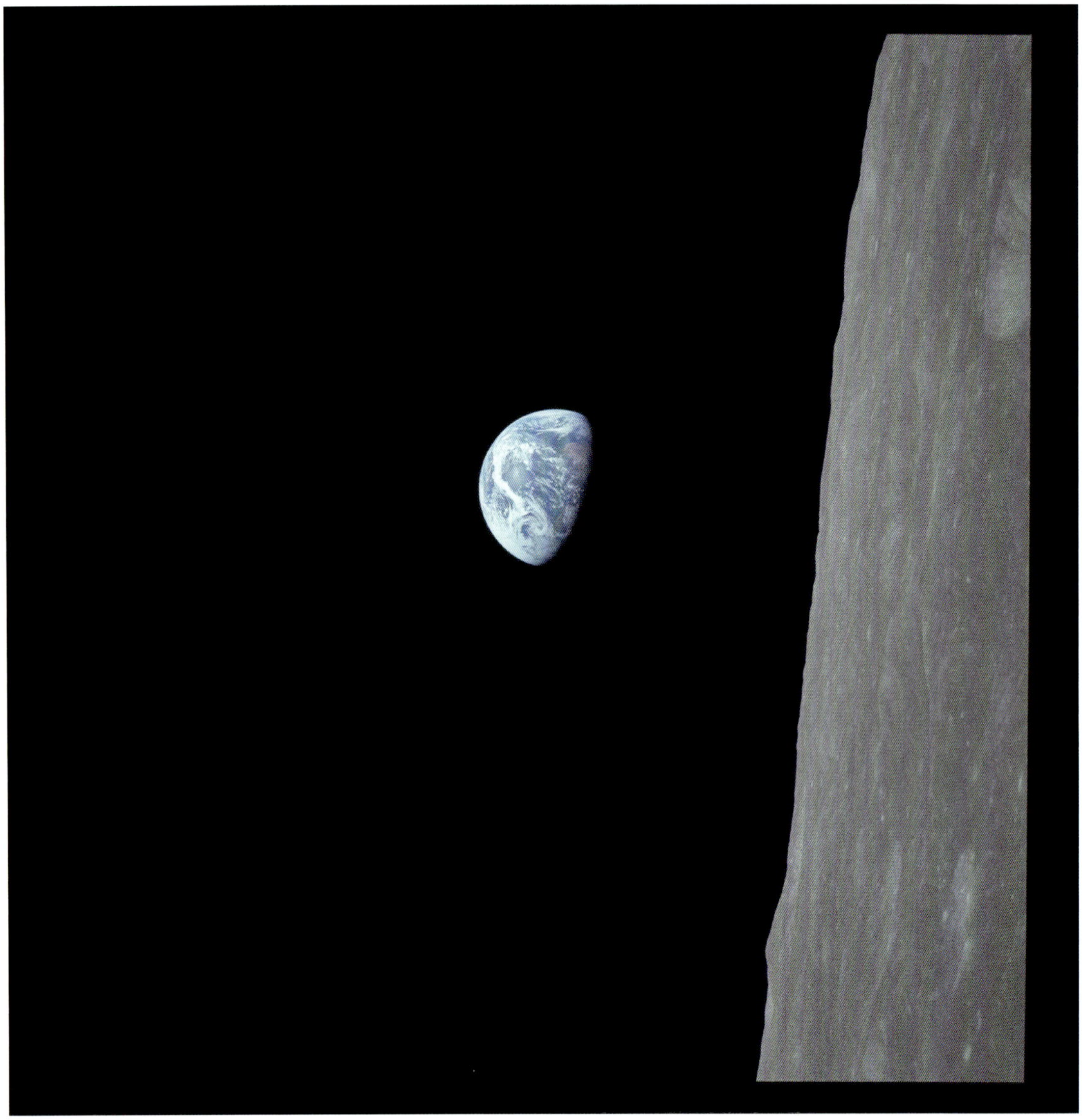

Earthrise in its original orientation, as seen by the crew of *Apollo 8*
Courtesy NASA

brown jewel-like icon amongst a quite featureless black vacuum. Islands know about limitations."

What did this image not change about seeing Earth? In picturing a "whole" Earth, something hidden always remains: the other side of the sphere. A photograph can depict only half of anything it represents, and it can represent only the superficial circumstances of light falling on surfaces. These are the ingrained limitations of the medium, and they are also the constraints of eyesight itself that are scarcely acknowledged in our attempts to secure certainties from vision, truths from light, enduring evidence from sight.

Brand's demand to see Earth from outer space not only centers the planet as a narcissistic image of cohesiveness, it also inscribes vision as the keenest means of understanding. Reacting against this presumption, the astronomer Carl Sagan, as part of the *Voyager* imaging team, conceived for NASA to take the 1990 image of what he called the "pale blue dot," a nearly indistinguishable, pixel-sized Earth embedded in the vastness of space. "Our planet is a lonely speck in the great enveloping cosmic dark," Sagan wrote. "In our obscurity, in all this vastness, there is no hint that help will come from elsewhere to save us from ourselves." Much of our ongoing climate crisis unfolds

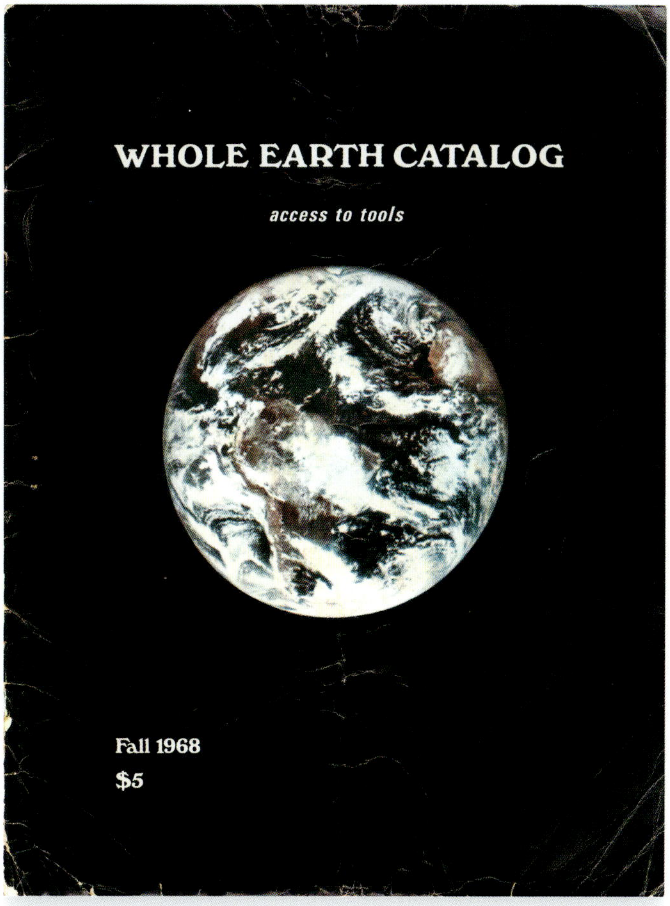

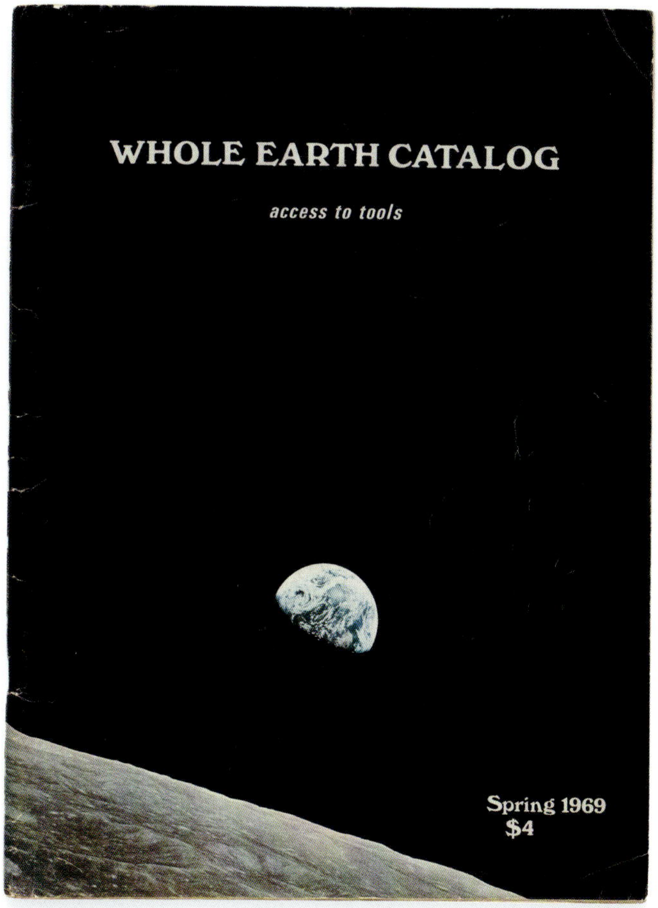

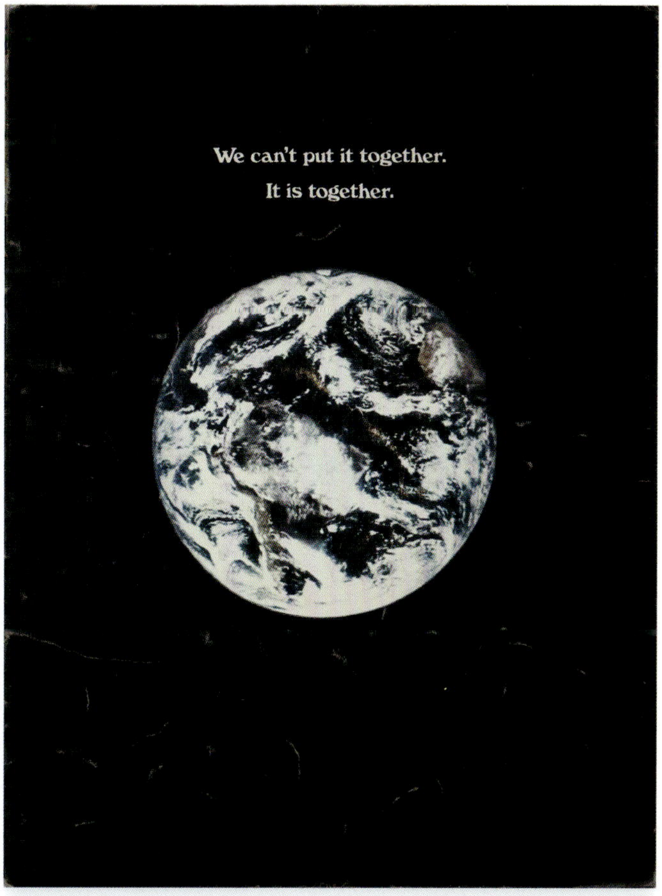

Left, top and bottom:
Cover and back cover of the *Whole Earth Catalog*, Fall 1968

Right, top:
Cover of the *Whole Earth Catalog*, Spring 1969
Photograph © The Museum of Modern Art and courtesy SCALA/Art Resource, NY

Opposite:
Tavares Strachan, *ENOCH* (display unit), 2015–17
© Museum Associates/LACMA

Could Stewart Brand have ever imagined how increasingly banal space imagery could become?

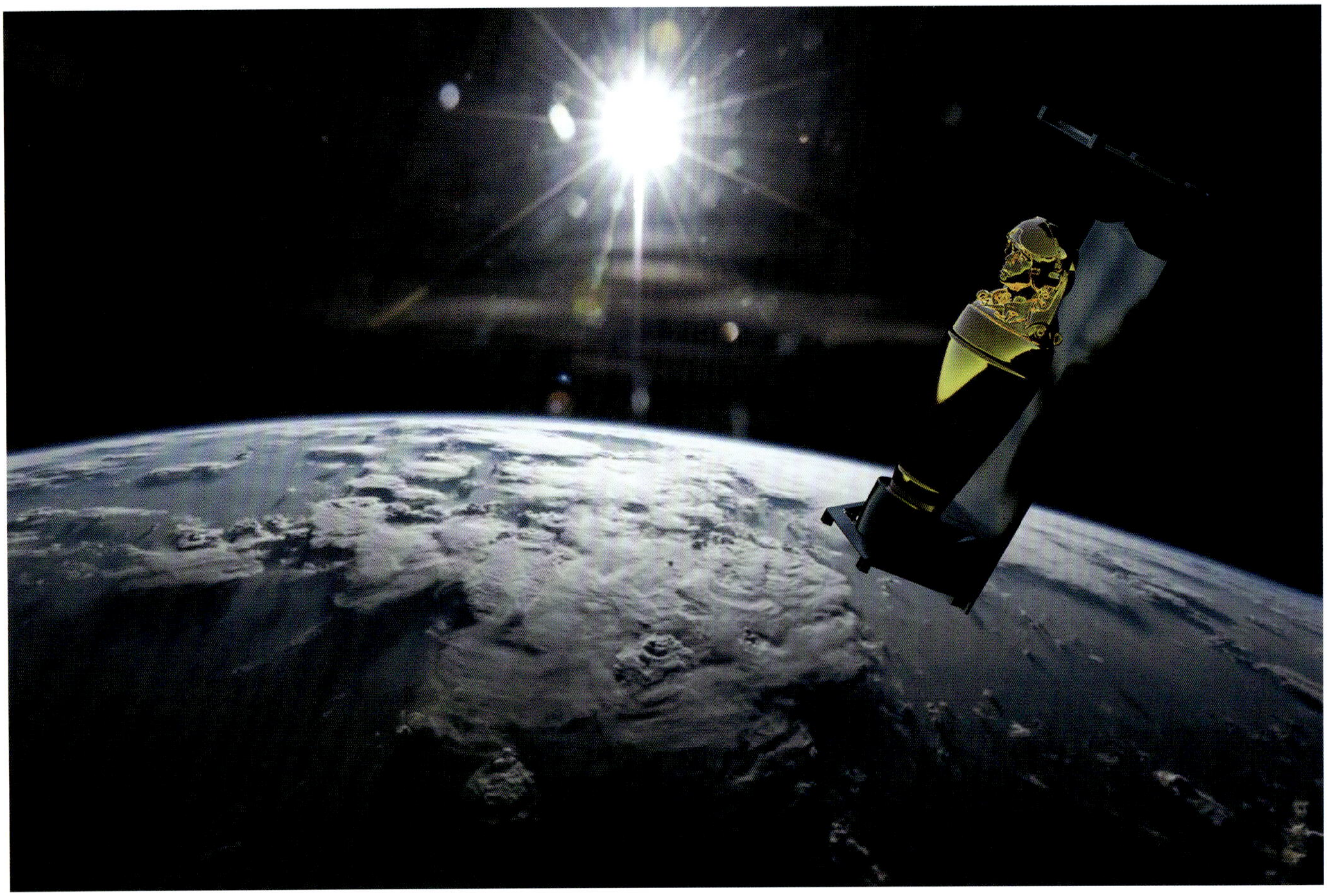

invisibly—excessive carbon dioxide pollutes the atmosphere resulting in rising, acidifying, and warming seas.

The question of Earth's visibility also extends to inequity. The contemporary artist Tavares Strachan's work often invokes invisible systems that underpin our knowledge of the world—DNA, molecules, Fibonacci numbers—in addition to the powerful biases that shape the reality of human consciousness. In his 2018 piece *ENOCH*, Strachan launched on a SpaceX rocket a satellite of a 24-karat gold bust dedicated to the first Black US astronaut, Robert Henry Lawrence Jr., who died in a crash at Edwards Air Force Base before he could be deployed to space. Though *ENOCH* brings Lawrence to metaphoric visibility as a crucial figure in the history of space travel, in orbit it is invisible to the human eye. When discussing his work *The Encyclopedia of Invisibility* (2018), which spurred his interest in Lawrence, Strachan remarked that "so much education all over the world is based on the idea that we're looking for things that we've already found." His *Encyclopedia* uses the familiar visual format of the *Encyclopaedia Britannica*, with small photographs and diagrams surrounded by printed textual entries, as ground for wall-sized renderings of the book's pages, themselves superimposed with technical diagrams, photographs, and texts of various sizes. It's an overwhelming palimpsest of information that speaks to what the systems philosopher Timothy Morton refers to as hyperobjects: systems too large to fully picture, such as the environment, the ecology, or Earth.

Could Brand, tripping on acid sixty years ago, have ever imagined how increasingly banal space imagery could become, that pictures of the cosmos would be circulated regularly in a desensitizing drip of social-media posts? (In the not-too-distant future, one might thumb through one's Instagram Stories and see hundreds of earthrises, the snapshots of billionaire influencers who cheerfully corrode the planet with their space tourism.) Stewart's belief in the power of a single photograph to awake in people a sublime feeling of accountability and enduring wonder has since been refuted. The question today, perhaps, is not how to effectively mobilize an image of the world but whether we can salvage hope from an overpowering world of images.

Eva Díaz a critic and professor of contemporary art history at Pratt Institute.

Lucas Foglia
Butterfly Effect

Lydia Millet

If you choose to confine them, painted lady butterflies will shred their wings to nothing trying to free themselves. Migrate or die is their creed.

Like the journeys of monarchs, those of painted ladies stretch over multiple generations in a relay of fleeting lives: A single flier does not make the whole trip but fades away as others take up the baton.

Those journeys—which occur in various forms across much of the globe, since painted lady butterflies are widespread—include the longest known butterfly migration. Beginning in the African savanna and ending in Northern Europe, its extent exceeds nine thousand miles round trip—the tiny insects flit across the forbidding reaches of the Sahara Desert and the expanse of the Mediterranean all the way up to Scandinavia. One butterfly can cover perhaps two thousand of those miles, living for about five weeks and laying, in the case of females, some five hundred eggs.

For his series *Constant Bloom* (2021–24), the photographer Lucas Foglia followed the butterflies from Kenya to Norway, accompanying the researchers of the Worldwide Painted Lady Migration Project who were tracing the complete route for the first time. He took pictures not only of the butterflies and their landing spots but also of people and other animals inhabiting those terrains.

As the planet heats up, the butterflies are finding fewer and fewer familiar touchstones in the landscapes they've relied on for millions of years. They peg their migration "to the brief blooms of wildflowers that follow seasonal rains," Foglia said. "They need blooming flowers to survive. But as climate change disrupts weather around the world, wildflowers don't bloom where or when they used to. So painted lady butterflies adapt. They find nectar in the flowers of our parks, farms, and gardens."

During his travels, he discovered people moving along similar paths, south to north, likewise struggling to adapt to the shifting conditions of their home. As the painted ladies crossed borders in pursuit of the future, so too did human migrants. In the wake of the closing of the land crossing between Greece and Turkey in 2020, Foglia said, the Mediterranean has become the deadliest human migration route in the world.

In the midst of a historic drought, researchers find butterflies on an outcrop over a vanishing glacier in Switzerland, where the moisture from melting ice sustains a green oasis on a high mountainside. A merchant ship makes its way past the island of Zembra—both of them minuscule in a vast, shining span of water—on a vector shared by painted ladies and people seeking refuge in Europe. From a boatyard in Tunisia to stacks of coffins on the other side of the sea—for migrants who had died in the passage and would be buried in unmarked graves—Foglia's photographs capture the interwovenness of faunal and floral, wild and built, ephemeral and eternal.

Lydia Millet is a novelist and conservationist based in the desert outside Tucson, Arizona.

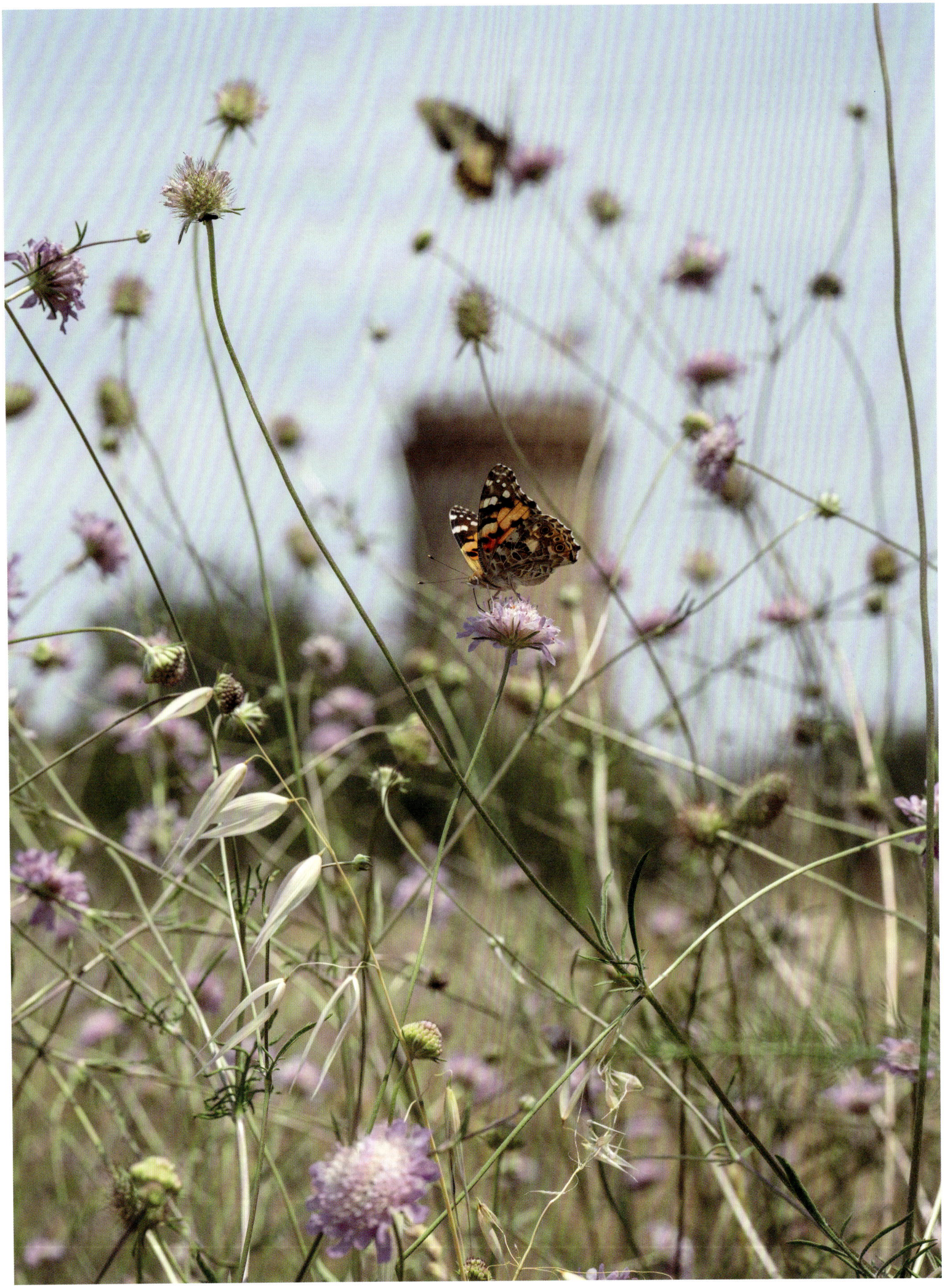

Page 119:
Painted Lady Butterfly on a Pincushion, Spain, 2021

This page:
Painted Lady Butterfly, England, 2021

Opposite:
Adam Building Boats, Tunisia, 2023

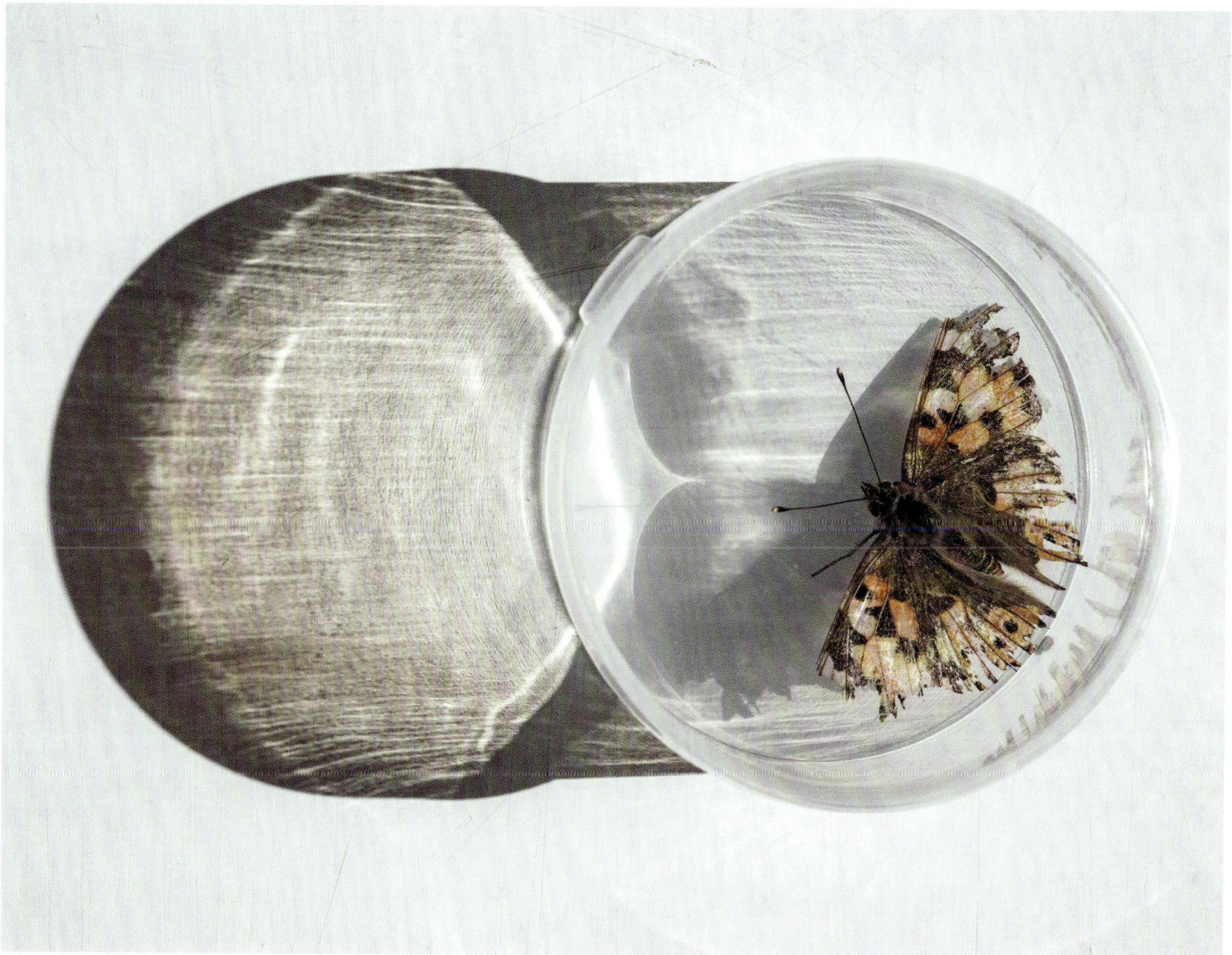

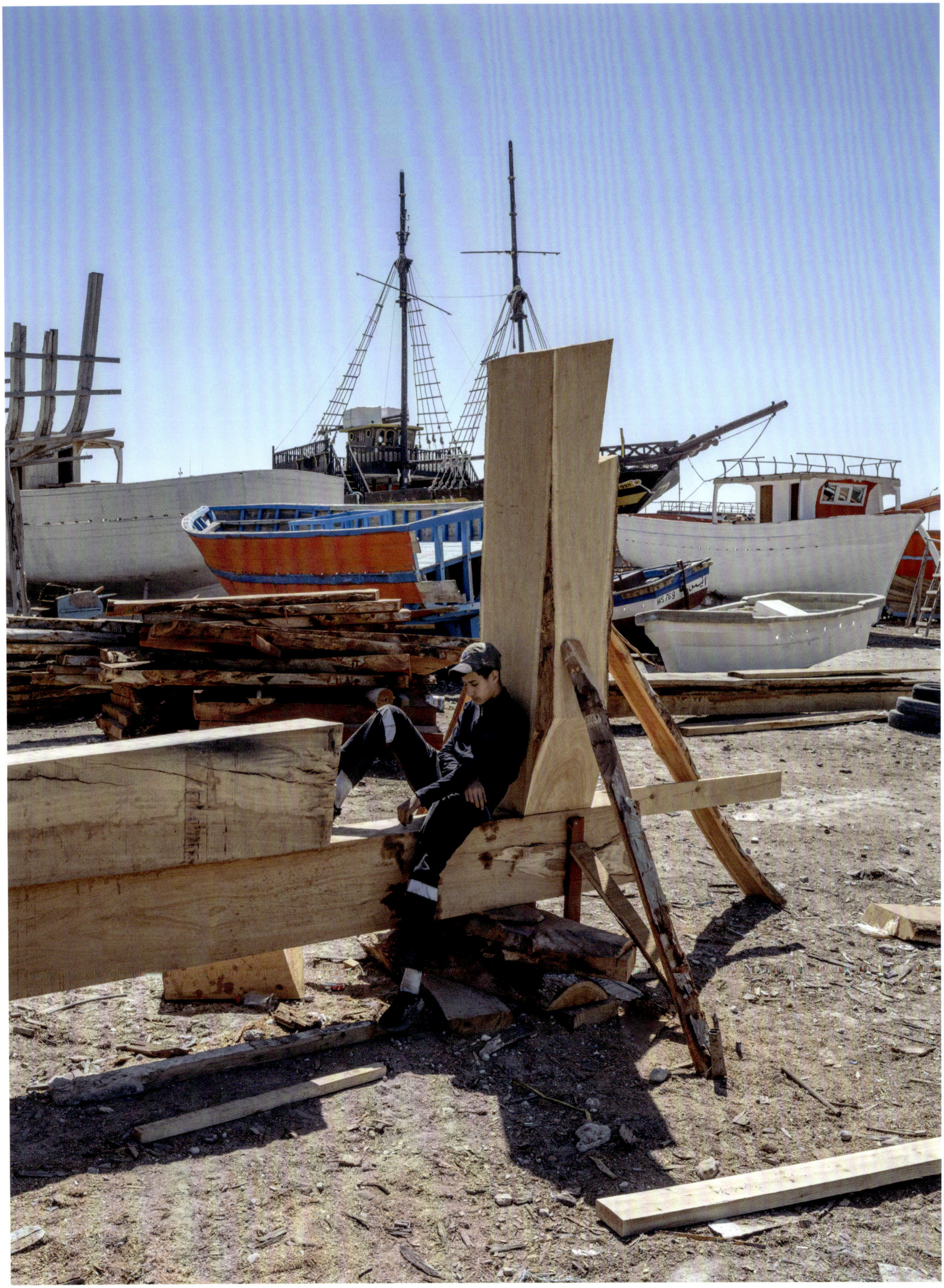

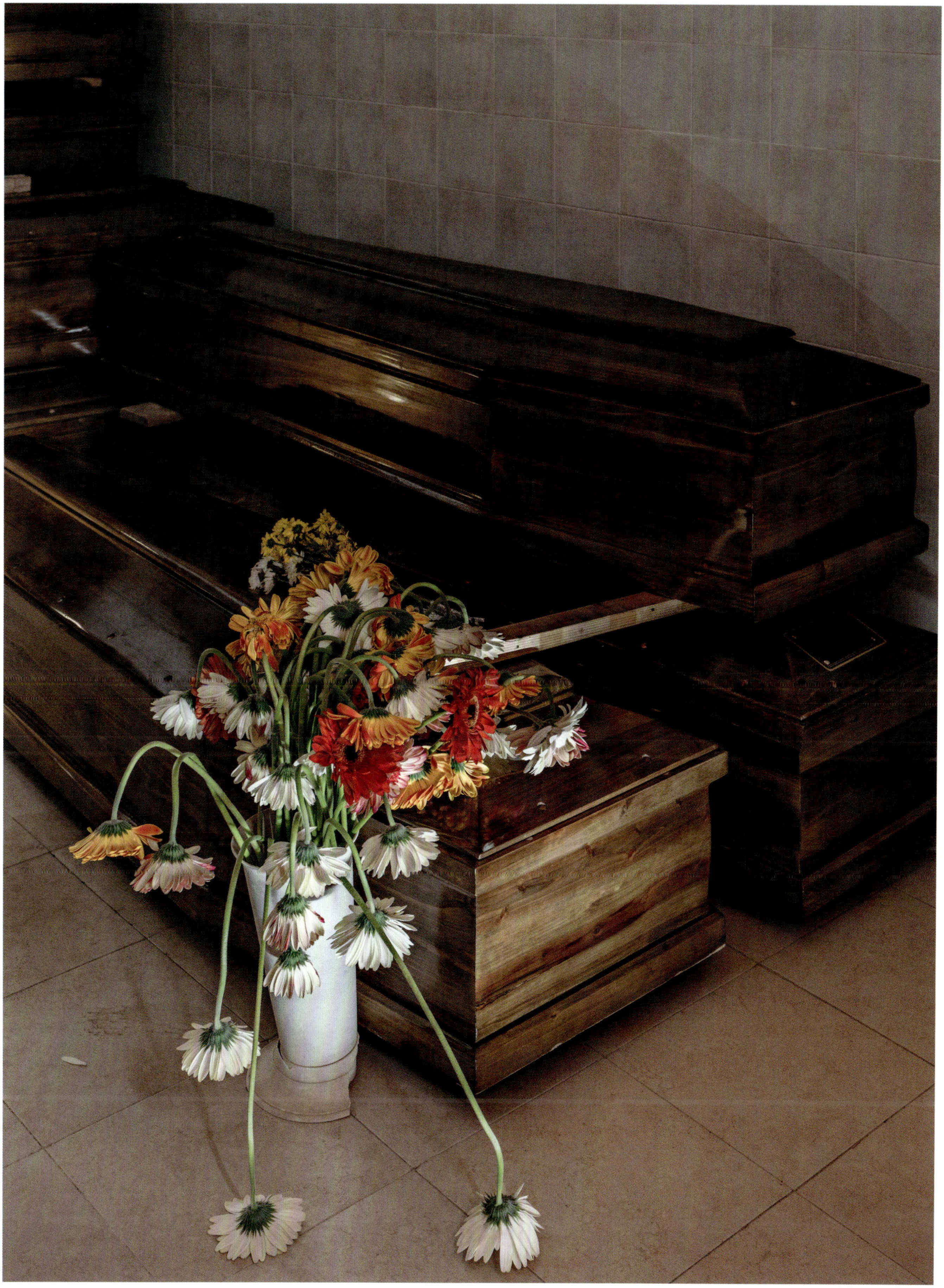

Opposite:
Migrants Who Drowned While Crossing the Mediterranean Sea, Italy, 2023

This page:
Raluca Collecting Butterflies for the Worldwide Painted Lady Migration Project, Switzerland, 2023

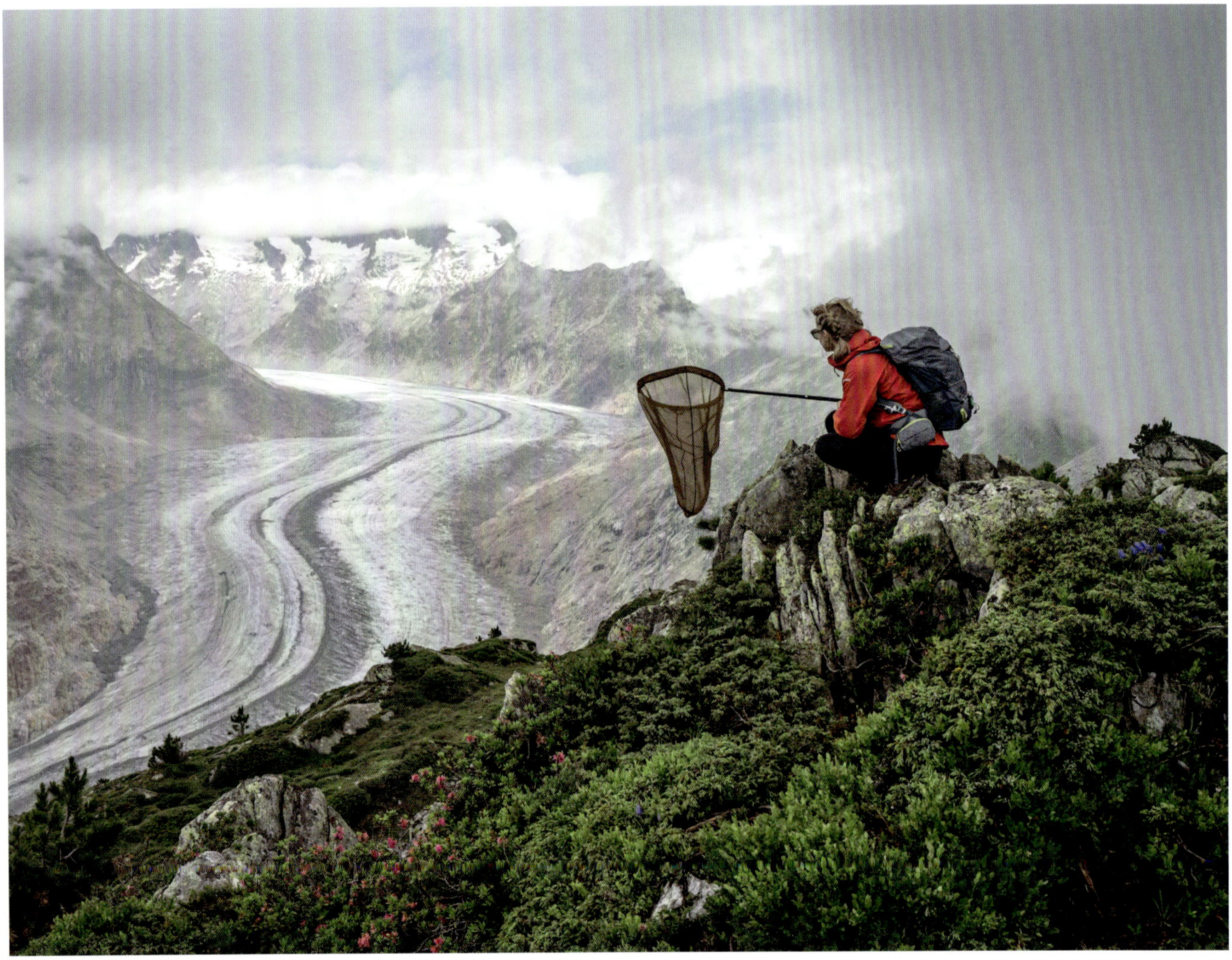

This page:
***Painted Lady Butterfly Wing with a Caterpillar,* Morocco, 2022**

Opposite:
***Merchant Ship Passing Zembra,* Tunisia, 2023**
Courtesy the artist and Fredericks & Freiser Gallery, New York

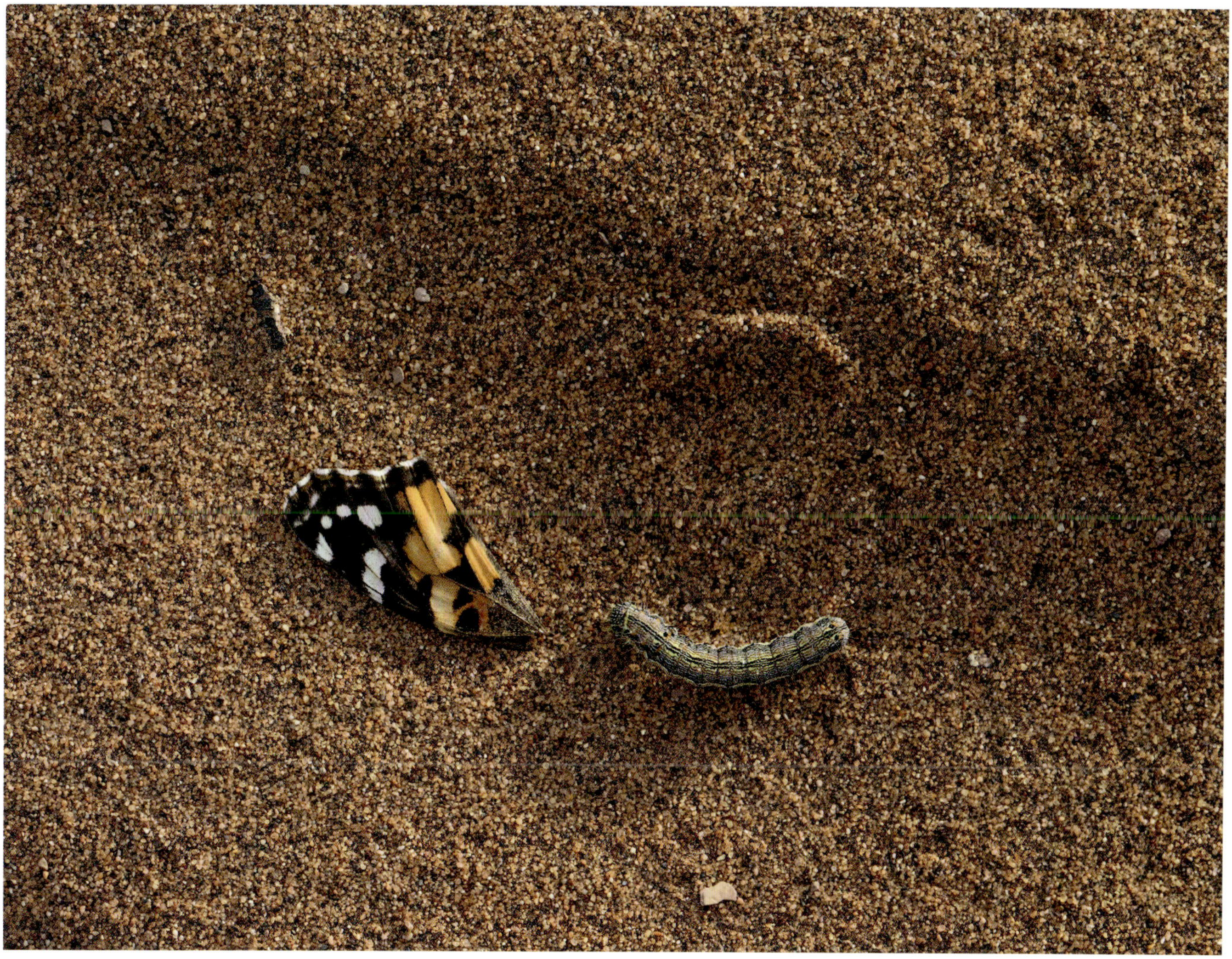

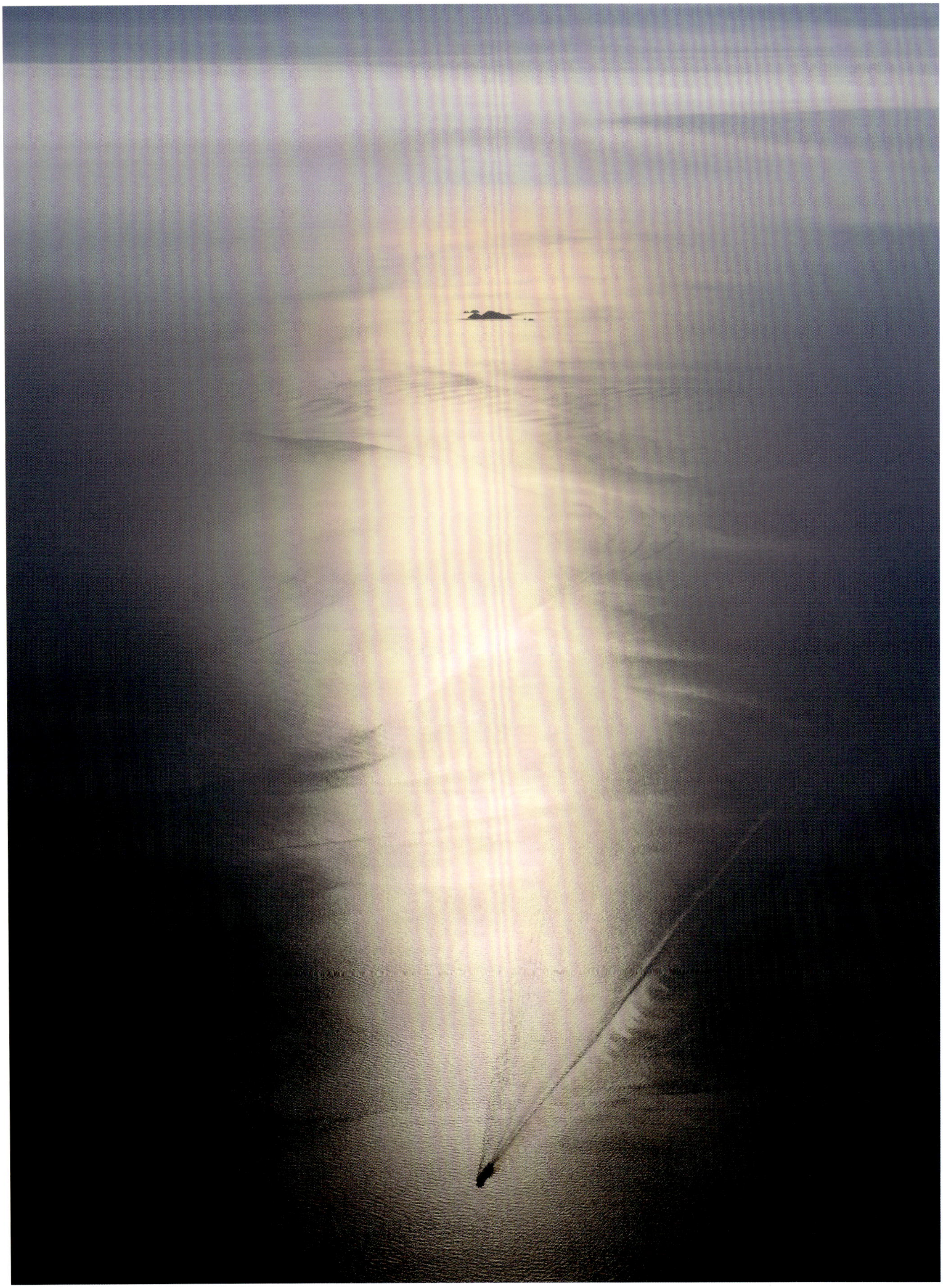

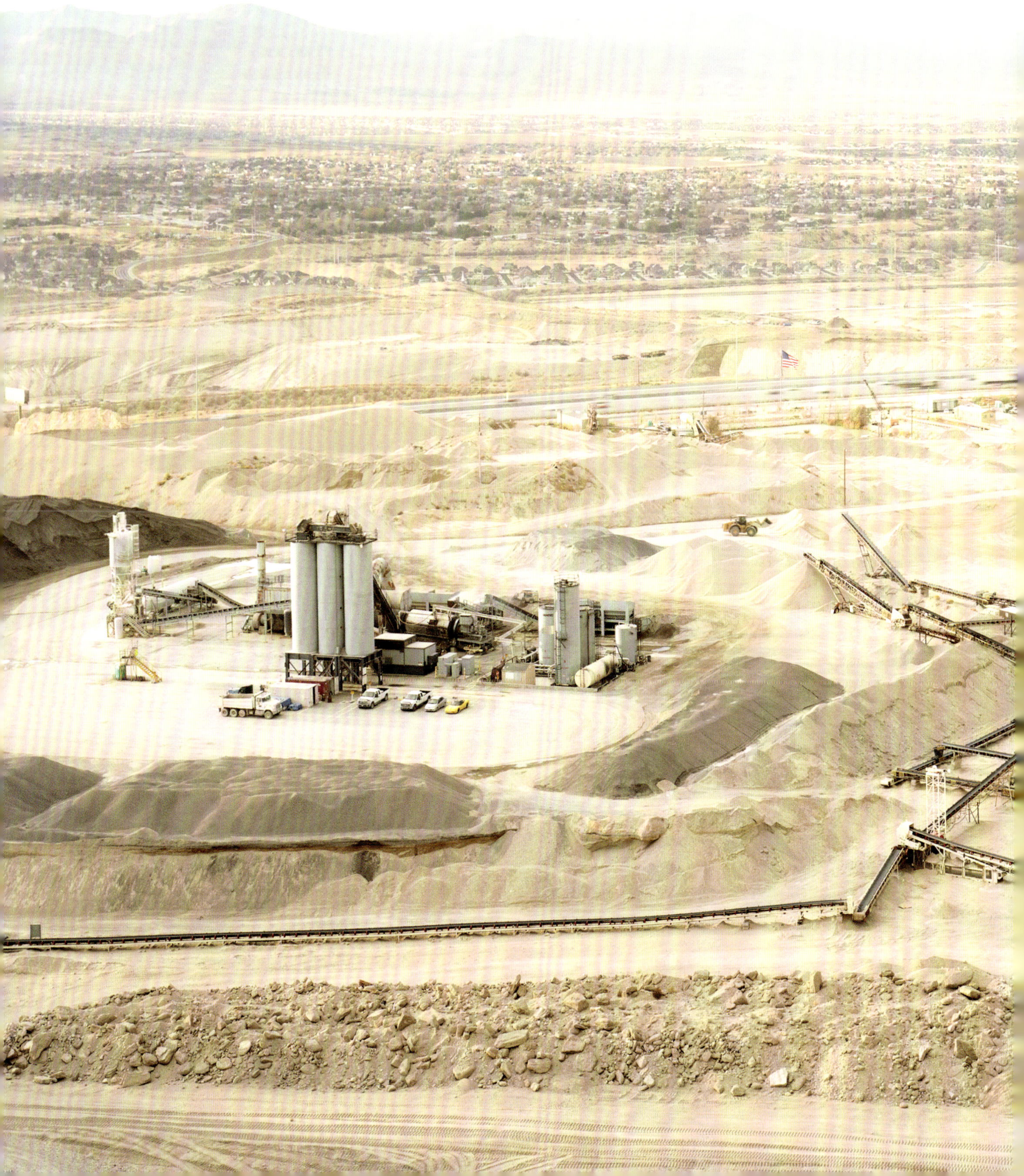

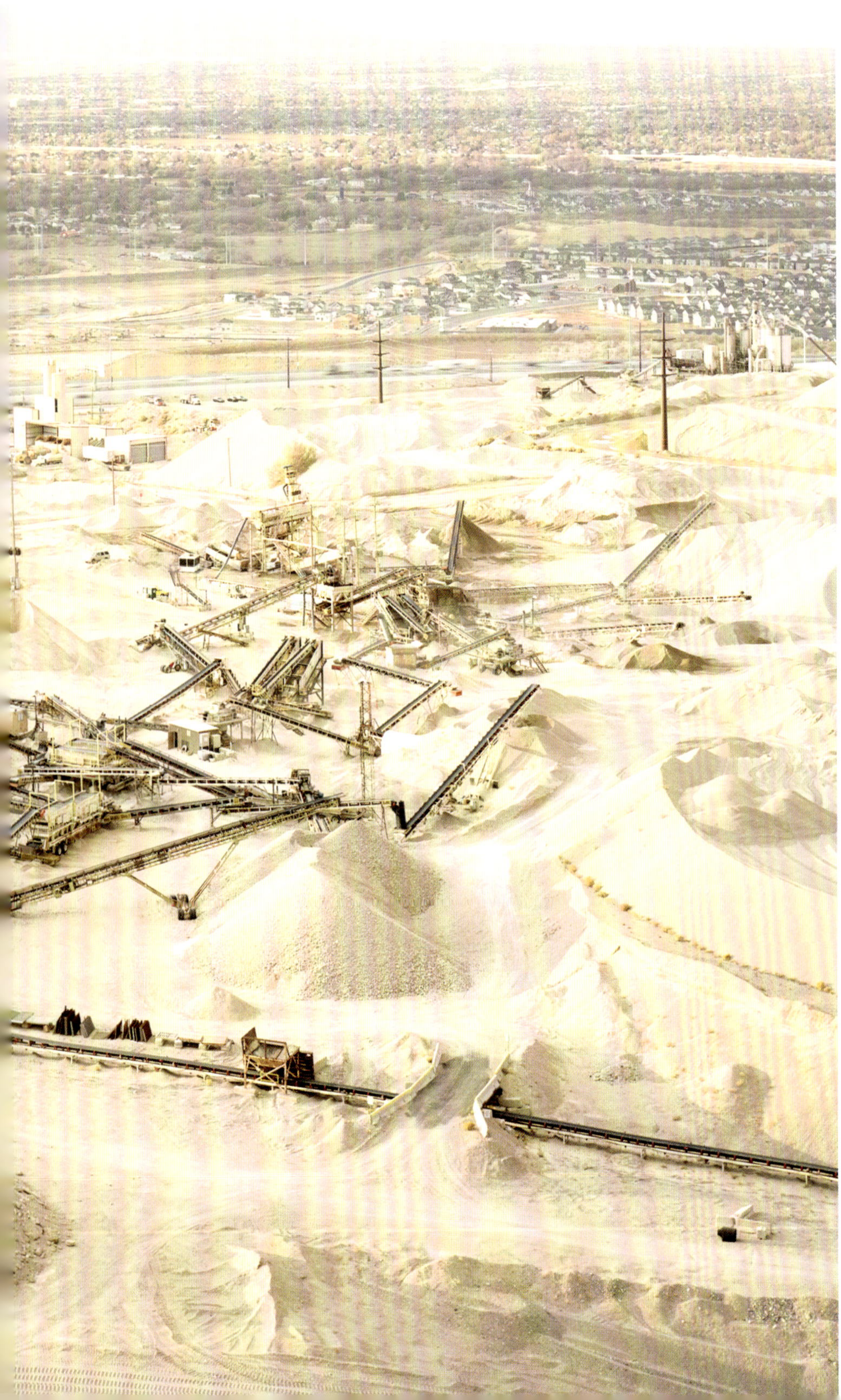

Victoria Sambunaris *Terra Infirma*

Sean J Patrick Carney

Staring out the passenger window at eighty miles per hour in the Intermountain West, you can clock three simultaneous time streams. Just yards beyond the glass, fence posts are a buzzing blur. Farther out, dust devils, bursts of sagebrush, sunbaked cisterns, and stolid cattle tumble along at a more grounded clip. At the absolute edges of perception, hazy geological spines and altocumulus clusters hold steady.

The driver rarely gets to appreciate these visual polyrhythms.

For a quarter century, Victoria Sambunaris has been the driver—most recently of "Mt. Fuji," as she calls her 2001 Toyota Land Cruiser with an odometer approaching 350,000 miles. Sambunaris spends months drifting east and west on Interstates 40, 70, and 80, or pitching north and south on the 5, 15, and 25. Mt. Fuji, though, ferries no passengers, just a spartan road kit: camping gear, two coolers, extra boots, and a hatchet. Also in tow: a 5-by-7-inch large-format field camera. Capturing images with this accordioned, wood-framed instrument requires anachronistic patience. Sambunaris might watch a site for days before releasing the shutter, waiting for specific conditions to reveal themselves.

Such a restrained approach to landscape and light is something Sambunaris gleaned from the early films of Terrence Malick. While shooting *Badlands* (1973) and *Days of Heaven* (1978), Malick insisted on filming during the "magic hour," the golden period that lasts, in practice, less than an hour at sunrise and sunset—an obsession that reportedly alienated production crews. Sambunaris exhibits her own unwavering fixation on light, though it's more meridian than Malick's. Shadows are short, if present at all. Every rock is bathed in even illumination. Gazing into a Sambunaris photograph

evokes the dislocating shimmer of standing in the desert at the sun's zenith.

Images of endless playas, hulking outcroppings, and terminal lakes reliably conjure the sublime of Carleton Watkins and William Henry Jackson. But Sambunaris is traversing a twenty-first-century, postcolonial West, one that, while still visually stunning, is fully networked by rail lines, roadways, and subdued rivers. These systems puncture the Rockies and Sierra Nevada, linking oil pipelines, bombing corridors, container yards, and open-pit mines to shipping channels carved into the Atlantic, Pacific, and Gulf coasts. Sambunaris bears slow witness, adding to a lineage of cultural landscape photography anchored by Dorothea Lange, Robert Adams, and Richard Misrach—what might be called a "forensic sublime."

"Our human landscape is our unwitting autobiography," the US geographer Peirce F. Lewis wrote in 1979. Sambunaris cites the passage frequently; it's a conceptual complement to Malick's formal influence. Indeed, the scars of extraction, transportation, and imperialism are diaristic. To subvert denial, Sambunaris seductively catalogs the personal effects of our collective belligerence so we might face them (as a joke might smuggle a brutal truth). Imagine Sophie Calle's undercover chambermaid, commissioned by the US Geological Survey.

The view of the American West through Sambunaris's camera is less animated than what she'd see out Mt. Fuji's passenger window, if she relinquished the wheel. But from a stationary point, quiet and methodical looking can access other time streams. Sambunaris's wide-open, topographic portraits unwrap ongoing histories. For patient viewers, this forensic sublime records how empire's contemporary tentacles of interstates, canals, and commercial rail lines were built, often violently, atop the bones of earlier infrastructures: overland immigrant and supply routes including the Mormon Trail, Oregon Trail, and Gila Trail; the Spanish colonial El Camino Real; and millennia-old Indigenous circuits such as the Chaco roads and Hohokam trade network.

And, still, at the absolute edges of perception, hazy geological spines and altocumulus clusters hold steady.

Sean J Patrick Carney is an itinerant artist and writer.

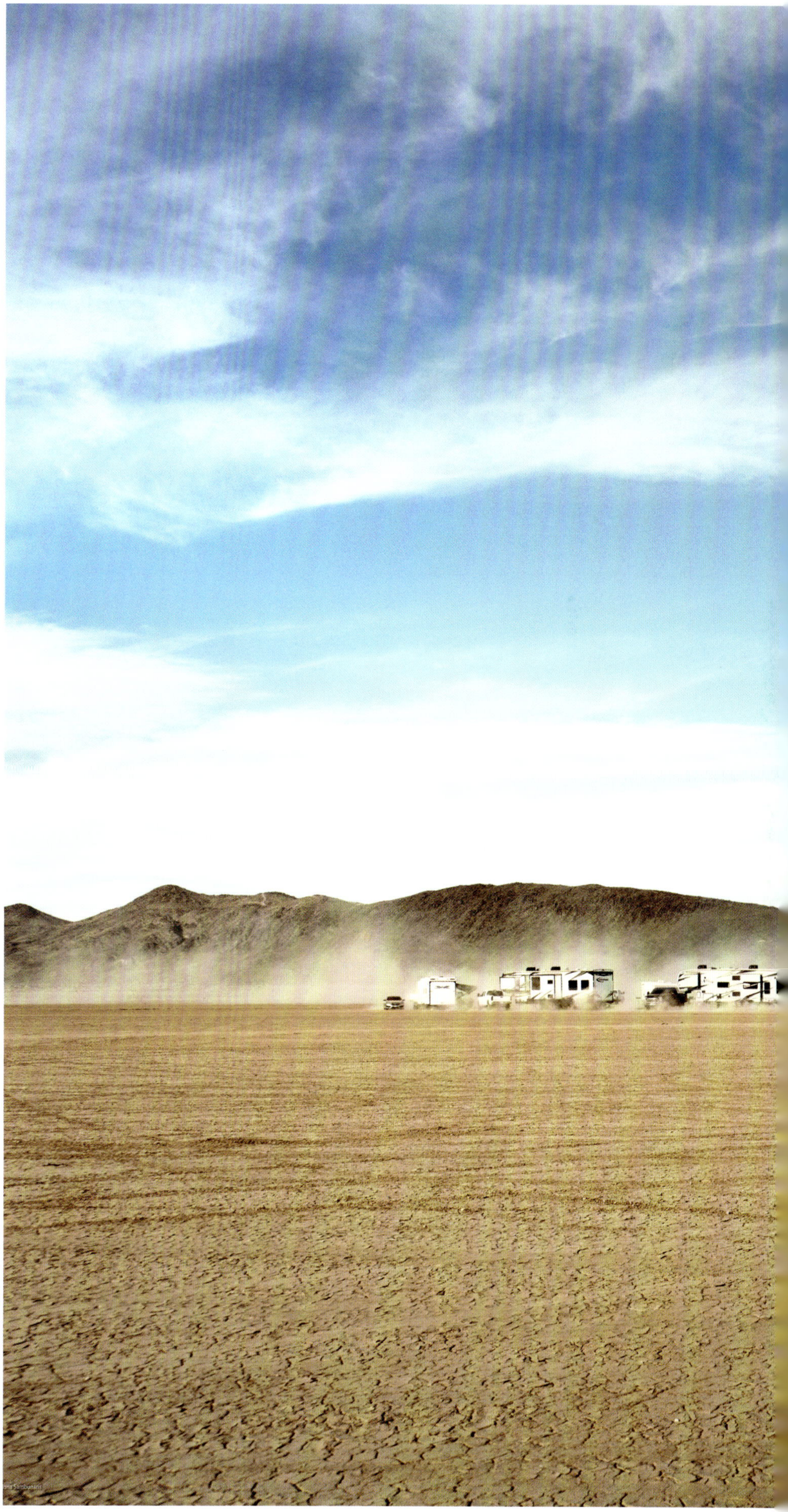

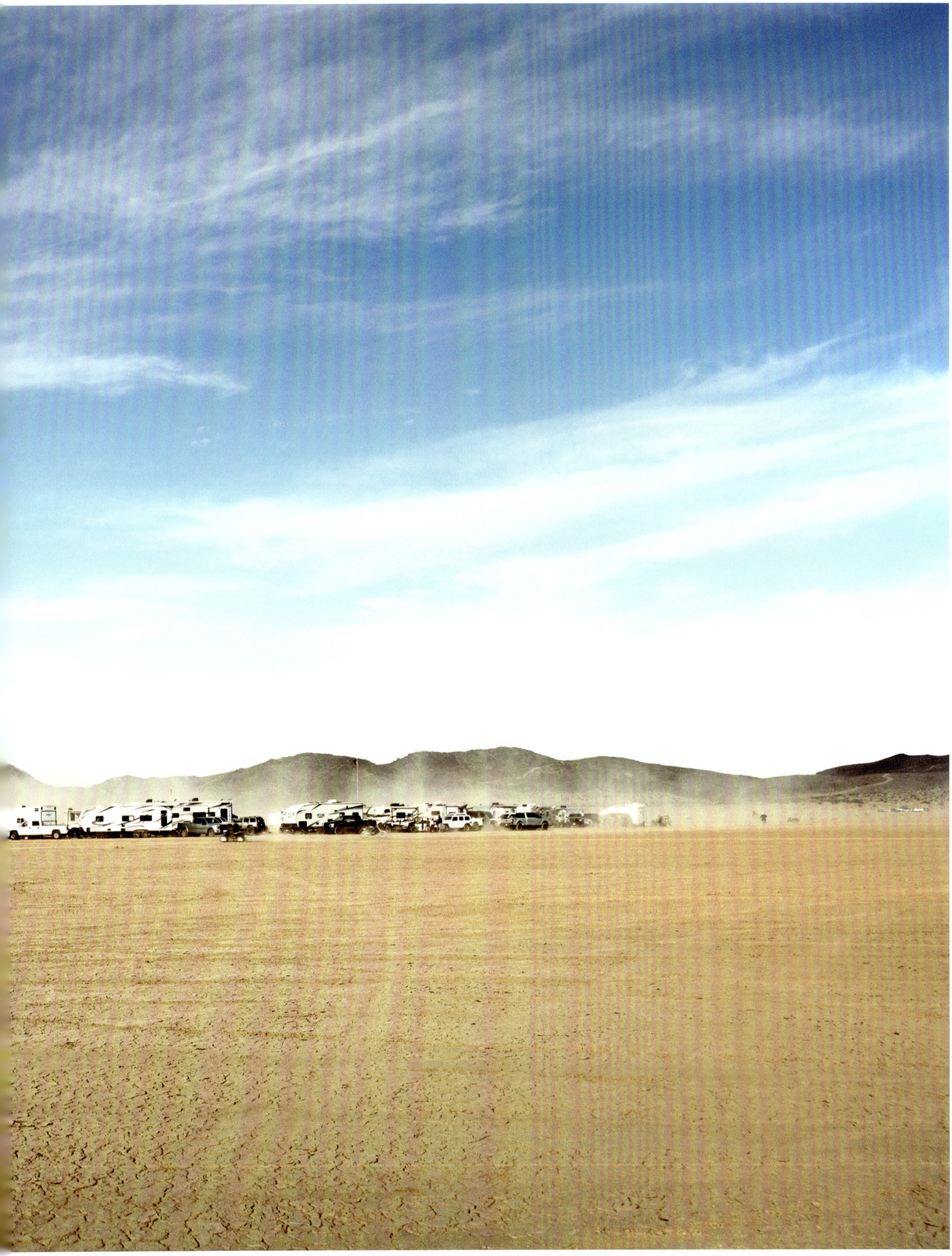

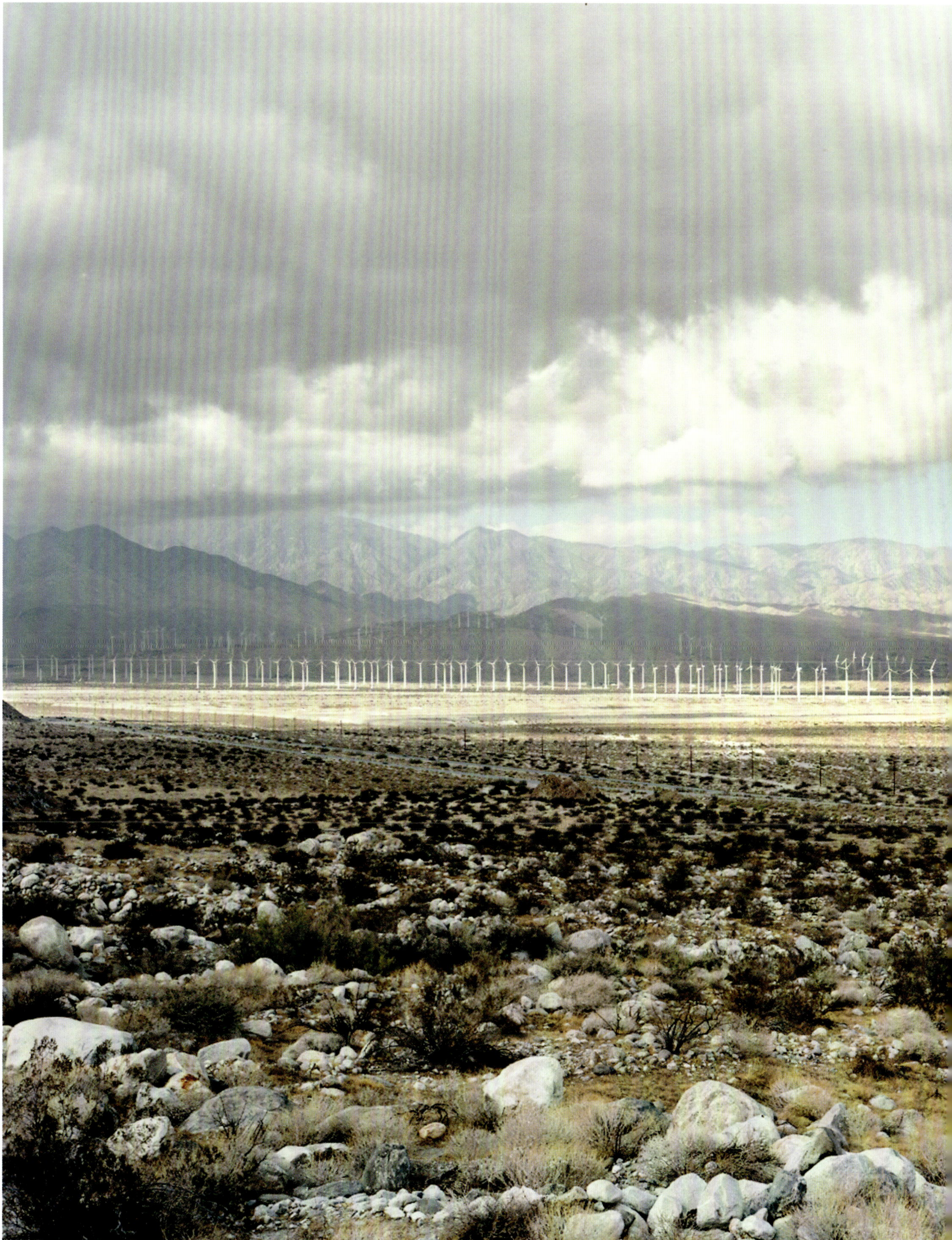
Victoria Sambunaris

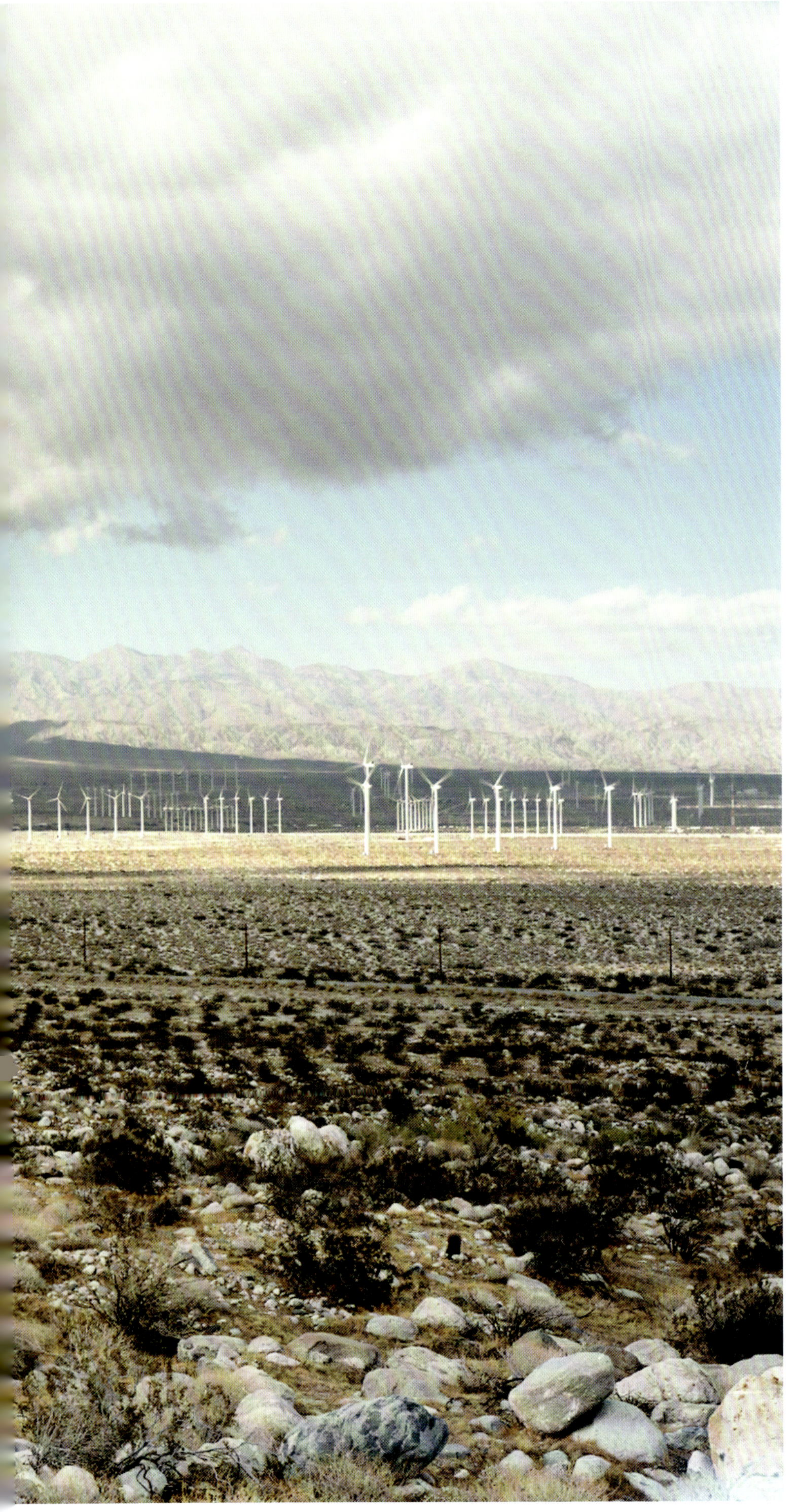

Pages 126–27:
Untitled (gravel pit), near Draper, Utah, 2017

Previous spread:
Untitled (caravan), Buttercup Valley, Utah, 2021

This spread:
Untitled (windmills), San Gorgonio Wind Park, Palm Springs, California, 2021

Untitled (train crossing Great Salt Lake), near Promontory, Utah, 2016

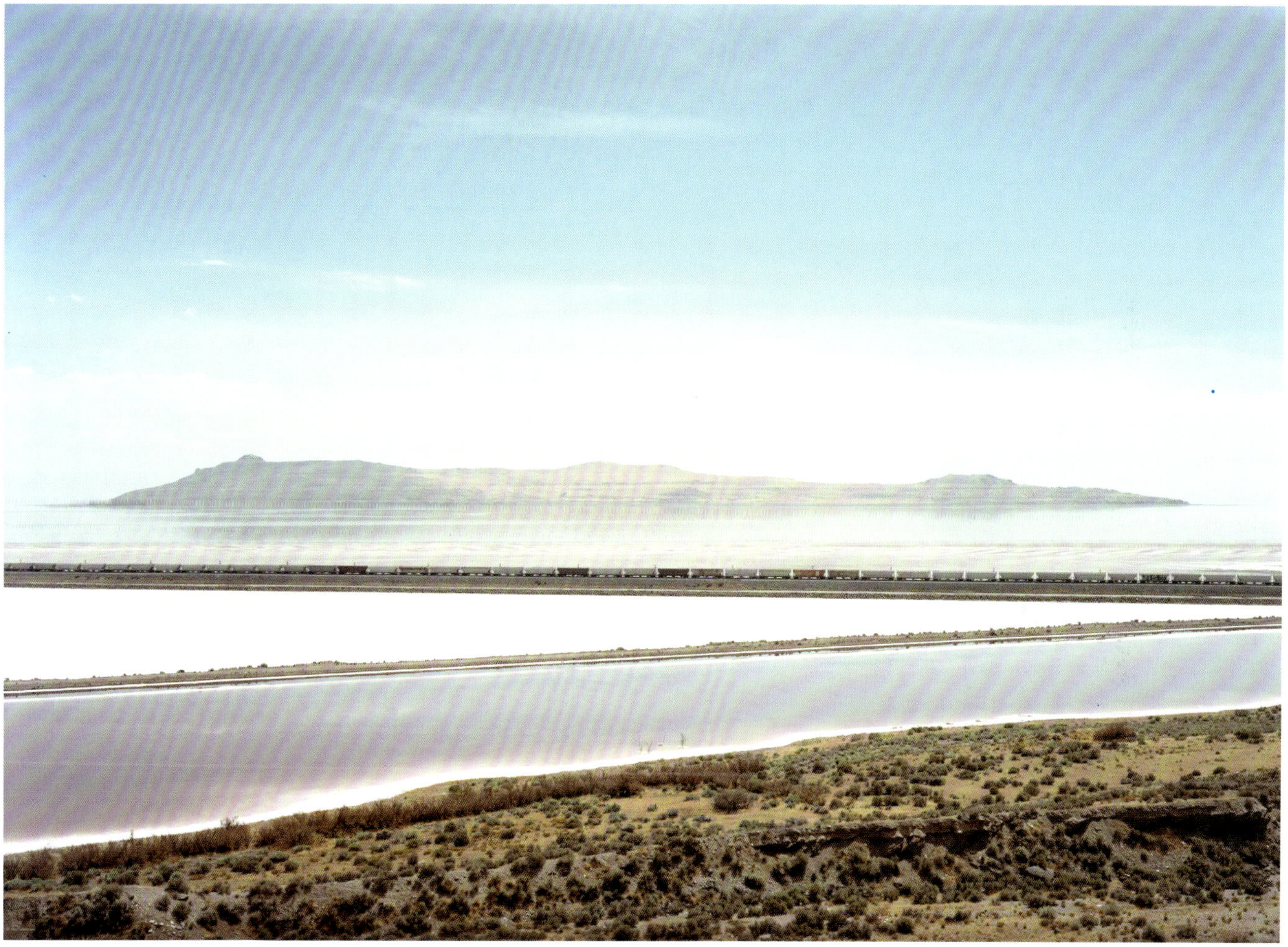

Untitled (container ship, CMA CGM Kingfish, Liberia), Houston Ship Channel, Texas, 2016

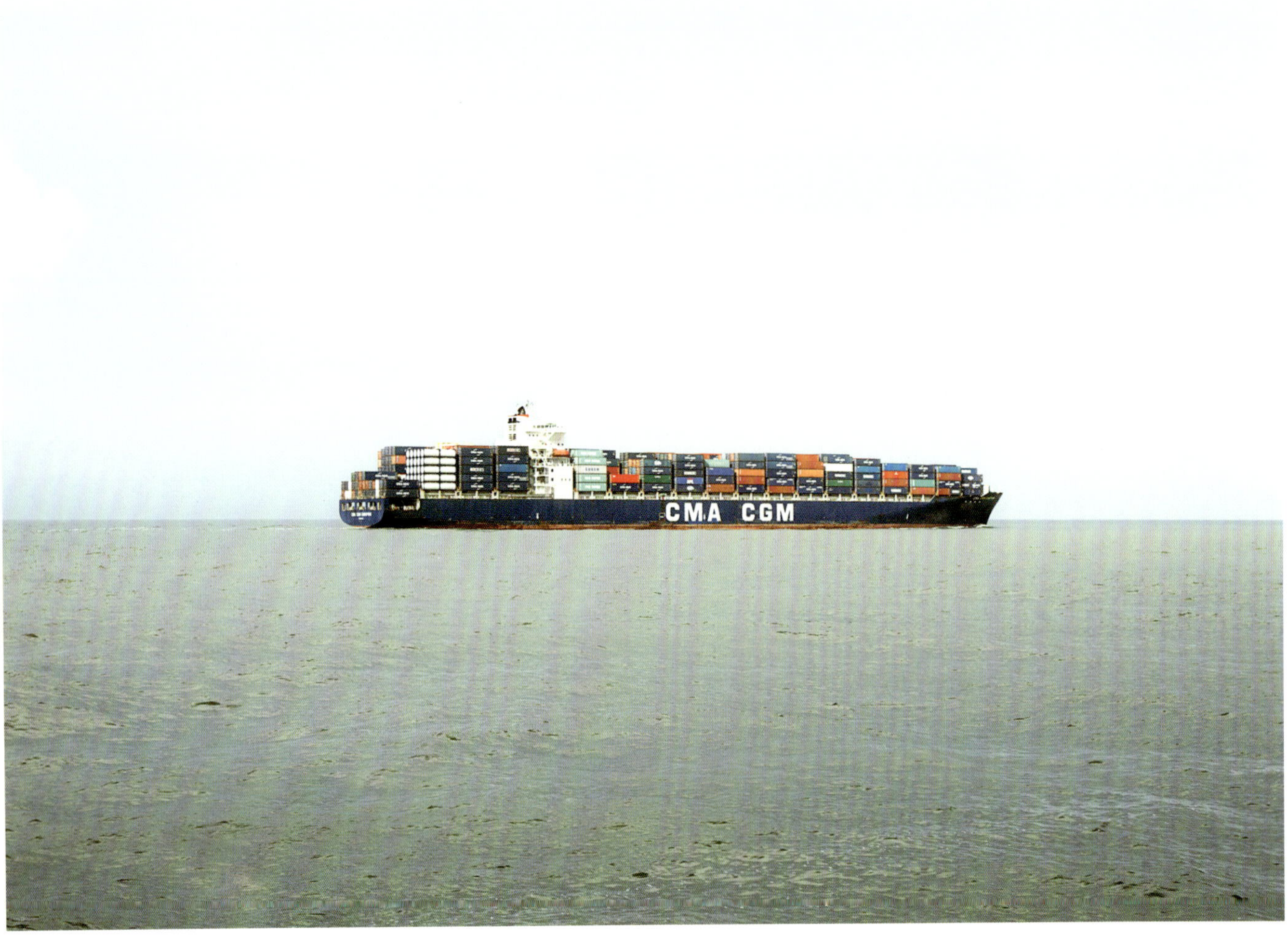

Untitled (train tunnel), Gore Valley, Kremmling, Colorado, 2023
Courtesy the artist and Yancey Richardson Gallery, New York

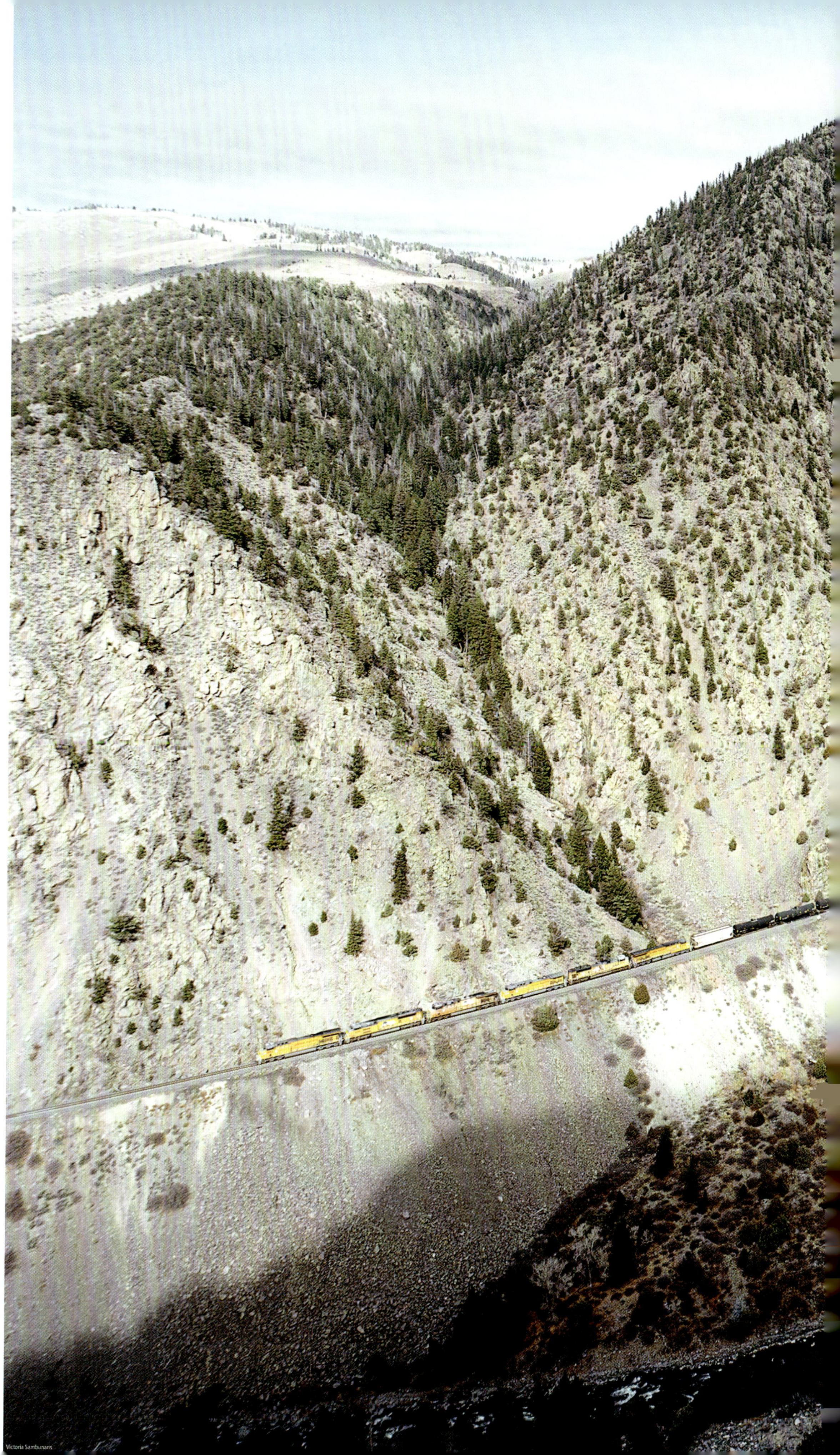
Victoria Sambunaris

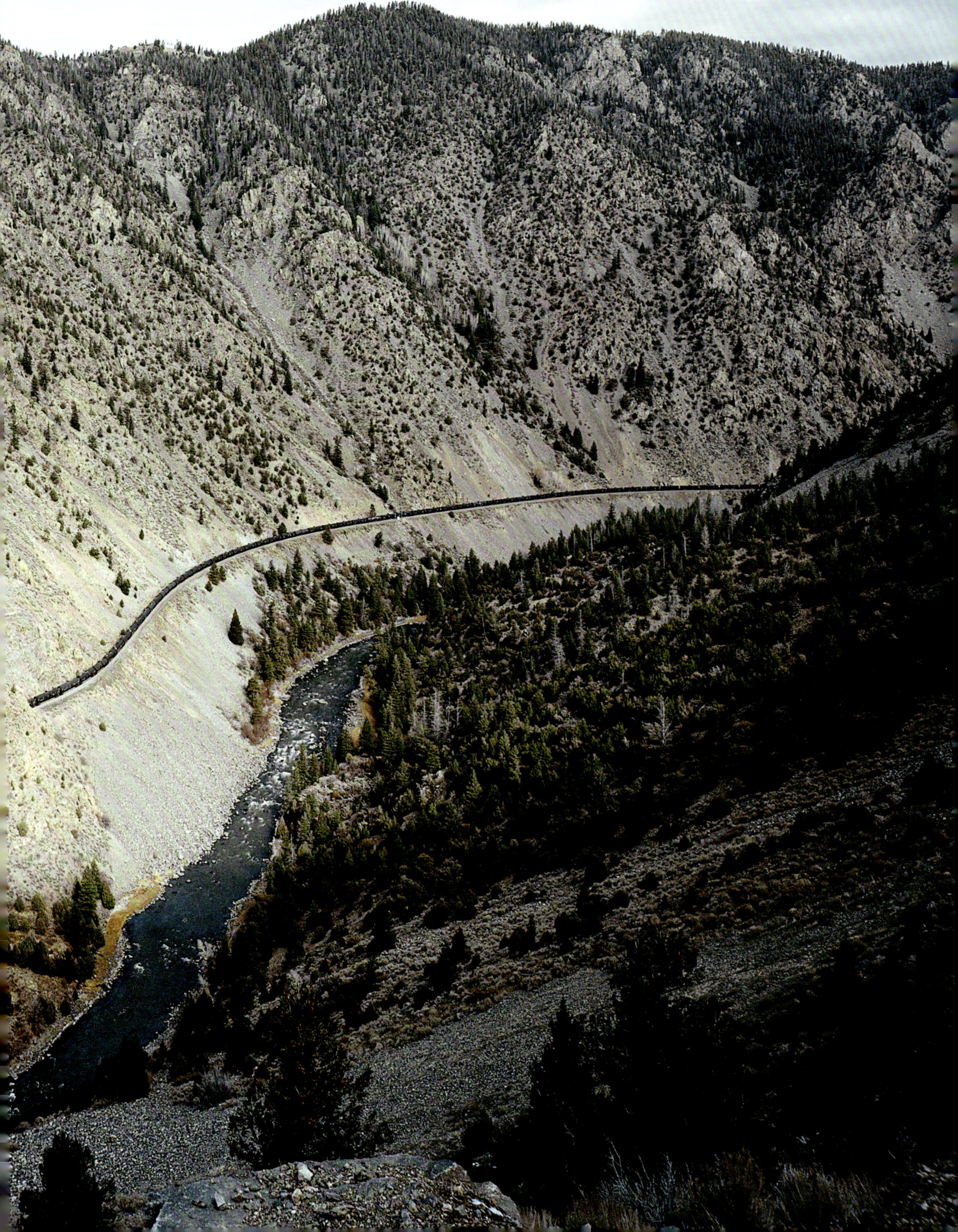

The PhotoBook Review

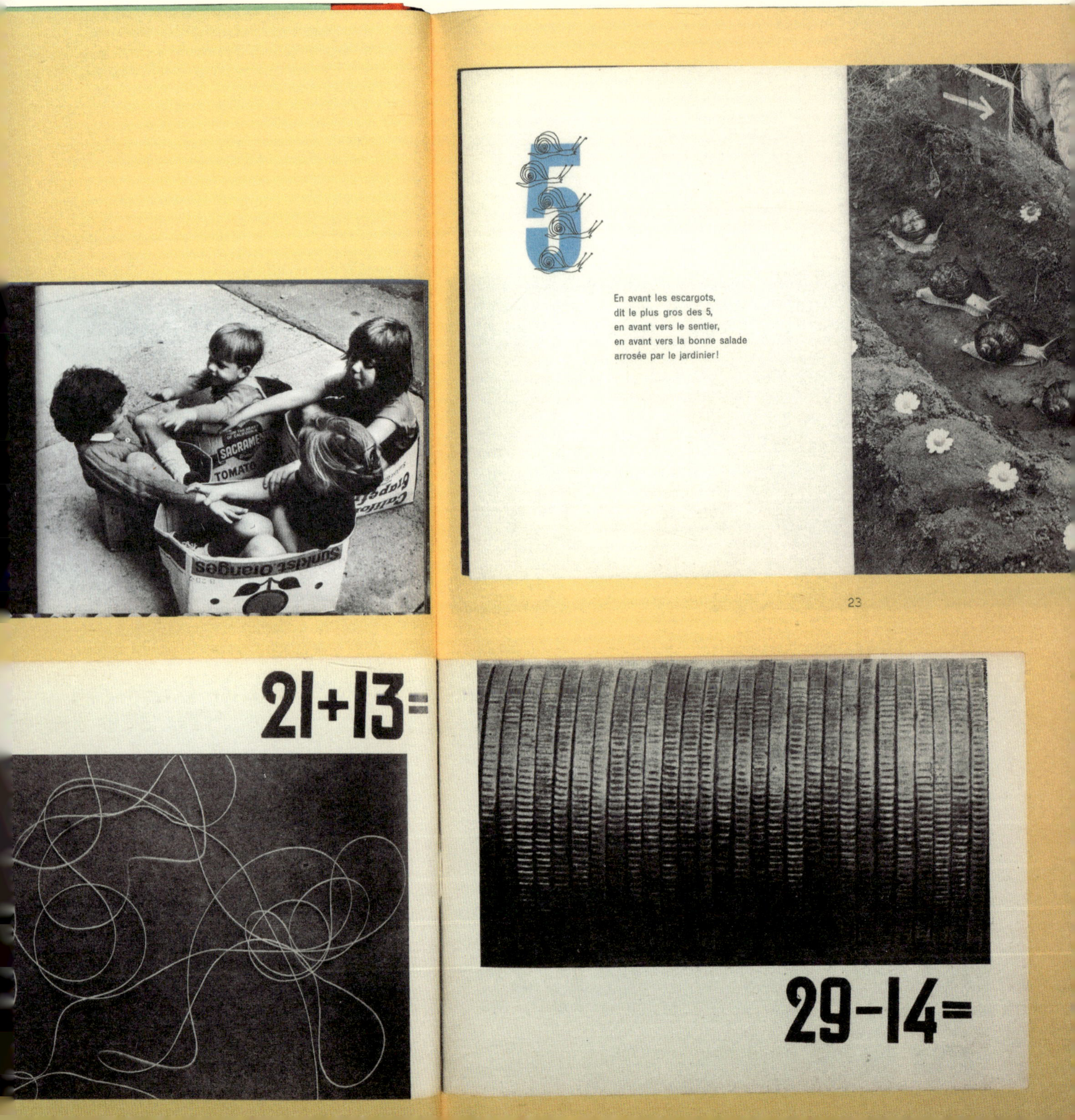

Tokyo Stories

Takashi Homma speaks with Marigold Warner about his photobook philosophy.

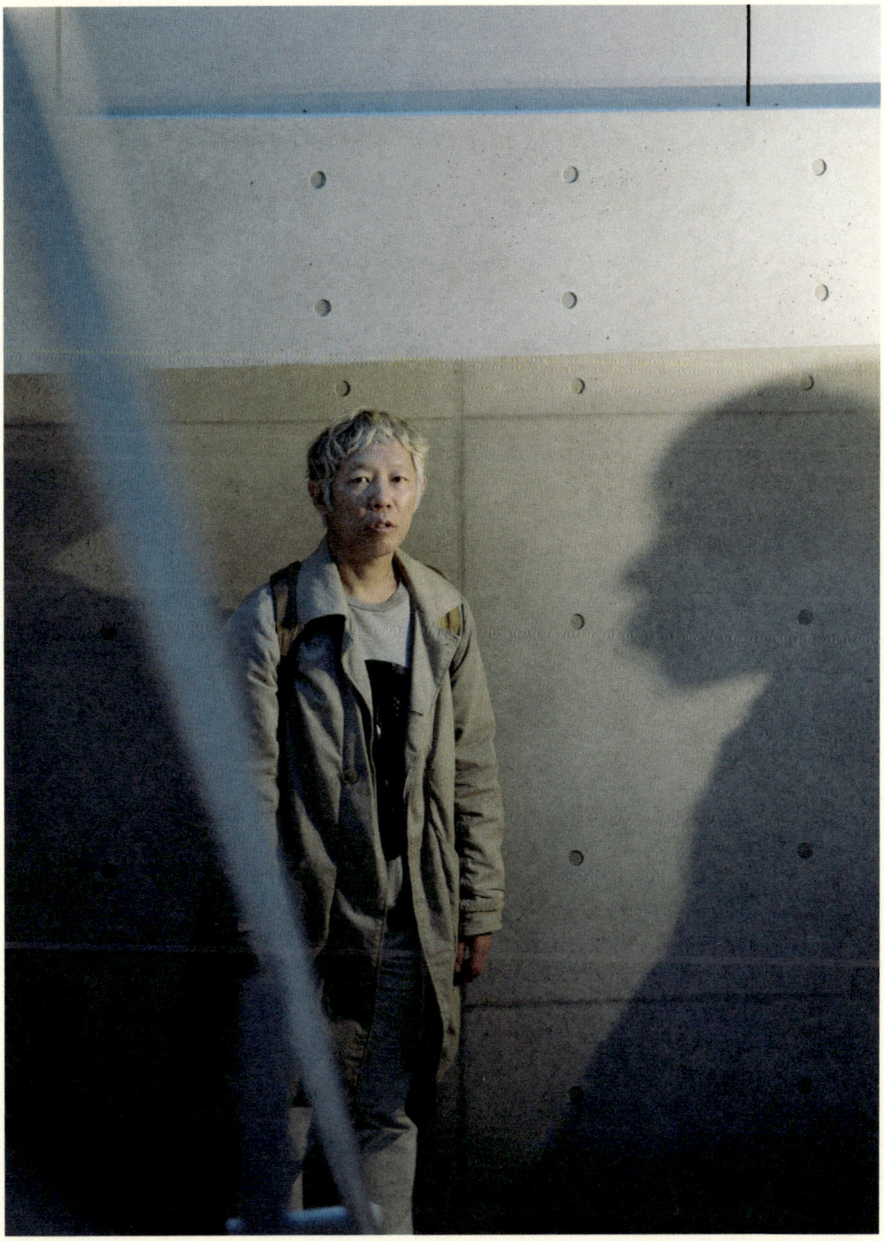

Takashi Homma made his name photographing street style in 1990s Tokyo, during Japan's so-called Lost Decade. Since then, he's continued to chronicle the vagaries of fashion and youth culture while also turning his distinct yet discreet eye toward suburban life, ocean waves, and radioactive mushrooms, becoming a pillar of contemporary Japanese photography. Now sixty-three, he has amassed an oeuvre of more than sixty publications, including zines, essays, exhibition catalogs, and, of course, photobooks, most recently *Portrait of J* (Dashwood Books/Session Press, 2025), a love letter to the ordinary people of Japan. Marigold Warner sat down with Homma at his office in Tokyo to talk about his evolving relationship with the medium, and the city itself.

Marigold Warner: **What was the first photobook you ever bought?**

Takashi Homma: It was a collection of photographs of Momoe Yamaguchi, a legendary pop idol in Japan. I bought it when I was in high school, and only later realized the photos were taken by Kishin Shinoyama. At the time I had no idea—the only reason I bought it was because I wanted to see photos of my favorite idol.

MW: **What about the most recent one you bought?**

TH: I haven't bought any books recently. I definitely don't buy as much as I used to. Half of this room was once full of books, but I've cut it down to a small collection. I think the biggest reason for that is the internet. I'm publishing a new text-based book on photography soon, and whereas before I'd have all these photobooks to dig through for references, now I can just look them up online.

MW: **Were there any books that you felt you absolutely had to keep?**

TH: The thinner photobooks, and the rare ones. Definitely not the big hardcovers from major publishers. I don't like things that feel too authoritative or prestigious, like they were made by an important person. Overseas, they call these coffee-table books. In the end, they just become interior decorations that sit on a fancy living-room table. I prefer the slim books that an artist might put out

just for an exhibition at that specific time. Jack Pierson once made this small, zine-like book called *Angel Youth* (1992). I bought it in the '90s, and I've kept it ever since.

MW: **Who do you see as a real master of bookmaking?**

TH: I've always respected Nobuyoshi Araki. He's published more than five hundred photobooks. A lot of people, especially designers and architects, want to make these grand, heavy books. What I like about Araki is that there's a kind of lightness to his work and attitude. As people become more famous, they get heavier, more serious, more rigid. But people like me and Araki—real Tokyo people—I think, crave a certain lightness.

MW: **Tokyo has been a subject of your books since you started out. How do you feel about your home city now?**

TH: It's love and hate. When I was in my thirties or forties, I probably had a different answer. I thought maybe I'd live abroad again, but at this age, it's more about what I can do now, within the current situation. Tokyo could be hit by a huge earthquake tomorrow. We all know it'll happen eventually. When it does, and if I'm still alive, I'll have no choice but to photograph it. That's kind of where I'm at now.

MW: **What do you think it is about Tokyo that attracts photographers to make work here?**

Page 137:
Spread from *L Is for Look: Children's Photobooks* (Spector Books, 2025)

Opposite:
***Takashi Homma, photographer*, 2016**

Bottom, left:
Cover of *Tokyo Suburbia* (Korinsha, 1998)

Bottom, right:
Cover of *Tokyo Olympia* (Nieves, 2023)

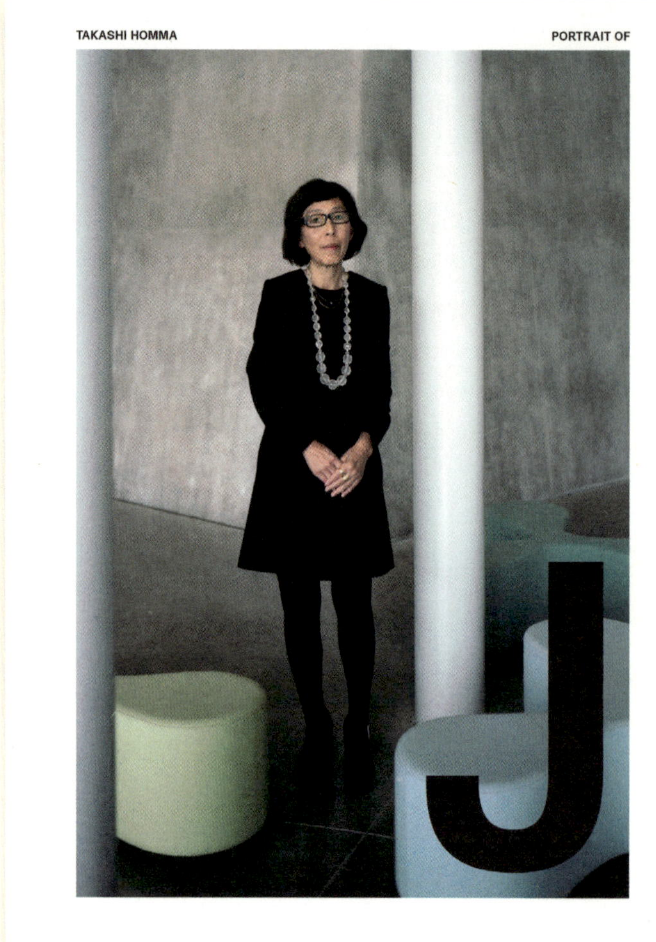

Above:
Cover of *Portrait of J* (Dashwood Books/Session Press, 2025)

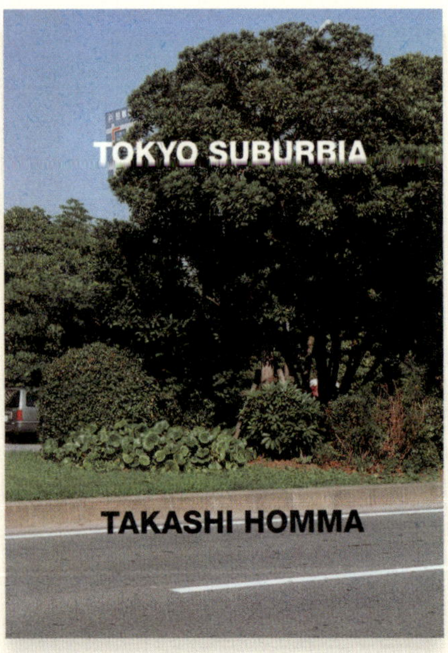

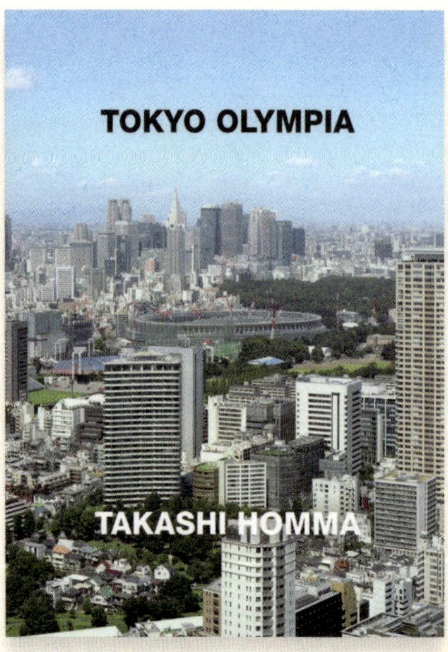

TH: In terms of the urban landscape, there's really no other capital with this level of scrap and build. I was just in Milan and Paris recently, and everything there is built from stone, standing for over hundreds of years. Take Shibuya, for example. This area of Tokyo is constantly under construction, changing so fast it feels like a different person. So, it's inherently photographic, because photography is best suited to capturing change. Most photographers, I think, take pictures because they love something, or they're emotionally attached to it. For me, it's different. For instance, I have a photobook of waves. Everyone always asks me: "Homma-san, do you surf?" I don't. Then they ask, "So, you like the sea?" Of course I like it, but that's not the reason I photograph it. Waves come and go, crashing in differently each time. They're never the same. I stand there, and when they come, I shoot. Each one is different. That's the concept that fascinates me.

MW: **Your latest book, *Portrait of J*, presents a collection of images you've been taking since 2002. You've photo-**

This page:
***Marina, model*, 2020**

Opposite:
***Moka, fashion stylist assistant*, 2024**
Photographs on this spread and page 138 from *Portrait of J* (2025)

Tokyo could be hit by a huge earthquake tomorrow. If I'm still alive, I'll have no choice but to photograph it. That's kind of where I'm at now.

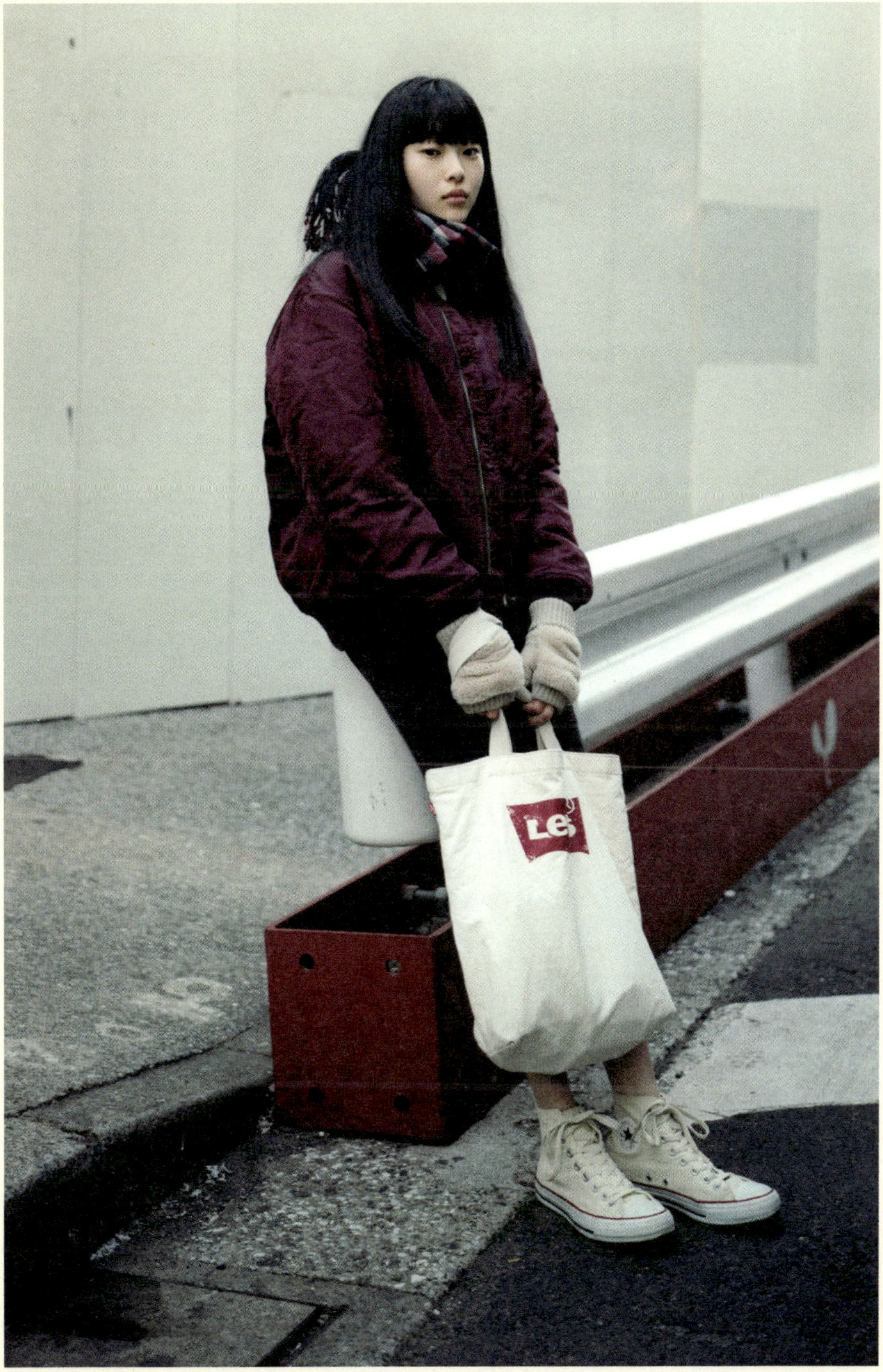

graphed celebrities, friends, children. Is there any particular shoot from the book that stands out to you?

TH: Not really. They're all equal to me. For me, famous people and my friends' children have the same value, and that's why they're placed on equal footing in the book. There isn't anyone in particular who stands out more than another.

MW: **How did you decide on the cover photograph then?**

TH: The cover photo is of the architect Kazuyo Sejima. Wolfgang Tillmans made a photobook of portraits, and his cover features the architect Rem Koolhaas. Mine is kind of a subtle response to that. I've also known Sejima-san for a long time, and I knew I definitely wanted the cover to feature a woman.

MW: **And why the title *Portrait of J*?**

TH: Because we're Japanese. Also, there's a guitarist named John Williams who released an album called *Portrait of John Williams*, in 1982. I thought that was really cool, and that the title was something I could use someday.

MW: **You published the book with Dashwood in New York. Was there anything you wanted to communicate about Japan to an international audience?**

TH: That's a very Japanese-minded question. Japanese interviewers always ask questions like, "What do you want to communicate?" Well, whatever the artist wants to say is already contained within the work. They made it because they didn't want to put it into words. Still, if I had to say one thing, last year Japan's population dropped by almost a million. If this continues, Japan will soon experience a super-aged society unlike anything the world has seen. The Japanese could even become an endangered species. In that sense, I think this book could be important.

MW: **Has the way you make or think about books evolved from when you started?**

TH: When I started, publishing a book wasn't something you could just do. You couldn't make a book unless a publisher

wanted you to, which is completely different from now. These days, every year there are so many publishers asking me to make something. I just respond to those opportunities and keep publishing. When I was in my twenties, I remember thinking it would be enough if I could publish just one photobook. I never imagined I'd end up publishing sixty.

Since I started, I've always decided on about 90 to 95 percent of everything myself. The sequence, the title, the cover—everything. That's been consistent since my very first book. There are still lots of photographers, especially in Japan, who just throw all their photos at the editor or designer and let them build the whole book. There are definitely a lot of really talented editors and designers here, but I'm more interested in the conceptual side of creating the whole thing, rather than just being a photographer. Wolfgang Tillmans is similar in that sense. He always says in interviews that the actual photographing part is quick. The real time is spent thinking deeply about how to present the work, how to exhibit it, or how to make it into a book. I think that's natural, but in Japan it's different. When I first started working that way, Japanese critics and editors said terrible things about me. Kōtarō Iizawa, a once-prominent critic who has totally lost his influence now, once said something like, "Inside Homma, there are two people, a photographer and an editor. And that is not good."

MW: **In your view, what makes a good photobook?**

TH: First of all, it needs to be easy to read and easy to open. Some designers get too obsessed with special bindings, putting it in some annoying plastic case, or tying it up with strings. I like books where you can access the photos directly, and light ones, like zines. When I was living in London in the early '90s, there was a photobook store that sold these really thin books of about sixteen or twenty-four pages called "loose books." One of them was by Nigel Shafran, I think it was photos of his wife before they got married. It's too thin to really call a photobook, but it's good. That's what makes a great photobook—when it's good on its own terms.

MW: **Some of your older photobooks are now sold as rare items at high prices. What do you think of that?**

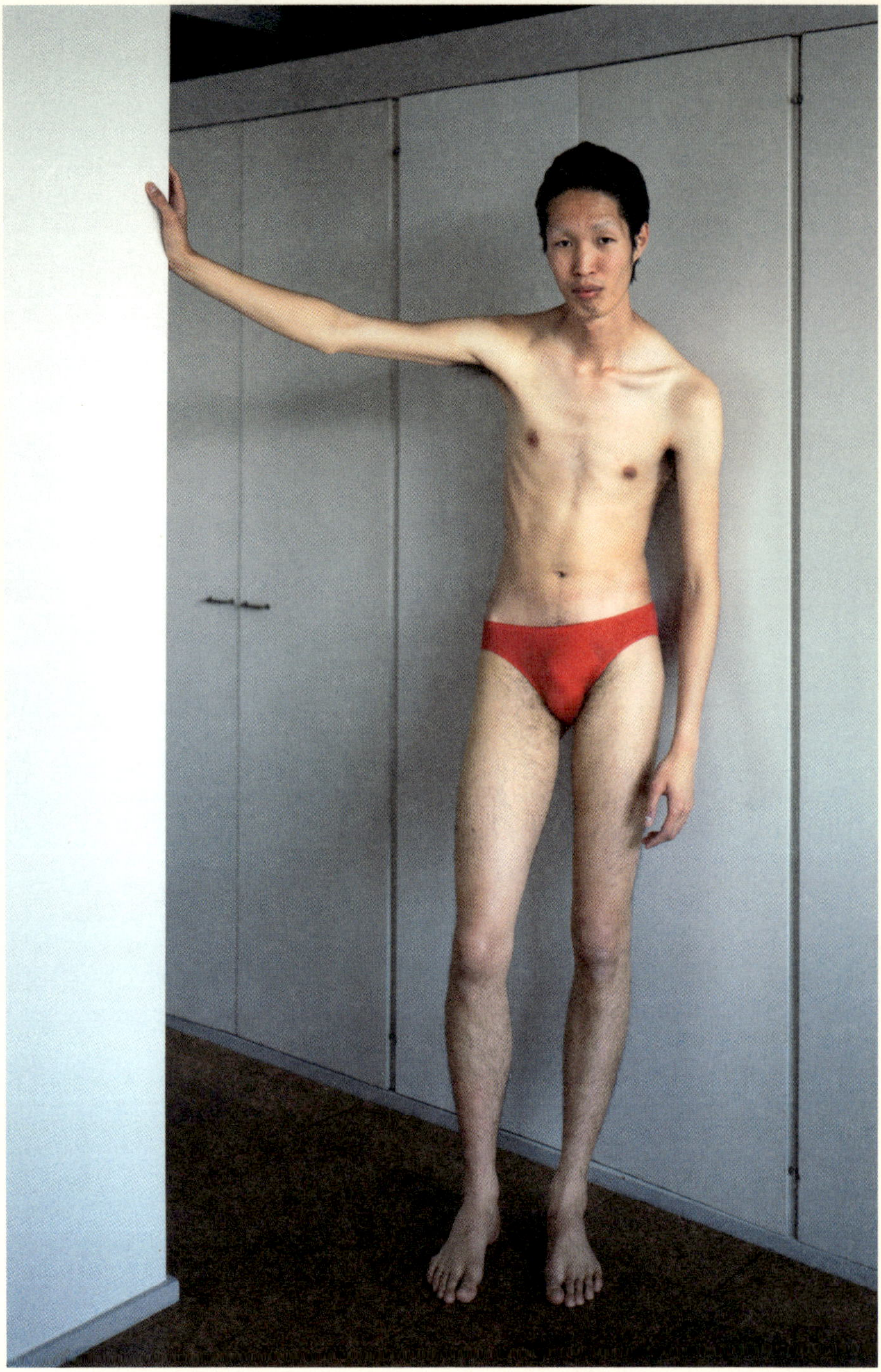

TH: Photobooks don't usually get reprinted, that's just how it is. So, they naturally become rare. Even though I've published over sixty photobooks, I've hardly received any royalties. Most of the time, it's payment in copies.

MW: **I suppose making books isn't something you do for money.**

TH: I was just talking about this the other day, and the question is always, "Why do you do it," right? For me, it's just part of daily life, like eating or exercising. It's not something I have to do. It's something that has to happen.

Marigold Warner is a writer based in Tokyo.

Tiny Tales

The untold story of children's photobooks.

Hannah Stamler

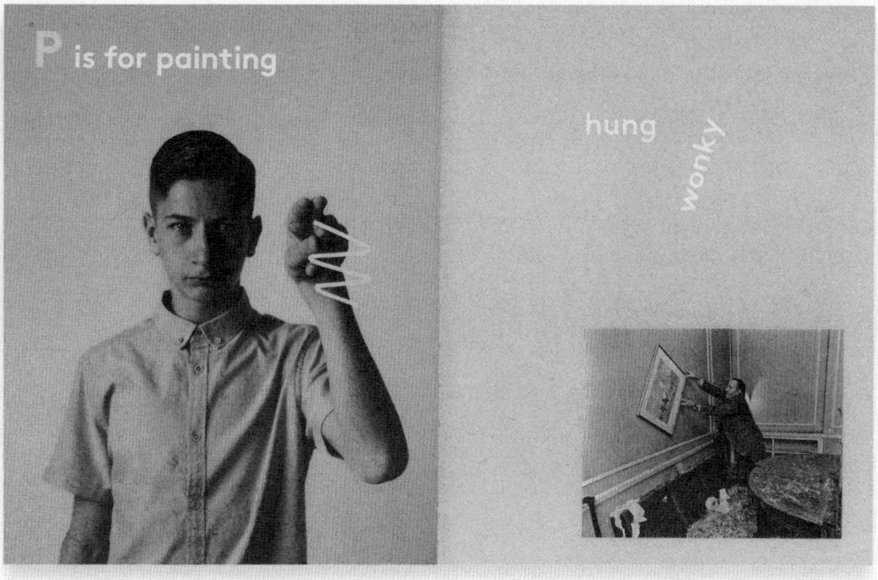

Top:
Spread from Adam Broomberg and Oliver Chanarin, *Humans and Other Animals* (Tate Publishing, 2015)
© Late Estate of Broomberg and Chanarin

Bottom:
Spread from Tana Hoban, *Look Again!* (Macmillan, 1971)
© Estate of Tana Hoban

As early childhood education expanded in the twentieth century, so did the demand for picture books. With greater importance came greater scrutiny. If picture books were essential to child development, then grown-ups needed to get the genre right. What combination of words and images would best awaken and excite young minds?

For Lucy Sprague Mitchell, a cofounder of New York's influential Bureau of Educational Experiments—now the Bank Street College of Education—it was clear that children craved stories grounded in the sensations of real life. Like other progressive educators, she believed that toddlers were natural empiricists and promoted an experiential, hands-on style of learning. Preschoolers were, she argued in 1921, captivated by the "here and now." Instead of escapism and make-believe, fairy princesses in faraway lands, their books should begin with "the familiar and the immediate."

Mitchell's realist maxim inspired one of the first important photographic picture books, according to *Click! Photographers Make Picture Books*, a current

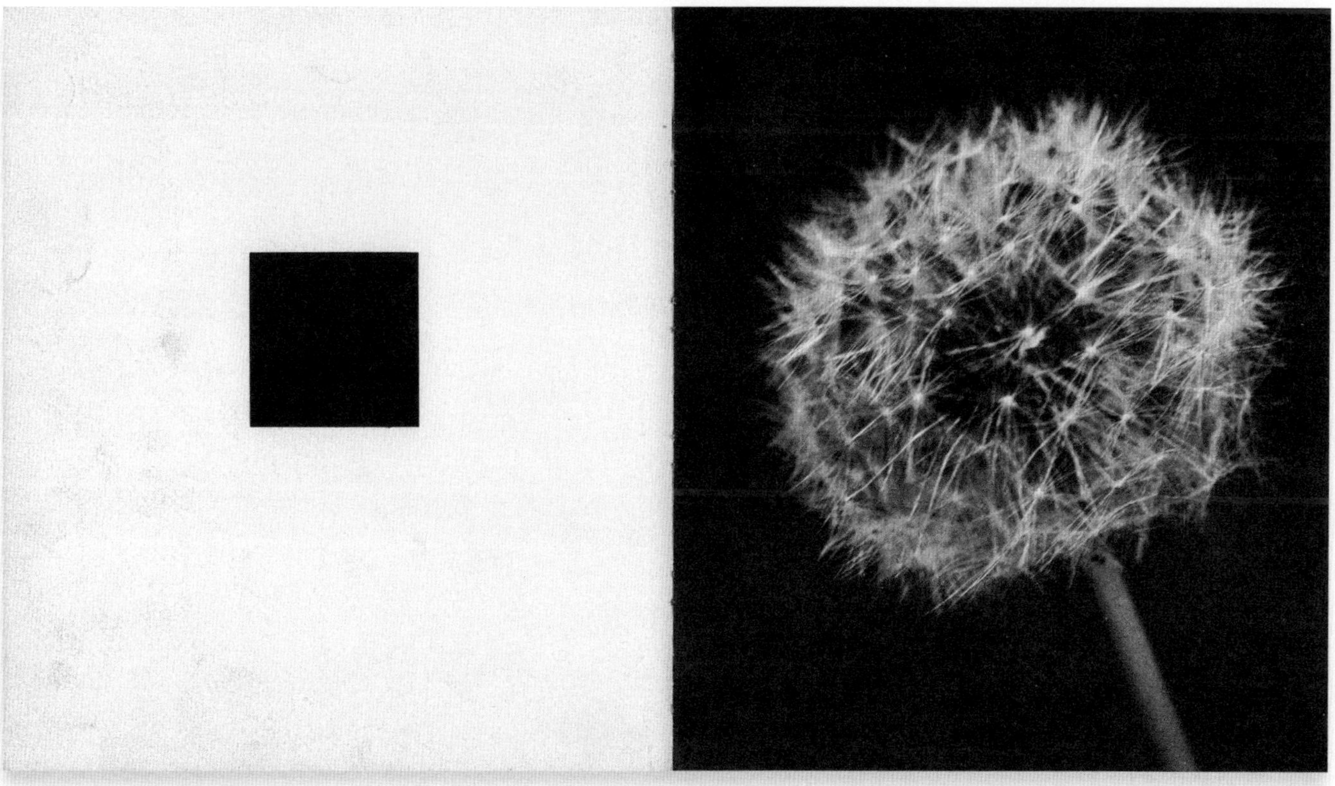

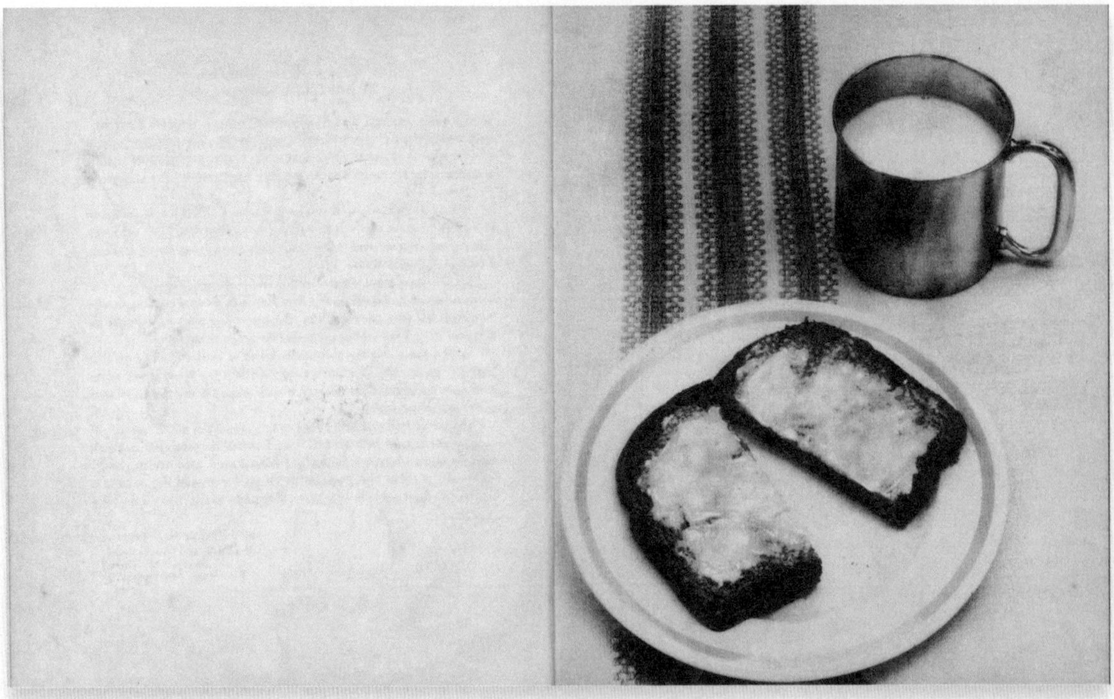

Spread from Edward Steichen and Mary Steichen Calderone (then Martin), *The First Picture Book* (Harcourt Brace & Company, 1930)

exhibition at the Eric Carle Museum of Picture Book Art, in Amherst, Massachusetts. As the curator Leonard Marcus explains, among the Bank Street devotees was Mary Steichen Martin (later Calderone), a public health advocate and the daughter of Edward Steichen. Convinced that photography could be used to innovate children's literature, Martin urged her father to collaborate with her on a picture book for two-year-olds. The result, published in 1930, is an ode to the objects in the average middle-class American home. Called simply *The First Picture Book*, it features stylishly composed black-and-white images of more than twenty domestic items—from a teddy bear to a hairbrush—paired with textless pages to encourage children to look closely, name what they see, and invent their own stories.

Click! follows on the heels of *L Is for Look: Children's Photobooks*, a touring exhibition first presented at Photo Elysée in Switzerland last fall and similarly preoccupied by the connections between histories of photography and education. And as outlined in its catalog, a beautiful volume published by Spector, the teachers and followers of Bank Street were not alone in seeing photographs as ideal vehicles for transmitting early concepts: objects, letters, numbers, shapes. Modern educators and modernist photographers became close allies throughout the interwar years, especially in Germany. To Weimar's child-centered pedagogues, crisply taken pictures in the New Objectivity style were the best teaching aids because they most closely mimicked the child's pure, untrained sense of vision. This belief, the photography historian Olivier Lugon observes, points to a "fundamental ambiguity" in progressive educational theory: "On the one hand, the photographic image was supposed to help 'form'—and transform—children. On the other, it was put forward as a tool for restoring their original way of seeing."

Although progressive education would wane in the Cold War, photography remained a staple of early concept books. Tana Hoban, who is featured in both exhibitions, attuned children to their environment in pioneering books such as *Look Again!* (1971), a guessing game in which windows cut into right-hand pages depict abstract details that expand into full photographs when the page is turned, and *Count and See* (1972), where photographs teach children their numbers via countable scenes of daily life (fifteen cookies, five trash bins, et cetera).

Not all photographers working on children's books chose to adhere to strict realism. Many, in fact, defied Mitchell and followed fantasy traditions in youth literature, weaving photographs into fiction and fairytales. Could there be anything more delightfully absurd than William Wegman's Weimaraners, dressed in high heels and pointed hats to play the evil stepsisters and fairy godmother, along with the titular character, in his 1993 edition of *Cinderella*? Is it possible to conceive of a set of pictures more haunting than the quietly surreal photographs in Dare Wright's *The Lonely Doll*, a 1957 cult classic whose treatment of girlhood alienation and abjection prefigures the work of Cindy Sherman and Laurie Simmons?

Whether one is drawn toward the documentary or the fabulist, questions about photography and children's media have, arguably, never been more compelling to consider. For the AI-native toddlers of today, being raised in the semiotic slop playground of social media and YouTube, the line between the observable and the imagined, the authentic and the illusory, is far murkier than for prior generations. As collective society increasingly loses its grip on the "here and now" that progressive educators once sought to bring into children's books, one wonders: What lessons are photographs teaching the kids of today?

Hannah Stamler is a historian, writer, and educator based in New Haven, Connecticut.

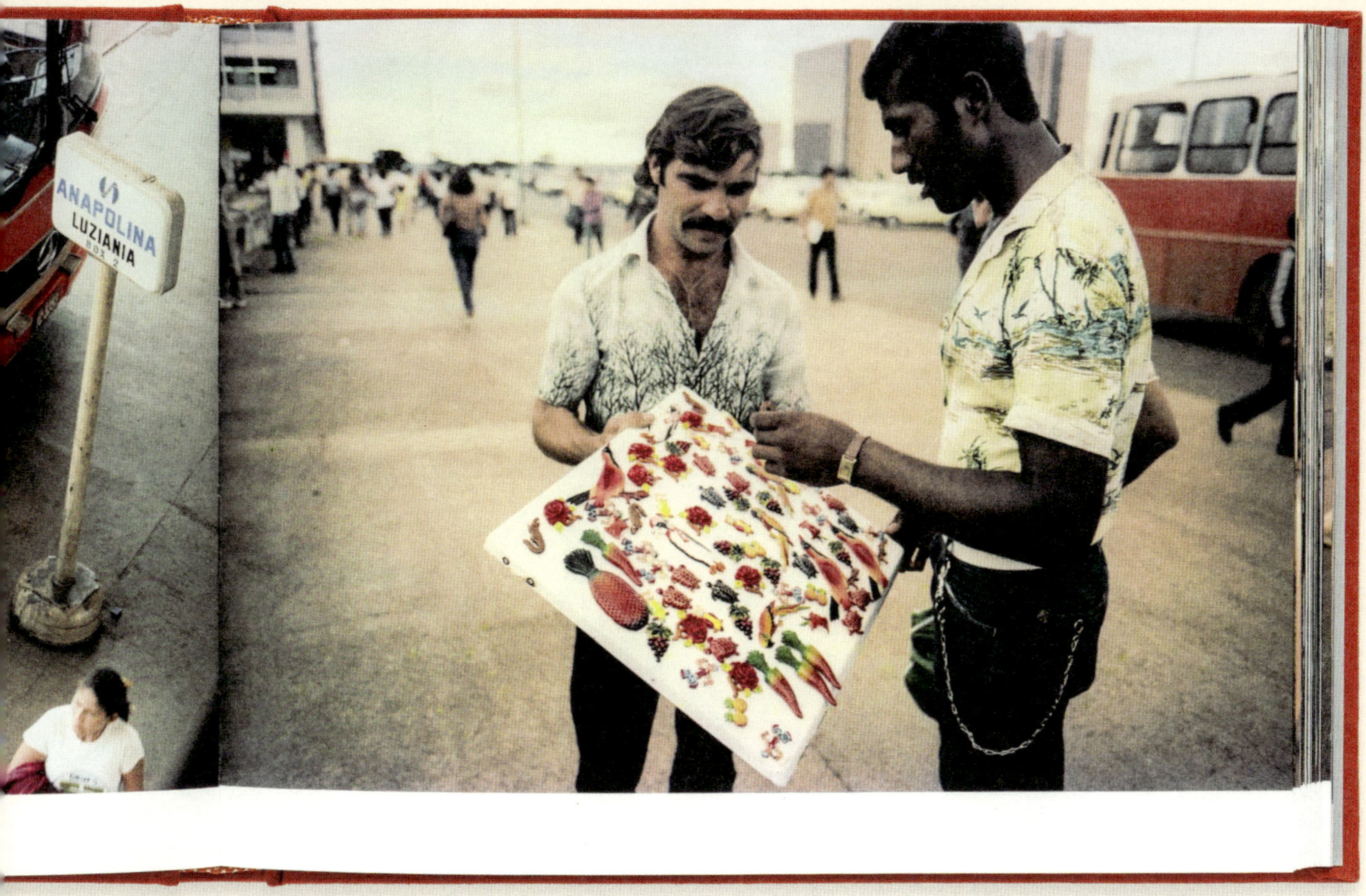

Close Encounters

A small but prolific publishing house in Brazil wants to make books that are like a movie coming to life.

Silas Martí

Walking down São Paulo's bustling Paulista Avenue on a crisp spring afternoon, Rony Maltz tells me how he lost all interest, and all hope, in photojournalism, a job he held for many years before founding {Lp} Press, a boutique publisher of artist-driven photobooks, with his business partner, Carolina Cattan, in 2015. Since then, this native *carioca* from Rio de Janeiro has also become a true *paulistano* of São Paulo—hard-edged, nimble thinking, and still passionate about every grain of film or glossy digital wonder he prints in books that have made waves in the heady photography scene of Brazil's biggest city.

"The scope of a newspaper photograph began to feel too narrow," Maltz said, "like a game where the pictures were the answer to a riddle." He adds that his company's name comes from *livros possíveis*, Portuguese for "books that are possible." "I see photography as the antithesis of that narrowness: not the bearer of a message, but something more ambiguous, more plural. It's about building something bigger, anchored on a collection of images," he explained.

Maltz leapt headfirst into publishing and has released thirty books to date (in

2018, he challenged himself to publish one zine a week—and succeeded). From a multivolume series by Joaquim Paiva, renowned in Brazil for his warm strain of conceptual photography and vast image collection, to lesser-known artists such as Vincent Rosenblatt and Patricia Goùvea, his books take a deft approach to narrative structure, forgoing straightforward storytelling for deep dives into rhythm: expansion and contraction, light and dark, polar opposites that make the pages vibrate as you flip from one spread to another. Reading them, your pulse quickens.

Central to {Lp}'s projects are what Maltz calls "hinge images," photographic moments that build bridges from one thought to the next, something he compares to a movie coming to life. "It's about cohesion, all of it coming together, the noise of turning the page, the smell of the book itself," he said.

In Rosenblatt's *Rio Baile Funk* (2022), we can almost smell the hot sweat on the skin of dancers. This chronicle of Rio de Janeiro's underground funk soirees is an explosion of pictorial energy, emanating from scenes of sweet flirtation unfolding under the glare of angry strobe lights amid the orgasmic huff and puff of the dance floor and its blinding neon. For Maltz, it's all about building an atmosphere: the feeling of an encounter before the heat picks up.

Or maybe not. The pocket-size *Do Amor* (2022) is all about the smartphone's cold, deadening screen. Over the course of the pandemic, Goùvea documented her chats with unlovely men, from late-night DMs to dick pics, to create a bleak yet playful account of superficial relationships in the ghosting era. It's a mirror into our century's special species of loneliness. Yet, like most of {Lp}'s books, it makes you feel a little less alone.

Opposite: Spread from Joaquim Paiva, *Rodoviária de Brasília* (2021); this page, top: Cover of Vincent Rosenblatt, *Rio Baile Funk* (2022); bottom: Spread from Patricia Goùvea, *Do Amor* (2022)

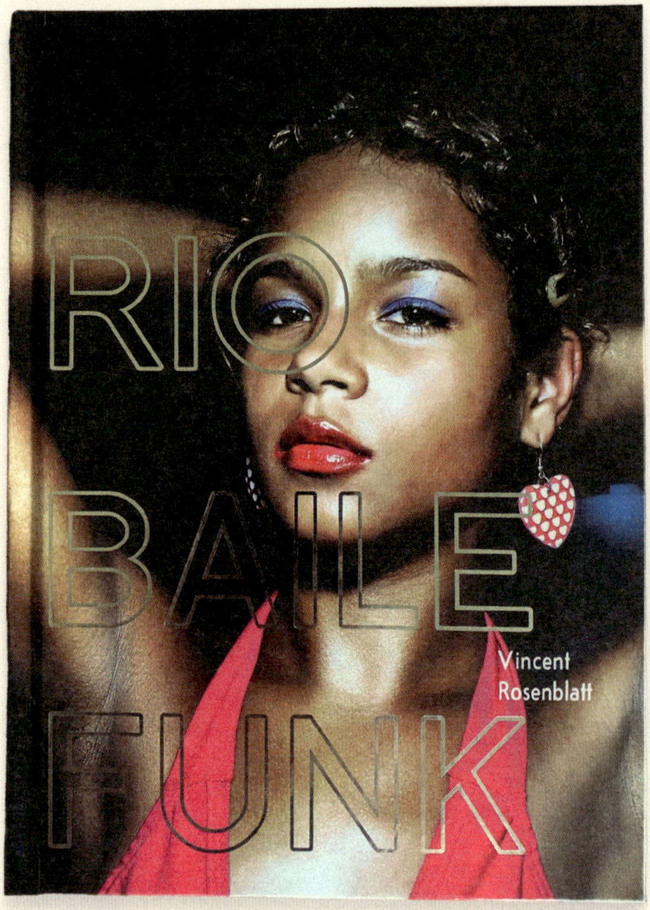

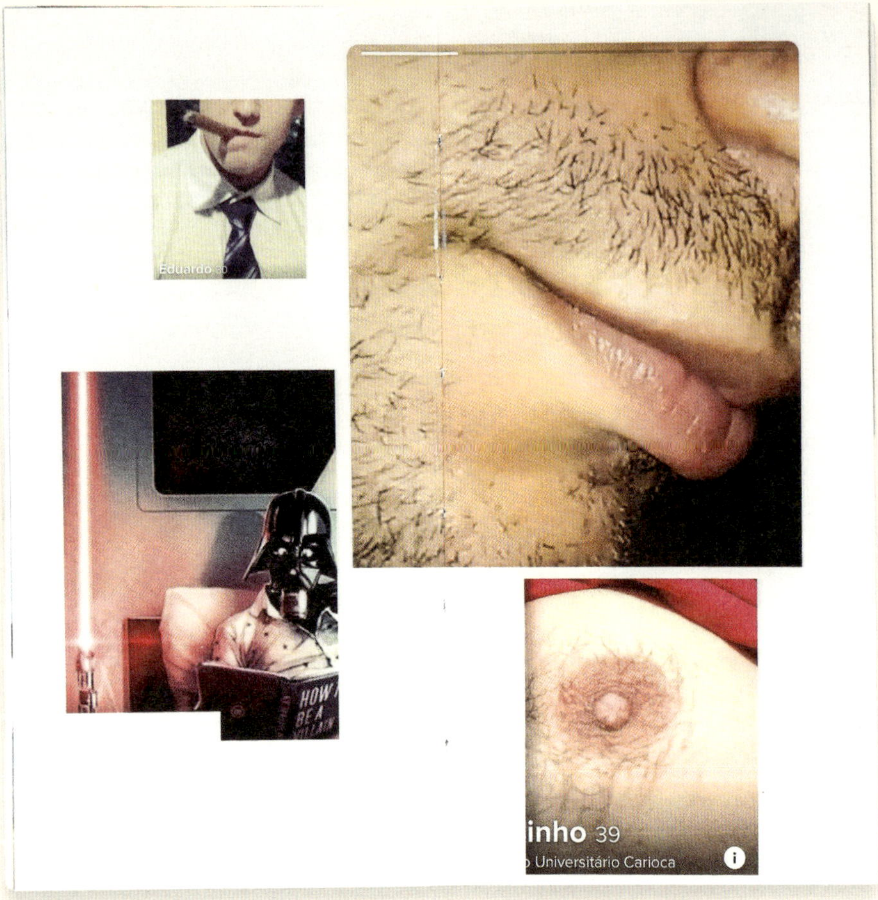

Silas Martí is a writer based in São Paulo and the head of the culture desk at *Folha de S.Paulo*.

Meet the Press

Sue Medlicott and Thomas Bollier discuss the world of photobook printing.

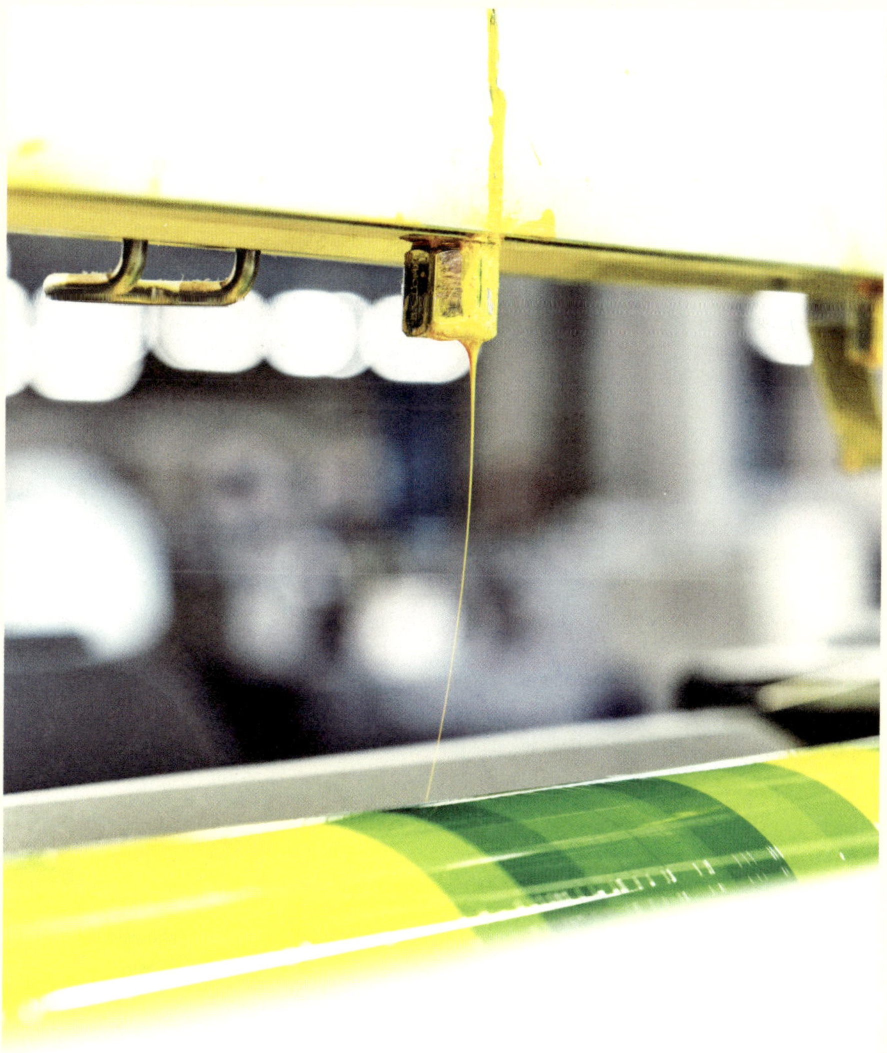

Since the days of Gutenberg, printing has remained a highly specialized skill—especially photographic reproduction. The production manager Thomas Bollier recently called up Sue Medlicott, a veteran of photobook printing, to talk shop about this fast-changing industry.

Thomas Bollier: **How did you get started in printing photography books?**

Sue Medlicott: I wanted to be a book designer. At Smith College, one of my professors said, "If you want to get into grad school at a place like Yale, go and work at Meriden Gravure Company." I walked in the front door, took one whiff of the fumes coming out of the back room, saw the funky setup, and fell in love. And I got the job.

TB: **What was your role there?**

SM: Basically, I hung out in those press-rooms all day. The first book that I got to watch was the reprint of the National Gallery's *Alfred Stieglitz: Photographs & Writings*. I still think that's one of the great books of all time. At Meriden, I got to learn about the mechanics of printing. It was pretty unusual for a woman to be doing it, frankly.

TB: **You've witnessed a huge shift in printing, from using film and analog technology to make plates, and for all the prepress, to using computers and digital technology.**

SM: The transition to digital was rough, but we got through it.

TB: **Where do you like to work these days?**

SM: Lately, I've been getting projects done in Japan again. It's just a different approach, and one that feels right to me.

TB: **In terms of quality and attention to detail?**

SM: Exactly.

TB: **What separates a just-okay book from a great book to you?**

SM: A lot of people get sucked into these fancy productions, with eighteen gate-folds and all this stuff. It doesn't make it a

This page and left: die Keure Printing, Bruges, Belgium, from *The Last Book* (Loose Joints, 2025)
© Thomas Prior 2026, and courtesy Loose Joints

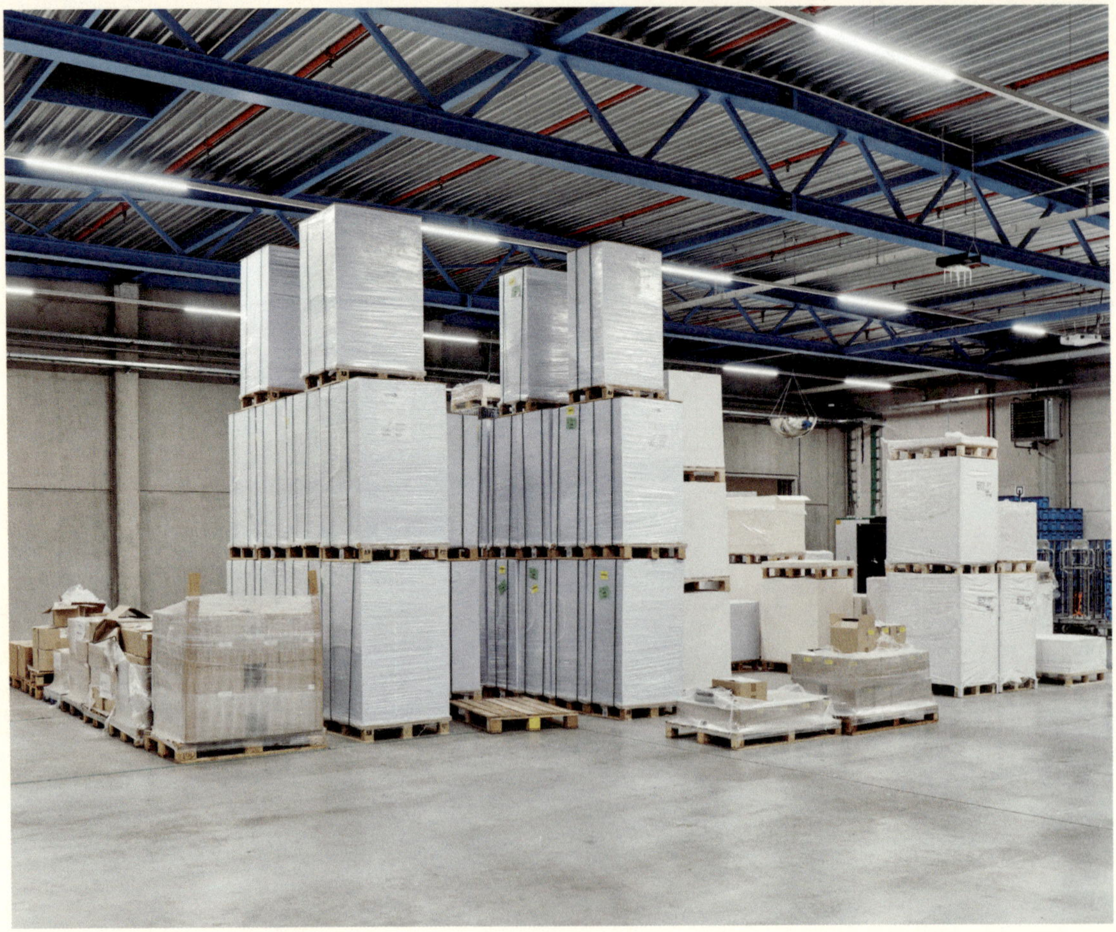

great book. I always check the binding first. Everybody's gotten to be a pretty good printer, but I just don't see great binding anymore.

TB: **It's a challenge.**

SM: When I find a book that's bound well and thoughtfully laid out and the materials are great—like, the paper is beautiful—and then they knock it out of the ballpark with a really good set of separations, that's exciting. They know what a picture should look like.

TB: **Are there any recent books you picked up that you felt this way about?**

SM: No! I'm still looking, and I'm still trying to do one myself. The minute I think I've done a perfect book is probably the day I should just say, "Oh, I've got to quit."

TB: **You've worked with a lot of small specialty printers in Italy, where there's one person overseeing everything, but also with companies in China that have dozens of presses. How do you bring the same sort of attention to books at more anonymous big businesses like that?**

SM: I find it really easy to work with the Chinese. If you go to smaller places in Italy, the printer often has an idea of what it should look like, and it's not always what I think it should look like. When I go to China, I can get them to understand what it is that I'm looking to do. It might be out of their wheelhouse, but they always find a way to do it. They rarely disappoint. But it takes a long time. It's a relationship.

TB: **The relationship is very important.**

SM: It's everything. I never go through a broker. I want to talk to the people who are on the floor. I bring them an old book and say, "How can we get this?" And they work with me. If I would take it to Europe or the United States, forget it. They will say, "That can't be done." I think what happened in the United States is going to happen in Europe. All these craftsmen are going to retire, and I don't think there are young people that are going to come up and take their places.

TB: **It seems like there are young people who are into the publishing side of things but not into the actual printing itself as a craft.**

SM: So many young people want to do the creative part, but they wouldn't be satisfied to sit and watch ten thousand sheets of paper go through the press, or help fold five hundred copies of something, and you keep doing the process over and over again. It's a really interesting personality trait, and it doesn't come together often. When it does—that's the production person you want. They don't get bored by all of this. Because, you have to admit, some of it is just like watching paint dry.

Thomas Bollier is an independent retoucher and print production manager.

Reviews

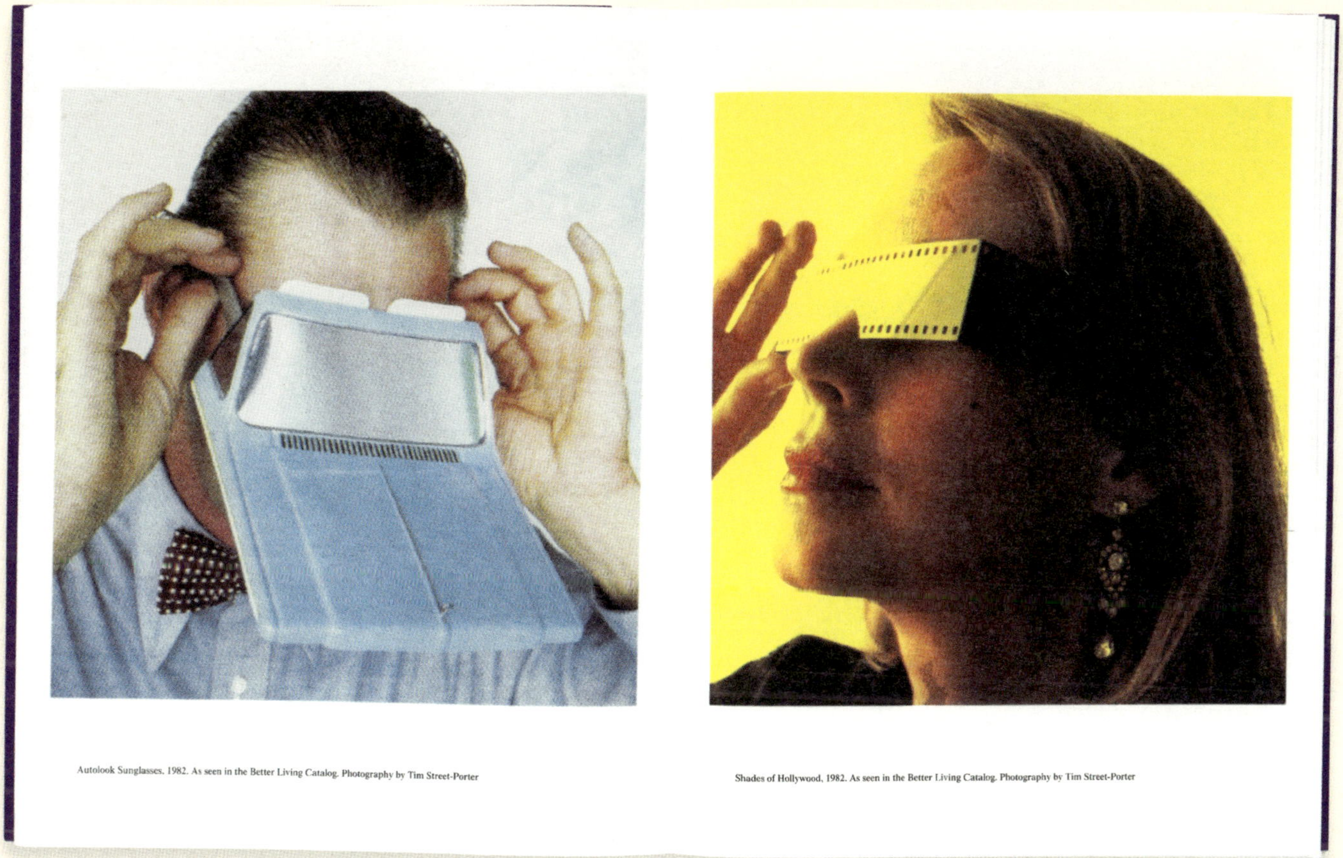

Spread from Pippa Garner, *Personal Ads* (2025)

Pippa Garner

Pippa Garner cultivated her eccentricity like a hothouse orchid. Or a hot rod. The artist was an inveterate product of California car culture: A former assembly-line worker for Chrysler and an expellee from the ArtCenter College of Design's automotive department, she toiled for decades in the art world's garage as a satirical illustrator for *Car and Driver* magazine and as a maker of conceptual sculptures, photographs, and screwball conveyances (for 1974's *Backwards Car*, she flipped the chassis of a Chevrolet so that it appeared to drive in reverse). She liked to transform preexisting things—appliances, attire, herself. "I did it for art," Garner wrote about her 1995 "sex change," as she called it. "My body has gone from a temple to a Winnebago." She didn't identify as Mr. or Ms., but *Misc.*

Long an artist's artist, Garner found broader recognition in her twilight years, the subject of many exhibitions, awards, and photobooks, most recently ***Personal Ads*** **(Art Paper Editions, 2025; 112 pages, $40)**, published a few months after her death, in December of 2024. The sleek paperback brings to mind a street peddler's trench coat, parted to flash a selection of dubious merchandise: high-heeled roller skates, "autolook sunglasses," a necktie made of a thick plait of hair, a list of T-shirt slogans ("FAQ: WTF?"). Winnowed by

the editors from thousands of slides, in collaboration with Garner, these photographs reveal the artist as a jauntily subversive commodity fetishist who, like her Pop precursors, both skewered and gleefully surrendered to the American cult of invention. —**Zack Hatfield**

Tessa Boffin

"The stakes are remarkably high," London-based photographer Tessa Boffin wrote in 1992. "There are so few embodiments of our desires and so many unfulfilled yearnings." Around the time that the UK government passed Section 28—a regressive legislative amendment that prohibited LGBTQ+ materials from being published or taught—Boffin doubled down on her commitment to picturing a liberatory lesbian erotics.

Tessa Boffin **(Stanley/Barker, 2025; 104 pages, $68)** is itself a fetish object of sorts, sheathed in black leather and dangling a quartet of ribbon bookmarks. Within the publication, the photographer Sunil Gupta details his collaboration with Boffin on *Ecstatic Antibodies: Resisting the AIDS Mythology*, in 1990, three years before Boffin's early death. The sex-positive exhibition and book included lesbians, whose frequent mischaracterization as being extrinsic to the HIV/AIDS epidemic overlooked their risk factors, experiences of Thatcher-era homophobia, and queer coalitional politics. It's a subject taken up by Boffin's *Angelic Rebels: Lesbians and Safer Sex* (1989), an allegorical sequence in which a butch springs from wadded plastic wrap to embrace a seraphic femme. A photo-comic Boffin made in 1993, *The Sailor and the Showgirl*, takes a more didactic tack: The artist-as-high-femme-showgirl advocates for safer sex practices with a then-girlfriend dressed in seaman attire.

Wary of how documentary photography can "naturalize" sexuality, Boffin constructed her tableaux guided by the belief that artifice and play were meaningful sites of queer identity formation. Sometimes the result falls flat. Tongue-in-cheek images of a pelt-clad woman carrying a quiver, under the section titled "Quim" for the lesbian erotica magazine of that name, seem a rather perfunctory nod to the era's "sex wars." But then there's the magic of *The Knight's Move* (1990): In this filmic progression, portraits of lesbian icons of yore that appear scattered in a London cemetery (and cruising ground) are supplanted by living, costumed participants in a Sapphic courtly romance. In the jump cut between history and fantasy, so much feels possible. —**Cassie Packard**

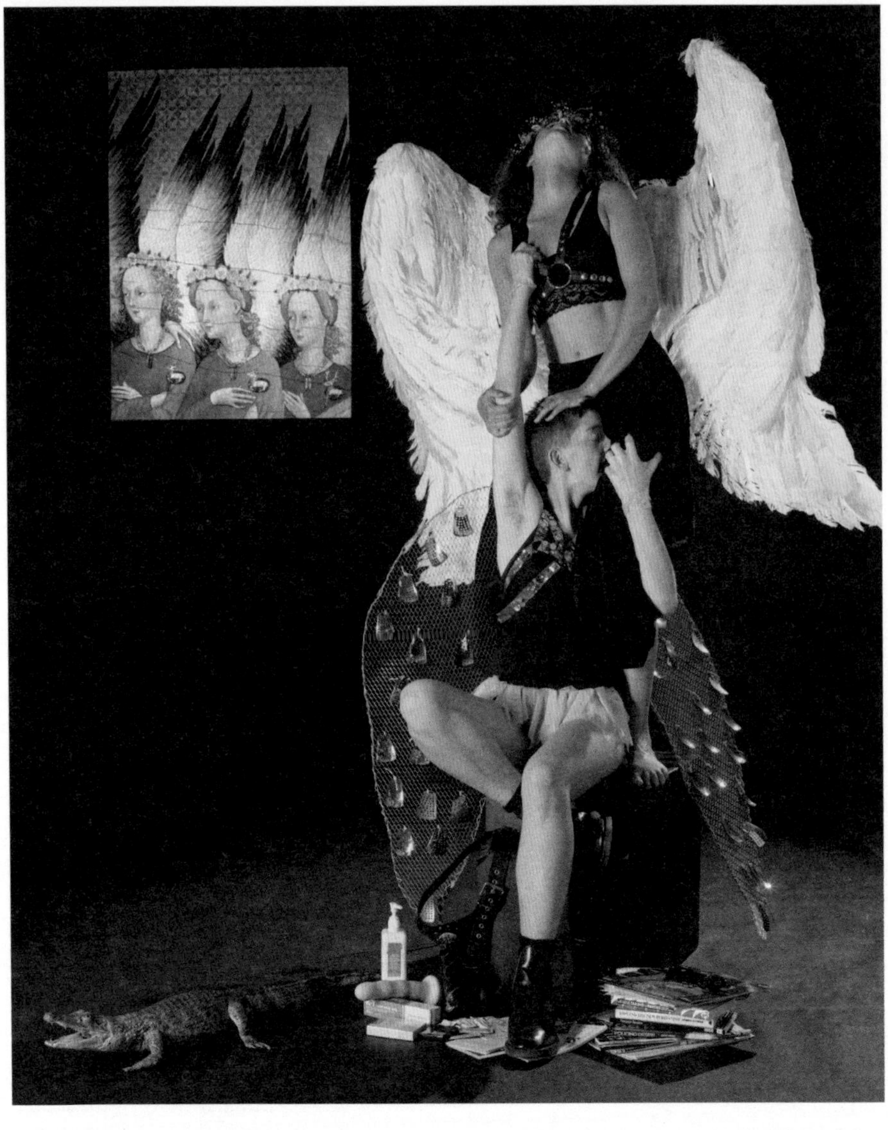

Tessa Boffin, from the series *Angelic Rebels: Lesbians and Safer Sex* (1989)

Yves Saint Laurent

The history of Yves Saint Laurent is, inevitably, the history of modern fashion photography. Not only were the designer and his collections documented by every important photographer of fashion, but two of the most famous and frequently anthologized fashion photographs are of Saint Laurent designs. Both appear in ***Yves Saint Laurent and Photography*** **(Phaidon, 2025; 160 pages, $69.95)**. The first, Richard Avedon's unavoidable *Dovima with Elephants*, is, incidentally, the picture of a gown Saint Laurent created while working at the house of Dior in 1955. Two years later, when Dior died of a

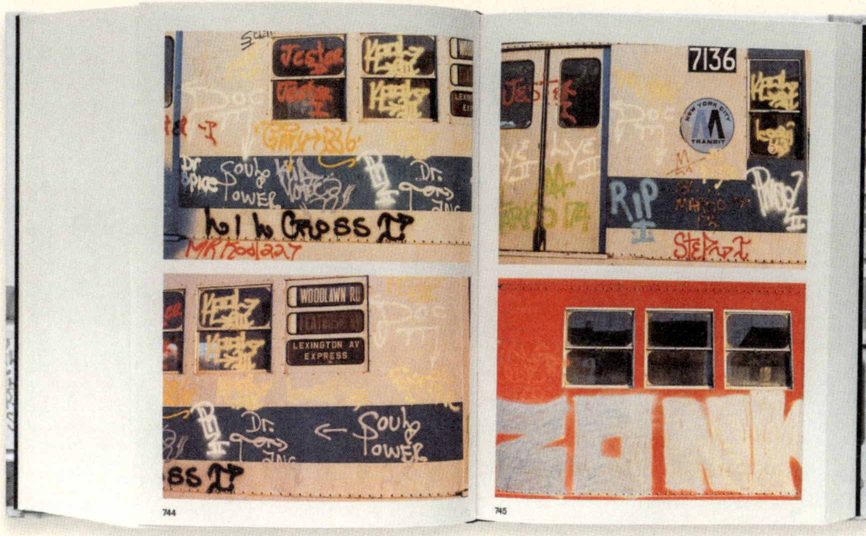

heart attack, Saint Laurent, just twenty-one, became the house's artistic director—the new Dior, celebrated within the rarefied world of couture, unknown outside of it. That changed in January 1962, when Saint Laurent staged the first show under his own name and, not long after, became the first designer whose carefully cultivated image—what one of the book's writers calls "a uniquely personal, cool masculinity"—was key to his brand. Who else would have posed naked (in 1971, for Jeanloup Sieff) to promote a new eau de toilette?

The second major image here, Helmut Newton's 1975 photograph of a woman in a man-tailored suit standing alone, at night, in the middle of a narrow Parisian backstreet, appeared in *Vogue Paris* at the height of Saint Laurent's fame. Fifty years later, the image has lost none of its coiled power as the document of a couture outfit that was also an elegant rejection of gender as a straitjacket. Not every photograph here is as charged as Newton's—or Avedon's—but the range is rich, and each image represents both the photographer and the designer at their best. Saint Laurent closed his haute couture operations in 2002; he was dead six years later, at seventy-one. This collection can only sketch in that hectic career, but from Irving Penn to William Klein, Sarah Moon to Jean-Paul Goude, the photographers here give it shape and weight and an insinuatingly seductive allure. —**Vince Aletti**

Top:
Spread from Gordon Matta-Clark: *Passing through moving in and getting away with it* (2025)

Bottom:
Cover of *Yves Saint Laurent and Photography* (2025)

Opposite:
Spread from Mari Katayama, *Synthesis* (2025)

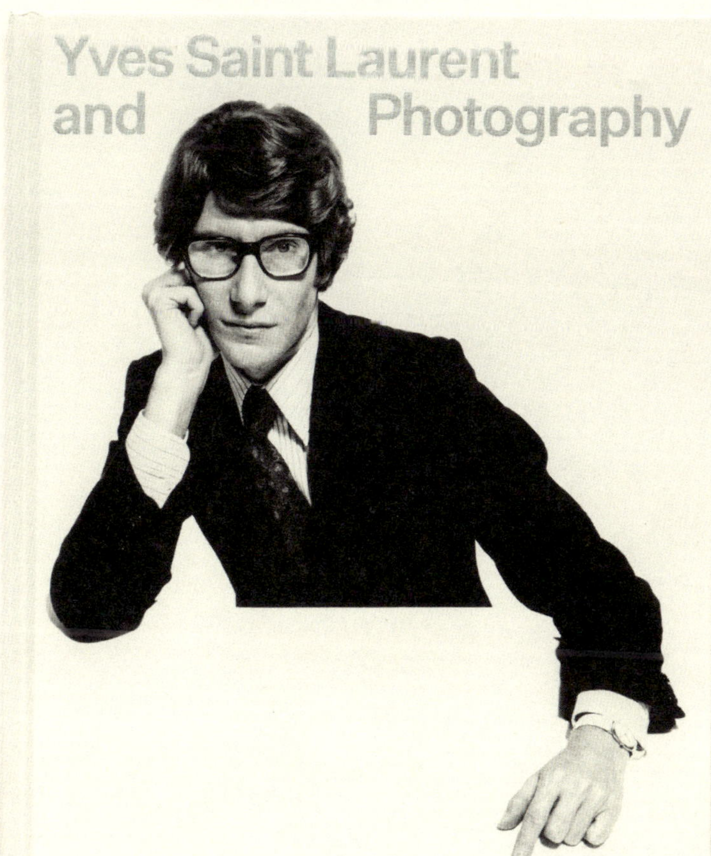

Gordon Matta-Clark

In the essay near the end of ***Passing through moving in and getting away with it*** **(Other Means, 2025; 1,008 pages, $85)**, which collects every photograph of New York graffiti that the artist Gordon Matta-Clark took across 1972 and 1973—more than fifteen hundred images—Antonio Sergio Bessa refers to Matta-Clark's "perplexing engagement" with this burgeoning aspect of the city. While Bessa's overview provides useful context otherwise, it seems odd to take Matta-Clark's interest as anything other than obvious: He was doing for the ephemeral work of others what he did for his own.

Matta-Clark used photography, film, and video to record his famous "voids"—sliced buildings that ranged from the brutal gash of *Splitting* (1974) to the elegant curves of *Office Baroque* (1977). The buildings that served as his medium were slated for renovation or destruction, and his cuts rendered them difficult, if not impossible, to enter. In a way, his documentation was simply practical. On a fundamental conceptual level, though, his multifaceted representations stoke a tension that arises as architecture passes through uselessness into image.

He could have left his art's survival to chance, as the mostly Black and Latino

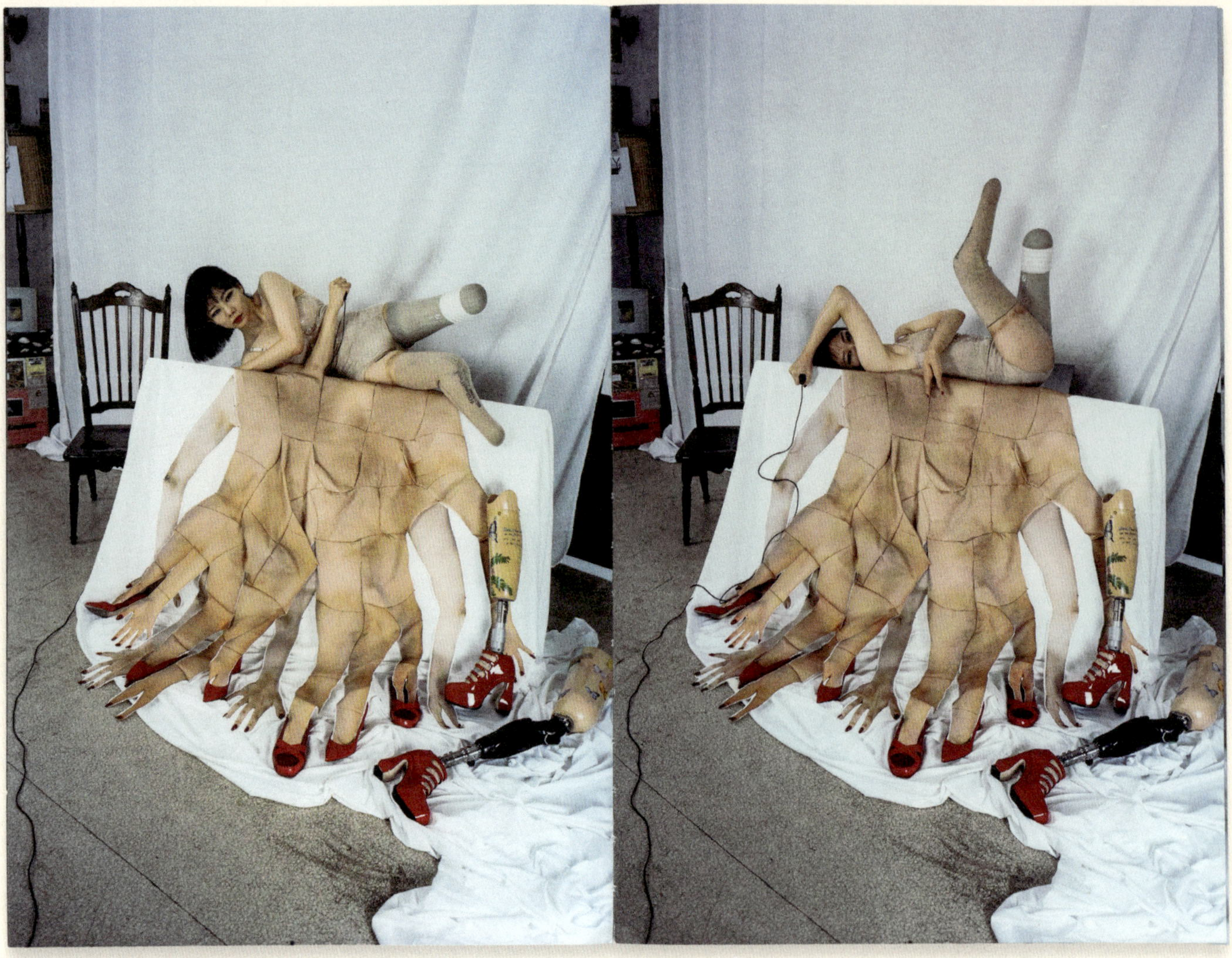

teenagers whose work he captures in *Passing through* had. Impermanence for them was a given, a spur to invention: getting more tags up, or getting them in places no one else would dare to reach. The sheer variety and inventiveness of drawn lines on offer in *Passing through* is astonishing, a quality deepened by Matta-Clark's often painterly framing. Clearly, the artist found in graffiti a continuity with his own interventions, which, in taking the city as surface rather than material, managed the same tension between architecture and image while avoiding uselessness, while remaining possible to live in.

—**Phil Coldiron**

Mari Katayama

"Every time I come into contact with nature's beauty and strength, I feel as though my work and my modified body are not a part of the landscape," Mari Katayama, who has prosthetic legs due to a childhood illness, writes in ***Synthesis*** **(MACK/SPBH Editions, 2025; 96 pages, $55)**. In the book, Katayama—known for the intricate handsewn objects, textiles, and collages that she incorporates into self-portraits—presents nine series, all photographed over the past six years in her home studio in Gunma, Japan. Each photograph is run at full bleed, with Coptic-stitch binding allowing the spreads to crack open and flatten out. The dense, effervescent chaos of Katayama's studio (a repudiation of the Japanese art of decluttering) is alternately the focal point of her compositions and an implication eating at their edges, peeking out behind makeshift backdrops. In carefully composed environs, Katayama engages a form of self-portraiture in which her position shifts between subject and object among the sprawl.

In one series, *red shoes* (2023), a pair of prosthetic legs clad in red platform heels appears strewn next to a wearable multilimbed sculpture draped over a white sheet backdrop; Katayama balances over the stuffed handmade appendages, her right hand clenching the shutter release cable, using her constructions and compositions to illustrate the troubled thresholds and boundaries she is working to bridge. In *Tree of Life* (2024–25), the series that concludes the book, a large photographic tapestry of a forested landscape covers one wall, and mirrored floors and walls throw its projection across the frame. Katayama here plays the role of a caryatid, holding up a refracted sky.

—**Mira Maxwell**

Endnote
Dana Lixenberg

For decades, the Dutch photographer Dana Lixenberg called New York home, spending the longest stretch in a building on Broadway that once housed Mathew Brady's studio. *American Images*, a survey of her work—including her era-defining portraits for *Vibe* in the 1990s—is on view at the Maison Européenne de la Photographie in Paris until May 24.

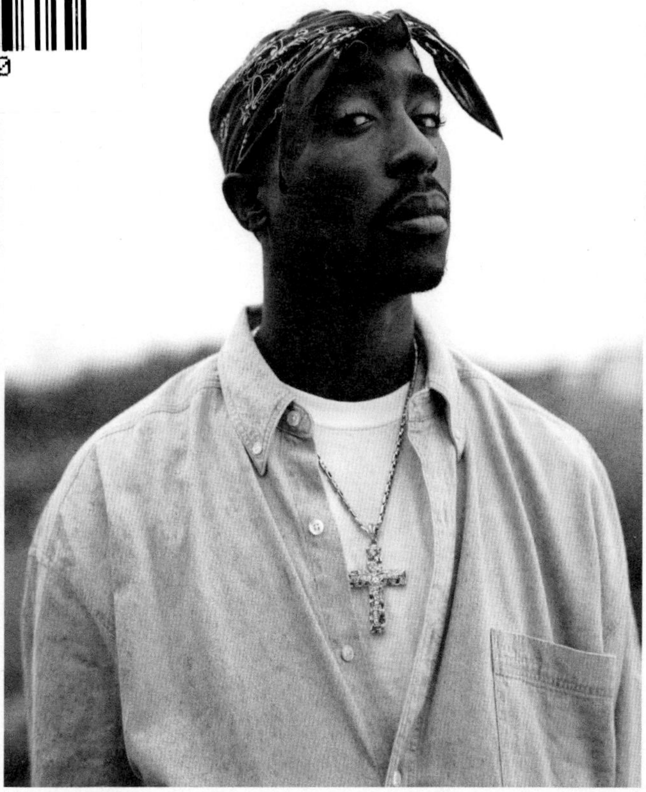

Tupac Shakur, 1993
Courtesy the artist and Grimm, Amsterdam

What made you decide to move to New York in 1989?
After high school in 1982, I came to New York as an au pair for a year. I took my first photography class at Parsons, and from that moment, I knew this was what I wanted to pursue. After art school in London and Amsterdam, I returned to the city I had fallen in love with.

You became a regular photographer for *Vibe* at a storied moment for hip-hop.
Vibe came about just after I had made a series of portraits in the Imperial Courts housing project in Watts, in the aftermath of the Rodney King uprising. South Central LA was highly mythologized, and my goal was to look beyond the one-dimensional representations in the media.

I was introduced to Tony Bogard, a Crips gang leader, who then introduced me to his community. That's when I decided to start working with a large-format camera, the same one I use today.

***Imperial Courts* (1993–2015), as this work became titled, would become a decades-long project of returning to the community. But at that time, you showed the early work to George Pitts, *Vibe*'s director of photography?**
Yes. George and the editor in chief saw the work and decided on the spot that they wanted to publish a portfolio of it. And I said, "Sure, definitely. But not in a journalistic context." It was a very elegant presentation, paired with a poem by Ntozake Shange. After that, I became a regular contributor. The first big assignment I did for them was Tupac.

How did *Vibe* work then? Were these small productions?
You had a kind of access that's really hard to find today. It was the pre-digital era: no social media, and print still carried a lot of weight. With *Vibe*, creatively, it was a very nurturing relationship. Some of the productions were big, like Jay-Z or even Tupac. The Tupac shoot looks like a very quiet, sort of concentrated moment, but there was actually a lot of noise and entourage around us.

Do you feel in the moment when you "have it"?
When everything clicks and I'm inspired by the subject, I can feel it in my gut. There's a much better chance I'll be happy with the results. But I won't know until I see the contact sheets. The texture and tone of the image are crucial. Like with the Tupac portrait, where the front eye is less in focus than the eye behind—it's very delicate. Or the image of Biggie, where you can almost hear him breathe.

The photograph of Kate Moss in the show must have been early in her career.
Yeah, it was right outside of my house on the Bowery, where I was living at the time. She showed up with a little plastic bag, no makeup artist or anything. She just had done the Calvin Klein campaign. You could tell how incredibly photogenic she was. I loved the little pimple on her forehead.

The title of your book and exhibition is *American Images*. Much of the work is from the 1990s, and obviously America is in a complicated—to put it lightly—place right now. How do you see the title operating?
Titles are tricky. I tend to prefer short, descriptive ones. Simply put, these are images from America. But the work also challenges the way the country is represented. I guess the word "images" is intentionally a bit ambiguous. It can suggest something not fully real.